THE BOOK OF NAMES

OF

NAMES

J. N. HOOK

A GROLIER COMPANY

FRANKLIN WATTS
New York | London | Toronto | Sydney
1983

Library of Congress Cataloging in Publication Data

Hook, J.N (Julius Nicholas), 1913–
The book of names.

1. Names, Personal—United States.   2. Names,
Geographical—United States.   3. Names, Personal—
United States—Anecdotes, facetiae, satire, etc.
4. Names, Geographical—United States—Anecdotes,
facetiae, satire, etc.   5. English language—Etymology
—Names.   I. Title.
CS2481.H66   1983   929.4'0973   83-12375
ISBN 0-531-09805-2

ACKNOWLEDGMENTS

John Algeo, for material in "On the Street (Circle, Drive, Lane Trail) Where You Live," from "Changing Fashions in Street Names," *Names*, March, 1978.

Leonard R. N. Ashley, for information about original names of actors and actresses. In "Flicks, Flacks, and Flucks," *Names*, Dec., 1975.

Associated Press, August 22, 1982.

Baer's Agricultural Almanac, 1981, for information in "No Submachine Guns?"

Ronald L. Baker and Marvin Carmony, for material in "13 Sources of Place Names," "Local Legends about Town Names," and "The Name Is Now Correct," from *Indiana Place Names*, 1975.

William C. Barge and Norman W. Caldwell, for information about place names, from "Illinois Place Names," *Journal* of the Illinois State Historical Society, 1936.

William C. Barnes, for information about place names, from *Arizona Place Names*, 1935; revised by Byrd H. Granger, 1960.

Ira Berkow, for information in "You Know Names from Maxwell Street," from *Maxwell Street*, Doubleday, 1977.

Blackwood's Magazine, March, 1842, for the anecdote in "Ask for Him by His Right Name."

Stephen N. Bowen, for material in "The Bowen Theory of Executive Advancement," from "The Executive Name Game," *Dun's Review*, 1973.

Erwin C. Brody, for information in "How Do Authors Name Their Characters?" from "Meaning and Symbolism in the Names of Dostoevsky's *Crime and Punishment* and *The Idiot*," *Names*, 1979.

R. V. Dietrich and L. T. Reynolds, for information in "What's Your Last Initial?" from an article in *Names*.

Lester F. Dingman, for information in "Not All Names Are Considered to Be Proper" and "One Run, One Miss, One Error," from *Naughty Names*, ed. Fred Tarpley.

Audrey R. Duckert, for the anecdote in "Mr. Reardon Couldn't Be There," material in "Wonderful People with Strange-Sounding Names," and material in "Nicknames for Places," *Names*, 1973.

Pierre DuPont, for the letter in "From One Pierre to Another."

The Encyclopedia Brittannica, 1975 Edition.

C. L. Ewen, for the list in "Those Good Old English Names," *History of Surnames of the British Isles*, Genealogical Publishing Co., 1968.

Gary S. Felton and Lynn S. Felton, for lists in *"A as in Alfa,"* *Names*, 1977.

Thomas P. Field, for information about place names, from *A Guide to Kentucky Place Names*, 1961.

Henry Gannett, for information about place names, from *American Names*, 1902; second ed., 1947, 1977.

Charles N. Gould, for information about place names, from *Oklahoma Place Names*, 1933.

Halliwell's Filmgoers' Companion, 7th Edition, Scribners, 1980.

Kelsie Harder, for information about place names, from *Illustrated Dictionary of Place Names*, 1976.

Harper's Magazine, for material in "News Affects Naming," Copyright © 1975 by *Harper's Magazine*. All rights reserved. Reprinted from the January 1976 issue by special permission.

Edward N. Hook, for material in "License Plates Can Be Goofed Up, Too," "Not a Sissy Name," and "What Ever Happened to Six-toed Pete?" From personal correspondence.

John C. Huden, for information about place names, from *Indian Place Names of New England*, 1962.

Information Please Almanac, 1981, for information about original names of famous people, state names.

Gary Jennings, for information in "What's in a Name?" and "Unusual Ways to Select Surnames," from *Personalities of Language*, 1967.

Thomas A. Johnson, for material in "8 Stems from *Roots*," from "*Roots* Has Widespread and Inspiring Influence," *New York Times*, March 19, 1977.

Benzion C. Kaganoff, for material in "Names That Are Acronyms" and "Unusual Ways to Select Surnames," from *A Dictionary of Jewish Names and Their History*, 1977.

Ephraim Katz for information in *The Film Encyclopedia*, Putnam's, 1982.

John Leighly, for material in "Bringing the Holy Land to America," from "Biblical Place-Names in the United States," *Names*, 1979.

Frederic Luther, for "Did Anybody Confuse Him with General Electric?" and "Could Johnny Carson Have Been Wrong?" From personal correspondence.

John McNamara, for information in "How Do You Name a Boat?" from "Reflections of Nautical Onomastics," *Names*, 1979.

Peter Mattiace, for information in "The Town Whose Mayor Can't Pronounce Its Name," Associated Press feature, Nov. 16, 1981.

H. L. Mencken, for information in "H. L. Mencken's Unusual Names for Girls," "Not Everybody Pronounces Enroughty as Darby," "The Rabbit Who Became an Irishman," "Unusual Ways to Select Surnames," and

"What Do You Call Someone Who Lives in Moscow?" *The American Language*, 1965 edition, *Supplement One*, 1966 edition, *Supplement Two*, 1962 edition.

Lynell Mickelson, for information in "You Mean There's More than One Barbara Walters?" from the Knight-Ridder newspapers, July 4, 1982.

William Least Heat Moon, for an anecdote in "The Nameless Ones." From *Blue Highways*, excerpted in *Atlantic Monthly*, Sept., 1982.

Names, the quarterly publication of the American Names Society. See listings under individual authors.

New Yorker, for information in "For Colored Girls..." in "Talk of the Town," August 2, 1976.

Don Nilsen, for names in "Cutiepie Commercial Names" and in "Take-offs."

Lowell Nussbaum, for "Remember General Beauregard?" Indianapolis *Star*, Jan. 25, 1976.

Newbell Niles Puckett, for material in "Names of Slaves" and "Names Adopted by Free Blacks." From *Black Names in America*, 1975.

Robert L. Ramsay, for information about place names, from *Our Storehouse of Missouri Place Names*, University of Missouri Bulletin, No. 7, 1952.

William A. Read, for information about place names, from *Florida's Place-Names of Indian Origin*, 1934.

Zvonko R. Rode, for material in "Zvonko Rode's 15 Sources of Jewish Family Names." *Names*, 1976.

Phillip R. Rutherford, for material in "Cricket, Croesus, Brownie Car," from "Come Ride with Me, Lucille," in *Naughty Names*, Fred Tarpley, ed.

William Safire, for the pun in "Don't Tell His Wife," from *New York Times Magazine*, July 11, 1982.

Raymond Schuessler, for quotations in "Namely Bloopers," from "Oops! All-time Great Bloopers," *Modern Maturity*, April-May, 1982.

Elsdon C. Smith, for material in "More Facts about Smiths" and "Is That Name Scottish or Irish?" *American Surnames*, 1969, and *New Dictionary of American Family Names*, 1973.

H. Allen Smith, for material in the chapter on Smiths, from *People Named Smith*, 1955.

George R. Stewart, for miscellaneous information in the sections on place names, "We Name Almost Every Place We Know" and "The Big Apple and Smaller Apples." *Names on the Land*, 1967 edition, and *American Place-Names*, 1970.

Surnames in the United States Census of 1790, for information in "Is That Name Scottish or Irish?" and "Unusual Surnames from the 1790 Census." Genealogical Publishing Co., 1971.

Karen Taylor, for material in "Mrs. Alice Jones...," from the Indianapolis *Star*, 1982.

Barbara Tuchman, for material in "Name-Trouble for Historians," *Atlantic Monthly*, Dec., 1975.

U.S. National Weather Service, for the lists of names of tropical storms in "He Called the Storm Maria."

U.S. Postal Service, for information about towns and cities, from *Directory of*

Post Offices, 1963, and *1982 National Five-Digit Zip Code and Post Office Directory*.

U.S. Social Security Administration, for information about surnames, from "Distribution of Surnames in the Social Security Number File," 1975.

TABLE
OF CONTENTS

PART I.
THE NAMES PEOPLE GIVE
THEIR DEFENSELESS CHILDREN

PART II.
THE NAMES WE INHERIT

PART III.
WE NAME ALMOST
EVERY PLACE WE KNOW

PART IV.

"The time has come," the author said,
"To talk of other names.
   Of cars—and pets—and baseball teams—
   Of suffragettes—and games."

PART I

THE NAMES PEOPLE GIVE THEIR DEFENSELESS CHILDREN

1

CHOOSING NAMES FOR GIRLS

BE SURE TO UNWRAP THE BABY
BEFORE YOU CALL ANYBODY

"Next time I'll unwrap the baby before I tell anybody what its name is," Mrs. Donna Schimmer said.

"You have a lovely boy," the Eugene, Oregon, nurse told Mrs. Schimmer as she wrapped the baby up and laid the little bundle on its mother's stomach. The time was 4:30 A.M. Maybe that accounted for the error.

The Schimmers immediately called friends in Los Angeles to tell them the news. The baby, they said, was named Clayton James.

Two hours later a nurse took the baby away to the nursery. When she unwrapped it, she saw that it was a girl.

Clayton James suddenly became Katherine Jane. The Schimmers had to make some more phone calls that morning.

BALLAD OF
BEAUTIFUL NAMES

Emily, Rachel, Bernadette,
Ellen, Astrid, Fawn,
Cecilia, Tamar, Christabel,
Lolita, Inez, Dawn.

Marguerite, Rita, Angeline,
Keiko, Moira, Mae,
Corinne, Denise, May-Ree-Lynn,
Mahalia, Pauline, Faye.

Heidi, Haidee, Isabel,
Kathryn, Lucette, or Joy
(In Heaven yclept Euphrosyne).
Thank God you're not a boy.

HOW TO AVOID A
BABY'S NAME YOU DISLIKE

Use tact. That's what one husband, Raymond Roberts, did.

His wife, Alice, said, "If the baby is a girl, let's call her Lana."

Raymond detested that name but didn't want to argue.

"Great!" he said. "The first girl I ever dated seriously was named Lana. She was beautiful and intelligent and sexy. I've always liked that name."

Alice was silent for a few moments and then said, "Of course we should talk over some other possibilities. What do you think of Marie, or Claudette, or Melanie?"

NEW YORK CITY'S
FAVORITE GIVEN NAMES

"I think what we're seeing is parents are no longer going to the Bible to find names, they're going to the soap operas," according to Marvin Bogner of the New York City Department of Health. Bogner was quoted in an Associated Press article in 1982, as he reported on the names most often given to newborn babies a year earlier.

Most popular girls' names, in order, were Jennifer (first choice in every year since 1972), Jessica, Melissa, Nicole, Michelle, Elizabeth, Lisa and Tiffany (a tie), Christina, and Danielle.

Maria and Mary, which had been high on most lists since 1898, had dropped in 1981 to thirteenth and thirty-seventh. In 1898, according to the AP report, the most popular girls' names were Mary, Catherine, Margaret, Annie, Rose, Marie, Esther, Sarah, Frances, and Ida.

Baby boys in 1898 were most often named John, William, Charles, George, Joseph, Edward, James, Louis, Francis, or Samuel.

But in 1981 only three of those names were still in the top ten, which consisted of Michael, Christopher, David, Jason, Joseph, Anthony, John, Daniel, Robert, and James.

DO TEACHERS FAVOR
CONFORMISTS?

Herbert Harari, a psychologist at the University of California in San Diego, made a study in 1973 of whether children's first names affect the grades that teachers give.

Eight essays said to be of identical quality were duplicated and given to eighty fifth- and sixth-grade teachers to evaluate. Four of the papers bore names considered ordinary: Michael, David, Karen, and Lisa. The other four had less common names: Elmer, Hubert, Bertha, and Adelle.

Michael and David outscored Elmer and Hubert by a full letter grade. Karen and Lisa outscored Bertha by a small margin—a point and a half. Adelle's grades were reported as "not significantly lower."

Like other such research, this study should not be considered conclusive unless confirmed by further investigations.

HOW ABOUT
ETTA CANDY BARR?

Thomas Pyles, a noted linguist and student of Americana, must have had fun when he wrote for the magazine *Names* an article about his beloved Southland: "Bible Belt Onomastics or Some

Curiosities of Anti-Pedobaptist Nomenclature" (1959). He listed a number of pairings of given and last names that, in combination, proved amusing. The following are taken from his longer list:

Candy Barr
(also the stage name of a famous stripper)
Okla Bobo
Pinkie Bottom
Girlie Burns
Sandy Candy
Royal Child
Melody Clinkenbeard
Honey Combs
French Crown
Pamela Gay Day
Merry English
Charming Fox
Golden Gamble
Fawn Gray
Fairy Guy
Bunker Hill

Early Hawaiian McKinnon
Rocky Mountain
Virgin Muse
Percy Nursery
France Paris
Dill L. Pickle
(who sold pickles)
English Piper
Diamond Queen
Summer Robbins
Paris Singer
Lovie Slappy
Shellie Swilley
Drew Swords
Etta Turnipseed
Early Wages
Pleasant Weathers

H. L. MENCKEN'S
UNUSUAL NAMES FOR GIRLS

H. L. Mencken, that great collector of oddities of the American language, listed several hundred girls' names that were found in newspapers of the 1930s and 1940s, mainly in the South and Southwest. Here are some of the especially remarkable ones:

Armadilla	Delector	Exum
Attaresta	Dewdrop	Fairy
Ava Marie	Dicey Mae	Faucette
Buena Vista	Dinette	Febe
Cementa	Dreamy	Flouzelle
Cherubim	Dullere	Flowanna
Chlorine	Echo	Fra
Coita	Elicious	Fragoletta
Credilla	El Louise	Gazelle
Dardanella	Endamile	Glanda

Gloriola
G'Ola
Gommeray
Halloween
Hygiene
Iceyphobia
Jaann
Jennyberry
Johnny-v
Kewpie
Kiwanis
La Duska
Ladye
La Lahoma
Larceny
(pronounced lar-CEE-nee)

Livera
Locust
Lush
Madame
Malta Jean
Mecca
Navelle
Nordamyrth
Okla
Ova
Pencilla
Phalla
Pleasantina
Polo
Qay
Ravola
Roseola

Rumba Jo
Satyra
Sing
Swan
Twitty
Ulyssia
Ureatha
Vasoline
Venajulia
Windi
Wroberta
Zdenka
Zoya
Zula Bell
Zylphia
Zzelle

Charlton Laird, in *Language in America*, adds the following:

Acid
Charm
Dawn Robin
Delyte
(also a name for men,
one of whom became a
university president)

Dimple
Dovey
Kitty Bit
Lance Amorus

Mary Sunshine
Orchid Favia
Pixianne
Satire
Tyty

WHY FREELOVE DIDN'T LAST

Although most of the Puritans had such ordinary given names as Mary and William, some parents liked to emphasize their religious convictions through the names they gave their children. A male might go through life as Persistence even if he gave up easily, and Preserved ⟨saved⟩ was sometimes teamed with an unsuitable surname, as was true of one Preserved Puddifoot.

Compound or hyphenated names were somewhat less common: Everlasting-Mercy or Avoid-Illness. Gary Jennings found these names in a 1658 jury panel list: Faint-Not Hewett, Stand-Fast-on-High Stringer, Search-the-Scriptures Moreton, Fly-Debate Roberts, and Be-of-Good-Comfort Small.

Jennings adds: "One poor girl was baptized Through-Much-Tribulation-We-Enter-into-the-Kingdom-of-Heaven Crabb. Her friends called her Tribby."

Among the jury panelists not mentioned by Jennings were Repentant Hazel, The-Work-of-God Farmer, Be-Thankful Playnard, God-Reward Smart, More-Fruit Flower, Fight-the-Good-Fight-of-Faith White, and Hope-for Bending.

Other Puritan names, likely to be masculine but sometimes feminine, include Thankful, Submit, Godly, Faynt-Not, Experience, Sorry-for-Sin, Tamesin (Tame Sin), and Prosper (short for Prosper-Thy-Works). Increase Mather, the son of one prominent Puritan pastor and the father of another, made Increase a familiar given name in his day.

Two men whose last names originally may have been Barbon, perhaps inevitably found it corrupted to Barebone. One of them was Jesus-Christ-Came-into-the-World-to-Save Barebone; the other, If-Christ-Had-Not-Died-for-Thee-Thou-Hadst-Been-Damned Barebone. The latter, it is said, was called Damned Barebone for short.

Some girls were named Faith or Faithful, Faith-My-Joy, Hope, Gracious, Charity, Prudence (a favorite), Blessing, Comfort, Constant or Constancy, Felicity, Virtue, Diligence, and Obediencia. Flora Loughead's *Dictionary of Given Names* has this to say about another name:

> **Freelove**...This name was bestowed upon girls of highly respected New England families in late Puritan days, evidently through a misconception of the practices advocated by the apostles of its creed; but enlightenment evidently came, for within a few years it was discarded abruptly.

WHAT WOULD SHE HAVE CALLED CHARLES BOYER?

Actress Jean Harlow, one of the movies' early voluptuous blondes, is said to have met Lady Margot Asquith, widow of a onetime British prime minister. Miss Harlow constantly mispronounced the lady's name, calling her "Mar-gott."

Finally the British lady said icily, "My dear, the *t* is silent, as in *Harlow*."

TWO HUNDRED FIFTY
SLIGHTLY OFFBEAT NAMES
FOR GIRLS

Excluded from this list are the most conventional names, such as Mary and Elizabeth, currently very popular names such as Jennifer and Karen, and seemingly far-out names such as Satinka and Semiramis.

Included are some old-fashioned names such as Abigail and Edwina that perhaps should be given another chance, a variety of rather infrequently used but attractive names such as Astrid and Mona, and other names, such as Benita and Almira, now popular with only certain segments of the population.

Where appropriate, some of the alternative forms or approximate synonyms are listed. A few pronunciations are given, although some individuals or groups may prefer a pronunciation not shown here. The usual national or linguistic origin is shown, but some names are also sometimes derived from other sources and may have different meanings. Many girls' names that came from ancient Greek or Latin have undergone changes in modern languages.

Abigail (Abbey, Abbie, Abby, Gail, Gale): Hebrew ⟨father's joy⟩

Adelaide (Adeline, Addie, Adele, Della): Teutonic ⟨noble and kind⟩

Adora: Latin ⟨adored⟩; Greek ⟨a gift⟩

Adorna: Latin ⟨she makes beautiful⟩

Adrienne (Adria, Adriana, Adriane, Adrianna, Adrianne): Greek ⟨girl from Adria, girl from the sea⟩

Agatha (Aga, Agata, Atka): Greek, or southern or central European ⟨good⟩

Agnella (Agna, Agnola; same as Agnes): Greek, Italian ⟨pure⟩

Aida (ah-EE-duh): Italian ⟨happy⟩

Alameda (ah-la-MAY-duh): North American Indian ⟨cottonwood grove⟩; Spanish ⟨parade, promenade⟩

Alana (Alanna, Lana): Celtic ⟨fair, harmonious⟩; Hawaiian ⟨light and airy⟩

Alberta (Albertina, Berta; feminine of Albert): Teutonic ⟨noble and bright⟩

Alda: Teutonic ⟨rich⟩

Alesia: Greek ⟨helper⟩

Aleta: Greek ⟨wanderer⟩

Alicia (uh-LEE-see-uh)
   (Alice, Alisa, Alison,
   Alyce, Elissa, Alys, Alika):
   Greek, Italian, Spanish,
   Swedish, Hawaiian ⟨truth⟩

Aline (uh-LEEN) (Alina):
   Teutonic ⟨noble⟩;
   Russian, Polish ⟨bright⟩

Alita (uh-LEE-tuh) (Leta,
   Adelita): Spanish ⟨noble,
   truthful⟩

Alma (AL-muh or AHL-
   muh): Latin ⟨nourishing,
   supportive, spiritually
   helpful⟩

Almira (Elmira, Mira):
   Arabic ⟨complete truth⟩;
   Hindustani ⟨clothing
   container⟩

Althea (Althaia, Thea):
   Greek ⟨wholesome,
   healing⟩

Amabel (Amabelle,
   Amabella, Amybelle):
   Latin ⟨beautiful loved
   one⟩

Amata (Ama, Amanda,
   Amy): Latin, Spanish
   ⟨loved one⟩

Amber: Arabic ⟨jewel⟩;
   Gaelic ⟨fierce⟩

Amelia (Amalie, Amelie,
   Emilia, Emilie, Emily):
   Latin ⟨industrious⟩, but
   with overtones of
   ⟨affectionate⟩

Amity: Latin ⟨friendship⟩

Anastasia (Anastassia,
   Nessa, Stacy, Stasey,
   Tasya): Greek
   ⟨resurrection, Easter, who
   shall rise again⟩

Andreanna: Greek ⟨a man's
   woman, fearless⟩

Angela (Angel, Angelica,
   Angeline, Angelique,
   Angelita, Angie): Greek
   ⟨angelic, heavenly
   messenger⟩

Annis (Annys): Greek
   ⟨whole, complete⟩

Ardeen: Latin ⟨ardent⟩

Ardis (Arda, Ardella,
   Ardelle, Ardelia,
   Ardene): Latin ⟨fervent,
   zealous⟩

Arnina (Arona; feminine
   for Aaron): Hebrew, of
   uncertain meaning
   ⟨mountain (?), singer(?),
   inspired(?)⟩

Astrid: Teutonic, especially
   Scandinavian ⟨strong in
   love⟩

Aurelia (Aurel, Aurelie):
   Latin ⟨golden⟩

Aurore (Aurora): Latin
   ⟨dawn⟩

Avis (Ava): Latin ⟨birdlike⟩

Aviva (Avivah): Hebrew
   ⟨springtime, youthfully
   fresh⟩

Babette (Hawaiian Babara:
   buh-BAH-ruh): Greek
   ⟨little Barbara, "stranger,
   foreigner"⟩; sometimes
   considered a diminutive
   of Elizabeth ⟨God has
   promised⟩

Benita: Spanish ⟨little Benedicta, "blessed"⟩

Bernadette (feminine of Bernard): Teutonic, French ⟨little strong one, little masterful one⟩

Bertha: Teutonic, French ⟨bright, beautiful⟩

Bonita: Spanish ⟨pretty and good⟩

Brenna: Celtic ⟨with raven tresses⟩

Brigid (Birgit, Bride, Bridget, Brietta, Brigette, Brighid, Brigida, Brigitta): Celtic, with forms in other languages ⟨protective, strong⟩

Camille (Camila, Camilla, Camellia): Greek, Latin ⟨assistant in religious ceremonies⟩

Cara: Gaelic ⟨friend⟩; Vietnamese ⟨precious jewel⟩

Carli: Teutonic, pet name for Caroline, feminine of Charles; also Carla, Carlita, Carlina, Karla ⟨little womanly one⟩

Carmel: Hebrew ⟨vineyard, fruitful field⟩

Carlotta: Italian form of Caroline, Carla

Cecilia (Cecelia, Cecile, Cecily, Celia; feminine of Cecil): Latin original means ⟨blind⟩, but St. Cecilia is the patron saint of music, hence ⟨musical⟩

Celesta (Celeste, Celestina, Celestine): Latin ⟨heavenly⟩

Chandra (CHAHN-druh): Hindi ⟨moon⟩

Charmaine (shar-MANE) (Charmain, Charma, Charmian): Greek ⟨joy, delight⟩

Claudia (feminine of Claude or Claudius; Claudette, Claudina, Claudine, Gladys): Latin ⟨little lame one⟩; sometimes interpreted as ⟨magnanimous⟩ because Emperor Claudius treated captives so well

Cora (Corena, Coretta, Corette, Corinna, Corinne): Greek ⟨maiden⟩

Coral: Greek, Latin ⟨coral⟩

Cordelia: Celtic ⟨daughter of the sea⟩; Latin ⟨warm-hearted⟩

Cornelia (feminine of Cornelius) (Cornella, Nella, Nellie): Latin ⟨queenly, womanly, enduring⟩

Dagmar: Teutonic, especially Danish ⟨glory of the Danes, joy of the land⟩

Damita (duh-MEE-tuh): Spanish ⟨little noble lady⟩

Daphne (Daphna): Greek ⟨laurel tree, laurel maiden, victorious⟩

Dawn: English
⟨dawn = Aurora⟩
Deirdre: Celtic ⟨sorrow,
compassion⟩
Delia: Greek ⟨from the
island of Delos; also short
for Cordelia, Adele⟩
Delphine (Delphina,
Delphinia): Greek ⟨calm,
serene; loving sister⟩
Desiree (DEZ-uh-REE):
Latin ⟨desired, desirable⟩
Dorene (Doreen, Dorena,
Dorenn, Dorine, Dorina):
Greek ⟨bountiful⟩
Dorinda: Greek ⟨she has
been given to us⟩
Dorisa (variant of Greek
Doris): Hawaiian ⟨from
the sea⟩

Edwina (feminine of
Edwin): Teutonic ⟨rich
friend⟩
Eldora: Teutonic ⟨gift of
wisdom⟩
Elfrida (Elfreda): Teutonic
⟨wise and peaceful⟩
Elise (variant of Elizabeth):
Hebrew ⟨God's promise⟩
Elma: Greek ⟨pleasant,
lovable⟩; English ⟨like an
elm⟩; Turkish (el-MUH)
⟨apple⟩
Elvira (el-VI-ruh): Spanish
⟨elfin⟩
Emilia (Emilie, Emily): Latin
⟨industrious⟩
Enid: Celtic ⟨pure in soul⟩;
English ⟨fair⟩
Enola (ay-NO-luh):

American Indian,
meaning unknown
Erica (Erika; feminine of
Eric): Greek ⟨the heather
flower⟩; Teutonic ⟨ever
regal⟩
Erlinda: Hebrew ⟨lively⟩
Ertha (Eartha, Erda):
Teutonic ⟨child of the
earth, earthly, earthy,
worldly, realistic⟩
Esmeralda: Latin ⟨adorned⟩;
Spanish ⟨emerald⟩
Eudice (ee-oo-DEES):
Modern Israeli form of
Hebrew Judith ⟨praise⟩
Eudora (Eudore); based on
Dora ⟨gift⟩): Greek
⟨splendid gift⟩
Eugenia (Eugenie, Gena,
Gina; feminine of
Eugene): Greek ⟨well-
born, of fortunate
parents⟩
Eula (Eulalia, Eulalie):
Greek ⟨sweet in speaking⟩
Eustacia (Eustacie): Greek
⟨rich in flowering; steady⟩
Evadne (ee-VAD-ne or ay-
VAD-ne): Greek ⟨sweet
singer⟩
Evangeline: Greek ⟨bearer
of good news⟩

Faith: Teutonic ⟨ever true,
always faithful⟩
Felcia (FEL-shuh): Polish,
from Latin Felicia
⟨happy⟩
Felicidad (Feliciana):
Spanish, from Latin

Felicia ⟨happy⟩

Fenella (Finella): Celtic ⟨white-shouldered⟩

Fiona: Greek ⟨violet⟩; Celtic ⟨fair-complexioned⟩

Flavia (feminine of Flavius): Latin ⟨light-haired⟩

Fleur (Fleurette): French ⟨flower⟩

Flora (Florence, Floria, Florinda, Floris): Latin ⟨flowers, blossoming⟩

Gabrielle (Gabriella; feminine of Gabriel): Hebrew ⟨heroine of God; God gives me strength⟩

Gari (feminine of Gary): Teutonic ⟨spear maiden⟩

Gerda: Scandinavian ⟨protected⟩

Gianina (juh-NEE-nuh), (feminine of Giovanni = John): Italian ⟨God is gracious⟩

Gillian (one of the most popular names in the Middle Ages; variant of Julia): English, from Latin ⟨youthful⟩

Gina (sometimes a variant of Eugenia): also Japanese ⟨silvery⟩

Gleda (GLED-uh): Icelandic ⟨make happy, gladden⟩

Glenna (feminine of Glen or Glenn): Gaelic ⟨from the valley⟩

Golda: Teutonic, Israeli ⟨golden-haired⟩

Greta: German, from Latin Margarita (Margaret, etc.) ⟨pearl⟩

Gwendolyn (Gwen, Gwendaline, Gwendolen, Gwendoline, Gwyn, Gwyneth, Wendy): Celtic ⟨white-haired, lady of the new moon⟩

Haidee (Haida): Greek ⟨modest⟩

Haley: modern U.S. ⟨clever, ingenious⟩

Helga: Scandinavian ⟨religious, pious⟩

Hilary (Hilaria): Latin ⟨cheerful, merry⟩

Iantha (Ianthe, Ianthine): Greek ⟨violet⟩

Ilona (Ilone): Greek ⟨a light⟩; Hungarian ⟨beautiful⟩

Ilse (Elsa, Else, Ilsa): Teutonic ⟨noble maiden⟩ (Also sometimes defined as a variant of Elizabeth)

Imogene (Imogen): Greek or Latin, meaning uncertain

Ingrid: Scandinavian, probably referring to Ingi, an early king

Iona (Ione, Ionia): Greek ⟨violet = Ianthe⟩ (Also Celtic, the name of a revered island where many Celtic kings are buried)

Irena (Irene, Russian Irina):
Greek ⟨peace⟩
Iris (Russian Irisa: i-REES-
uh): Greek ⟨rainbow;
goddess of the rainbow⟩
Isolde (Isolda): Celtic ⟨fair⟩
Ivy: Teutonic ⟨a clinging
vine, affectionate and
dependent⟩

Jacinta (jah-SIN-tuh;
Spanish: hah-SEEN-tah):
Greek ⟨hyacinth, purple⟩
Jamila (jah-MEE-lah):
Arabic ⟨beautiful⟩
Jasmine (In India, Yasmine,
Yasiman): Greek for the
flower of a climbing
shrub
Jocasta: Italian
⟨lighthearted⟩
Jocelyn (Jocelin): Latin
⟨playful, merry⟩
Joella (Joela, Joelle;
feminine of Joel):
Hebrew ⟨the Lord is
willing⟩
Johanna (feminine of
Johann = John): Hebrew
⟨God is gracious⟩
Joline (modern form of
Josephine, feminine of
Joseph): Hebrew ⟨she will
increase⟩
Juanita (Juana, Nita;
feminine of
Juan = John): Hebrew
through Spanish ⟨God is
gracious⟩
Juliet (Spanish Julieta: hoo-
lee-ET-ah; = Julia): Latin
⟨youthful⟩

Justina (Justine, Tina):
Latin ⟨the just one⟩

Kalila (kah-LEE-lah): Arabic
⟨sweetheart, loved one⟩
Kari: modern U.S. for
Carol, Caroline, or Carrie
⟨strong⟩; Hungarian form
of Karoly
Karla (Carla): also modern
U.S. for Carol, Caroline
⟨strong, womanly⟩
Kelilah (kuh-LEE-lah;
Kelula, Kyla, Kyle):
Hebrew ⟨laurel, crown,
victory⟩
Kenda: modern U.S. ⟨child
of cool, pure water⟩
Kristin (Kirsten, Kirstin,
Krysta): Scandinavian
⟨Christian⟩

Lala (LAH-lah): Slovak
⟨tulip⟩
Lara: Latin ⟨famous⟩;
Russian form of Larissa,
from Greek ⟨cheerful⟩
Lavinia (Lavenia, Lavina,
French Lavinne): Latin
⟨cleansed; woman of
Latium (religious city
near Rome)⟩
Leandra (feminine of
Leander): Greek ⟨lioness-
like⟩
Leila: Arabic ⟨dark beauty⟩
Leilani (lay-LAHN-ee):
Hawaiian ⟨heavenly child⟩
Leola: Teutonic ⟨dear⟩
Leonora (Lenora, Lenore,
Leonore): variant of

Eleanor = Greek Helen ⟨light⟩

Leticia (Letitia): Latin, now often Spanish ⟨joyous⟩

Lila: Hindi ⟨capriciousness of fate⟩; Persian ⟨lilac⟩; Polish, short for Leopoldine ⟨defender of the people⟩

Lilybet: Cornish form of Elizabeth ⟨God's promise⟩

Livana (lee-VAH-nuh; Levana): Hebrew ⟨moon; white⟩

Lola (diminutive of Lolita): Spanish form of Carol ⟨strong woman⟩

Lorna: Old English ⟨lost⟩; Latin (also Lara, Laureen, Laurel, Lauren, Lora, Loren, Loretta) ⟨laurel, victory⟩

Lucerne (Lucerna): Latin ⟨circle of light⟩

Lucita (loo-SEE-tah): Spanish ⟨(Mary of the) Light⟩

Luz (LOOS): also Spanish ⟨(Mary of the) Light⟩

Lydia: Greek ⟨girl from Lydia; cultured person⟩

Magda (MAHG-dah) (Magdalene, Spanish Madalena): Greek ⟨woman from Magdala⟩

Mahalia (Mahala: mah-HAH-luh): Hebrew ⟨woman, feminine tenderness⟩

Mara (MAH-ruh): variant of Hebrew Mary ⟨bitter⟩

Marcella (Marcelle, Marcelline): Latin feminine of Marcellus ⟨hammer⟩. Also said to be Teutonic ⟨intelligent contestant⟩

Margita: variant of Greek Margaret ⟨pearl⟩

Marta: variant of Aramaic Martha ⟨lady of the house, mistress⟩

Mavis (Mavia): Celtic ⟨singing thrush⟩

Meghan (Megan): Celtic ⟨strong⟩; Latin ⟨great⟩

Melina: Latin ⟨sweet as honey⟩

Melody (Melodie): Greek ⟨song, beautiful music⟩

Melvina (Melva): Latin ⟨sweet friend, sweet wine⟩

Merrie (Merry): English ⟨joyful⟩

Milada (MIL-uh-duh): Czech ⟨my love⟩

Millicent (Melicent, Mellicent, Millie): Latin ⟨sweet singer⟩; Teutonic ⟨good worker⟩

Minna (Minnie): Teutonic ⟨loving memories⟩

Mira (MEE-rah): modern Israeli for Miriam ⟨exalted⟩; sometimes considered a form of Mary

Miranda: Latin ⟨admirable, to be wondered at⟩

Mona: Latin ⟨solitary⟩; Teutonic ⟨lonely, far away⟩; North American Indian ⟨gathering the seed of the jimson weed⟩

Monica: Latin ⟨wise
counselor⟩

Morna (Myrna): Celtic
⟨tender beloved⟩

Nadia (nah-DEE-uh):
Russian ⟨hope⟩

Nadine: Russian ⟨hope⟩;
Greek ⟨charming⟩

Nanette (Nanetta): Hebrew
⟨little graceful one⟩

Natasha: Russian ⟨born on
Christmas⟩

Nelia (NELL-ee-yuh):
Spanish shortening of
Cornelia ⟨queenly,
womanly, enduring⟩

Nerissa: Greek ⟨daughter of
the sea⟩

Nola (Nolana): Latin ⟨little
bell⟩

Odele (Odell, Odelette):
Greek ⟨melody, song⟩

Olena (oh-LAY-nah;
Alena): Russian, from
Greek ⟨light⟩

Olga: Russian ⟨holy⟩

Olinda (Linda): Teutonic
⟨gentle⟩

Olivia (Oliva, Olive): Latin
⟨olive⟩ (a symbol of peace)

Onida (oh-NEE-dah): North
American Indian ⟨the
looked-for one, the
desired⟩

Oriana: Celtic ⟨golden,
dawning⟩

Pepita (pep-EE-tah):
Spanish from Hebrew

⟨she shall add, she shall
be fruitful⟩

Philantha: Greek ⟨she loves
flowers⟩

Philippa (feminine of
Phillip): Greek ⟨lover of
horses⟩

Phoebe (FEE-bee; Phebe):
Greek ⟨the moon goddess
(= Diana, Diane),
brilliant⟩

Pierrette (feminine of
Pierre = Peter): French
⟨little steadfast one⟩

Pilar (pee-LAR): Spanish
⟨pillar, foundation; refers
to Mary as the foundation
of the church⟩

Portia: Latin ⟨harbor,
gateway⟩

Ramona (Mona, Raymonde;
feminine of Ramon or
Raymond): Spanish or
Teutonic ⟨protector⟩

Rana (Ranee, Rani):
Hindustani ⟨queenly,
royal⟩

Ranita: modern Israeli
⟨joyful song⟩

Regina (Regine): Latin
⟨queenly⟩

Renee (reh-NAY): French
⟨reborn⟩

Risa: modern U.S. from
Latin ⟨laughter⟩

Roderica (Rica; feminine of
Roderick): Teutonic
⟨ruler, princess⟩

Rosabel: Latin ⟨beautiful
rose⟩

Rosaleen (Rosalie, Rosalind, Roselind, Rosina): Irish ⟨little rose⟩; Latin ⟨pretty rose⟩

Rowena: Celtic ⟨white-bosomed, white-clad, lighthaired⟩

Roxanne (Roxana, Roxane, Roxene, Roxie): Persian ⟨the new dawning⟩

Sabina (Bina, Savina): Latin ⟨girl of the Sabines⟩

Sabrina: from the name of an Anglo-Saxon princess

Sanura (suh-NOO-ruh): Swahili ⟨like a kitten⟩

Selena (Selene, Selina): Greek ⟨moonlight becomes you⟩

Serena: Latin ⟨girl with the tranquil heart⟩

Sigrid: Scandinavian ⟨beautiful conqueror⟩

Simone (Simona, Simonetta; feminine of Simon): Hebrew ⟨hearing gladly, obedient⟩

Sonia (Sona, Sonya): Greek ⟨the wise one⟩

Tabitha: Aramaic ⟨the gazelle, the graceful girl⟩

Talia (tuh-LEE-uh) (Talya): Hebrew ⟨the gentle dew from heaven⟩

Tamar (tuh-MAR) (Tamara, Tammie): Hebrew ⟨the palm tree⟩

Tania (Tanya): Russian ⟨the fairy queen⟩

Thalia: Greek ⟨luxuriant blossoms⟩ (In classical mythology, Thalia was the muse of comedy and was said also to be one of the three Graces.)

Theodora (Thea, Theda, Theo; feminine of Theodore): Greek ⟨God's gift⟩

Tilda (short for Matilda): Teutonic ⟨battle maiden⟩

Timmi (Timi, Timmy): modern U.S., from Hebrew Timothea ⟨she fears God⟩

Tonya (Toni, Tonia): Russian, from Latin Antonia (feminine of Antony) ⟨inestimable, beyond price⟩

Truda: Polish from Teutonic ⟨spear maiden⟩

Una (Ona, Oona): Latin ⟨unity, everything in one⟩; Hopi ⟨memory⟩

Undine: Latin ⟨of the waves⟩

Valda: Teutonic ⟨battle heroine⟩

Valentina (Valencia, Valerie, Valeria, Velora): Latin ⟨strong and healthy⟩

Vanessa (Vanni): Greek ⟨butterfly⟩ (Used by Jonathan Swift in his letters to Esther Vanhomrigh)

Velda: Teutonic ⟨wise⟩

Verda: Latin ⟨young, fresh, virginal⟩

Verna (Vernita): Latin ⟨spring-born, vernal⟩

Viviana (Vivian, Vivienne): Latin ⟨full of life⟩

Wanda: Teutonic, Slavic ⟨shepherdess, wandering one⟩

Wenona (wen-O-nuh): North American Indian ⟨firstborn daughter⟩

Wilda: Anglo-Saxon ⟨untamed⟩

Wilhelmina (Mina, Velma, Wilma; feminine of Wilhelm, William): Teutonic ⟨helmet, protector⟩

Willa: Teutonic ⟨resolute, firm⟩

Wilva: Teutonic ⟨determined⟩

Winifred; Teutonic ⟨friend of peace⟩

Yolanda (Yolande, Yolante): Greek ⟨violet, modest or shy⟩

Yvette (Yvonne): French, Teutonic ⟨carrier of the bow, archer⟩

Zada (ZAY-duh or ZAH-duh): Syrian ⟨the lucky⟩

Zara (Zarah, variant of Sarah): Arabic ⟨brightness in the east, princess⟩

Zelda (short for Griselda): Teutonic ⟨unconquerable heroine⟩

Zora (Zorah, Zorana, Zorina): Latin ⟨aurora=dawn⟩

Zuleika: Arabic ⟨fair and bright⟩

THE OLD MEN REMEMBER

When you and I were young, Maggie.

Who is Sylvia, what is she,
that all the swains adore her?

Nita, Juanita, ask thy soul why we must part—
Oh my darling, oh my darling,
Oh my darling Clementine—
lean thou on my heart.

My Bonnie lies over the ocean,
My Bonnie lies over the sea:
Sweet Leilani, heavenly flower,
Where Hilo Hattie does the Hilo hop,
Mademoiselle from Armentières,
You funny little Gigi,
Charmaine,
Lilli Marlene,
Oh bring back my Chloe to me.

How do you solve a problem like Maria?
Sweet Marie, come to me,
Maria Alena, Marianne,
All day, all night, Marian;
Though Mary is a grand old name,
and I loved Mary in the morning,
They call the wind Maria.

La vie en Rose:
Mexicali Rose, stop crying,
Honeysuckle Rose,
Rosemarie, I love you,
Sweet Rosie O'Grady, Rose of Tralee,
All my wild Irish Roses,
San Antonio Rose, Rosie the riveter,
Cracklin' Rosie.

Sunny.
Stella by starlight.
Estrellita.

Once in love with Amy—
I dreamed with my arms around Linda,
or Michelle, *ma belle*.
I dreamed of Jeanie with the light brown hair.
Jeannine, I dream of lilac time,
Dolores, Dolly (you're still glowin'),
Ida, sweet as apple cider,
Dinah, is there anyone finer,
Georgy girl,
Thoroughly modern Millie,

Nina, pretty ballerina,
Ravishing Ruby
—but always in love with Amy.

If you knew Susie like I knew Susie—
Wake up, little Susie. Wake up, Peggy Sue.
Lay down, Sally. Long tall Sally.
Wait till the sun shines, Nellie.
(It was from Aunt Dinah's quilting party
I was seeing Nellie home.)

Nola.
What Lola wanted, Lola got.

I lost my heart at the stage door canteen
—uh, something about Eileen.
I'll see you home again, Kathleen.
Good night, Irene.

Every little breeze seems to whisper Louise,
but poke salad Annie, sweet Betsy from Pike,
Mame, Annie Laurie, sweet Alice I like.

Frankie and Johnny were sweethearts—
Oh Genevieve, I'd have given the world.
Tangerine, with lips as red as flame.
You picked a fine time to leave me, Lucille.

Goodnight, ladies. Goodnight, ladies.
Do you remember, too?

2

CHOOSING NAMES FOR BOYS

The friends of young Pierre Fox of San Francisco kept making fun of his given name. His father, who had chosen it, was dead, and Pierre had no idea why a name so unusual in the United States had been selected for him. Learning that the governor of Delaware was also a Pierre, the boy wrote to him asking whether he liked the name and if he could suggest a good nickname for Pierre. Here is the governor's reply:

June 23, 1982

Dear Pierre:

    Thanks for taking the time to write to me about your name. My family taught me to be proud of my name, and you should be proud of yours, too. "Pierre" is a great name that goes way back in history, and you and I are lucky enough to be among the few people in the country who have it.

I can think of many other people named Pierre who are famous. Pierre Trudeau is the prime minister of Canada; Pierre Curie was a famous scientist; Pierre Auguste Renoir was a famous painter. And don't forget all those famous hockey players named Pierre.

My ancestors were French, and my namesake lived in France before the 1800s. Perhaps you have some French ancestors too, and that's why your dad chose your name.

My father's name is Pierre, and I have a son named Pierre. My son is twenty-two years old and very proud of his name. As for nicknames, I am called Pete, and that might be a good nickname for you.

You bet I will be your friend. There aren't many of us "Pierres" around, so we better stick together.

Your friend,
(s) Pierre S. du Pont

The governor might have suggested another appropriate nickname—Rocky, because Pierre, Peter, Pietro, and their equivalents mean ⟨rock⟩. One of the few puns in the New Testament is based on that fact. In Matthew 16:18 Jesus is reported as saying, "Thou art Peter, and upon this rock I will build my church."

"ASK FOR HIM
BY HIS RIGHT NAME"

A stranger in a Scottish village wanted to find Alexander White. He met a young woman and asked her,
"Cou'd you tell me fa'r ⟨where⟩ Sanny Fite lives?"
"Filk ⟨which⟩ Sanny Fite?"
"Muckle ⟨big⟩ Sanny Fite."
"Filk muckle Sanny Fite?"
"Muckle lang ⟨tall⟩ Sanny Fite."
"Filk muckle lang Sanny Fite?"
"Muckle lang gleyed ⟨squint-eyed⟩ Sanny Fite," shouted the stranger.

"Oh! It's Goup-the-lift ⟨stare-at-the-sky⟩ y'are seeking," cried the girl, "and fat the deavil dinna ye speer for ⟨and why the devil didn't you ask for⟩ the man by his richt name at ance?"

OUTDOORSY NAMES,
INDOORSY NAMES

If a baby boy is christened Jack or Sam instead of Theodore or Elbert, is the choice of name likely to influence his fortune?

William G. Gaffney (*Names*, March 1971) thinks that "names can influence character, personality, and occupation; and that (therefore) a parent can determine, or at least help to determine, his child's career by the *kind* of name he bestows."

As evidence Gaffney cites his study of U.S. Army officers' names—not the names of West Pointers but of those whose backgrounds and abilities had made it possible for them to work their way up through Officers Candidate Schools or by battlefield promotion. These men, much more frequently than in the general population, had simple names on their birth certificates—Jack, Tom, Bud, Bob, Sam, and the like—not John, Thomas, etc., and not Egbert or Lancaster, either.

His second study was of male college teachers. Very few Jacks or Buds, etc., were found there. Academic types (and presumably other indoor types) much more often than the law of averages would predict, had names such as Grove, Theodore, Lucius, Rodney, Prosser, Elbert, Wymberly, Linville, or Fordyce. "Children with unusual names tend to become bookish early in life and perhaps as a direct consequence, frequently end up as professors," Gaffney says.

He concludes, then, that his name dictates to a considerable extent a boy's future. There may be some truth in the conclusion, but we also have to remember that family background may be even more important. Parents who christen a boy Sam and parents who christen theirs Linville probably have different life-styles, different heritages, different educational levels (and hence different degrees of bookishness), and different aspirations. These factors affect first the choice of name and thereafter the boy's whole life.

THE BOWEN THEORY
OF EXECUTIVE
ADVANCEMENT

"An incredibly large proportion of the U.S. business leaders have very unusual first names. In fact, men with unusual names seem to rise to the front ranks of management out of all proportion to their numbers."

So Stephen N. Bowen (or S. Newton Bowen) said in 1973. His title was Director of Corporate Public Relations for TRW Inc., one of the nation's largest corporations.

Suppose, he said, that William Brown and T. Armstrong Ashburton are vying for a vice-presidency. "What will you bet that nine times out of ten Ashburton gets the nod? Obviously, he has an edge, a distinctive handle that separates him from the pack."

Bowen admitted that an occasional George, Bill, Bob, or Dick gets to the top—in General Motors, for instance. But in company after company, he said, top executives had less common names. (He looked at rosters of 1,000 companies.)

Cessna Aircraft—Dwayne, Delbert, Virgil, Pierre, Derby, and Max

Brown Foreman Distillers Corp.—Robinson, Rodman, Peyton, Mason, and Owsley Frazier and Owsley Brown II

Officers of various financial institutions—Gaylord, Freeman, Montgomery, Dorsey, Marriner Eccles, Pope Brook, True Davis

An initial instead of a first name is often effective, too. Bowen referred to O. Pendleton Thomas, I. John Billera, and J. Paul Getty. Repetition of the same initial isn't bad, either: W.W. Keller, H.H. Wetzel, and "R.R....does wonders for President Smith of Smith's Transfer Corp. But for ringing redundancy, my favorite is the chairman of Norman, Craig, and Kummel: Norman B. Norman."

The use of Junior or even Jr. is questionable, maybe even when a son is expected to inherit a company or a presidency.

Suppose that you are about to choose a name for a son (Bowen didn't consider daughters), and that family background suggests that he is likely to go into business. What should you name him?

Bowen suggested that you look at a list of forenames of the sort often appended to desk dictionaries. "Try names like Basil, Derek, Garth, Royal, Sterling, Yale, or even Zane. Each of those has a commanding aura to it almost guaranteed to make personnel managers snap to attention."

Bowen didn't mention what is sometimes another excellent choice for a first or middle name: the mother's maiden name. In all likelihood Armstrong in T. Armstrong Ashburton was little Tommy's mother's name. (By the way, what's a nickname for Armstrong? Army?)

NOT A SISSY NAME

In an Arizona gubernatorial primary, the first name of the incumbent (and eventual winner) was Bruce. One of his opponents attained a new low in mud-slinging by suggesting that that name was effeminate: "It surprises me that a state like Arizona, home of macho men, would ever elect a governor named Bruce."

A little knowledge of history might have helped him. The name gets its popularity from the Scottish national hero, Robert the Bruce or Robert de Bruce (1274–1329), who near Bannockburn on June 23–24, 1314, brilliantly outmaneuvered the English even though his Scots were outnumbered more than three to one. He drove out the English and as a result succeeded in establishing an independent Scottish monarchy that would last almost 300 years. In 1964, 650 years after that battle, Queen Elizabeth II of England renewed his memory by unveiling an equestrian statue of him at Bannockburn.

IF YOU HAVE
A HUNDRED SONS

An old Arabic saying is "If you have a hundred sons call them all Muhammad." A prolific Arab and his several wives and many concubines would thus presumably be paying great homage to the Prophet.

Whether any Arab ever followed this advice literally is

unknown. But a Scot did as well as he could in a similar attempt.

Many Scots in the early eighteenth century were resentful because a Stuart was no longer on the throne of Great Britain. James Francis Edward Stuart (1688–1766), son of the deposed King James II, and later the king's grandson, Charles Edward Louis Philip Casimir Stuart (1720–1788), became known in turn in England as "The Pretender." The latter, Charles Edward, was widely called by the Scots "Bonnie Prince Charlie." In Scotland these Stuarts were considered the legitimate rulers, and battles, such as the famous one at Culloden Moor, were fought in their behalf.

One fervent Scot, whose wife bore him fourteen sons, named each of them Charles Edward, in honor of the bonnie prince.

PERHAPS THE FIRST CHOICE
WAS BETTER

In 1943 (during World War II), a couple named Mittel in Astoria, New York, named their baby Adolf Hitler Mittel. Newspapers picked up the story, and public pressure became so great that the little boy was renamed.

This time the choice was Theodore Roosevelt Mittel.

Twenty-nine years later, in the *Bulletin* of the American Names Society, Robert N. Rennick reported the sad story of what happened to Theodore as he grew older. At the age of nine he was arraigned for pushing a six-year-old off a pier, causing the child to drown. At sixteen, when arrested as the leader of a burglary gang, he pointed an automatic at a policeman. But that gun, as well as a zip gun, was taken from him by another officer. Charged with eighty-five burglaries, Theodore Roosevelt Mittel was sentenced to a reformatory. Out on parole, he stole a truck, and a little later he was indicted on two counts of grand larceny and sentenced to Sing Sing.

TWO HUNDRED FIFTY
SLIGHTLY OFFBEAT NAMES
FOR BOYS

The names in this list were chosen in the same manner as the girls' names on pages 25–34. Excluded are the most conventional names such as John and William, currently very popular names such as Jason and Christopher, and seemingly far-out names such as Ablu and Guyapi.

Included are a few old-fashioned names that perhaps deserve renewed popularity, such as August and Orville, a variety of rather infrequently used but attractive names such as Baird and Emlyn, and other names, such as Ahmad and Casimir, now popular with only certain segments of the population.

Where appropriate, some of the alternative forms or approximate synonyms are listed. A few pronunciations are given, although these may vary with individuals or national subgroups. The usual national or linguistic origin is shown, but sometimes a name may also be derived from other sources and perhaps have different meanings. Note that many masculine given names are taken from surnames and place names, and for that reason do not supposedly describe or characterize, as do most feminine names.

Abel: Hebrew ⟨breath⟩

Adair: Celtic ⟨ford at the oak tree⟩ ⟨a descendant of Edgar "rich spear"⟩

Addison: English ⟨descendant of Adam "red earth"⟩

Adel (Adal): Teutonic ⟨noble⟩

Adrian (Adrien, Spanish Adriano): Latin ⟨from Adria (an ancient town in central Italy)⟩

Ahmad (AH-mahd; Ahmed): Arabic ⟨highly praised⟩

Alain (ah-LANE; French variant of Alan): Celtic ⟨handsome, cheerful⟩

Alano (ah-LAH-no; Spanish version of Alan): Celtic ⟨handsome, cheerful⟩

Alban (Alben, Albin): Latin ⟨white, dawn's early light⟩

Alden (Aldin): Anglo-Saxon ⟨old friend⟩

Aldous (Aldis): Teutonic ⟨old, wise⟩

Alek (Alik; Russian variant of Alexander): Greek ⟨he helps people⟩

Alger: Teutonic ⟨old spear, experienced spear, elf spear⟩

Alistair (Alastair, Allister; variant of Alexander): Greek ⟨he helps people⟩

Angelo (Angel): Greek ⟨messenger with good news, angelic⟩

Anson: Anglo-Saxon ⟨son of Ann⟩

Arden (Ardin): Latin ⟨eager, fervent, sincere⟩

Ardmore: Latin and Teutonic ⟨more ardent, more fervent⟩

Armand (Armando, Armin,

Armond, Ormond;
Russian Arman (ar-
MAHN): Latin, Teutonic
⟨armed, protective⟩
Arvin: Teutonic ⟨friend of
the people⟩
Ashley: Anglo-Saxon ⟨ash
tree grove⟩
August (Augustine,
Augustus, Austin): Latin
⟨imperial, exalted,
revered⟩
Averill (Averil, French
Avril): French ⟨born in
April⟩; Teutonic ⟨boar
battle⟩ (Also from an
English place name,
Haverhill ⟨oat hill⟩)
Avery (Aubrey; sometimes a
variant of Averil): Anglo-
Saxon ⟨ruler of the elves⟩

Baird: Celtic ⟨bard, minstrel⟩
Baldwin: Teutonic ⟨noble or
bold friend⟩
Barnabas (Barnaby):
Hebrew, Aramaic
⟨consoling son, son of
prophecy⟩
Barton: Anglo-Saxon ⟨he
holds the land⟩ (Also a
place name)
Beldon (Belden): Anglo-
Saxon ⟨on the hill⟩
Bellamy: Latin ⟨beautiful
friend⟩
Bennett (Benedict, Bennet):
Latin ⟨blessed⟩
Benton: Anglo-Saxon, a
place name of uncertain
meaning

Berggren (Bergren):
Scandinavian ⟨mountain
branch⟩ (Bergen or Bergin
is ⟨hill or mountain
dweller⟩)
Bertram (Bartram):
Teutonic ⟨bright raven,
he shall be famous⟩
Blair: Teutonic, Celtic ⟨boy
from the plains⟩
Blake: Teutonic. May mean
either ⟨dark⟩ or ⟨light⟩
Bond: English, Icelandic ⟨he
stays with the soil⟩
Boris: Slavic ⟨fighter,
stranger⟩
Bowen: Welsh ⟨son of Owen
"warrior"⟩
Bradford: Anglo-Saxon
⟨from the broad ford⟩
Brendan (Brandon,
Brendon, Brennan):
Scandinavian, but not
uncommon in Ireland
⟨aflame, inspirational⟩
Brice (Bryce): Celtic ⟨awake,
ambitious⟩
Burgess (Burges): Anglo-
Saxon ⟨from the town or
borough⟩
Burke (Burk): Teutonic
⟨fortress, stronghold⟩
Burton (Berton): Anglo-
Saxon ⟨village near a fort⟩
Byron: English ⟨from the
cottage⟩ (Often named
for the poet, George
Gordon, Lord Byron)

Carlos: Spanish form of
Charles ⟨manly⟩

Carmichael: Celtic
⟨Michael's stronghold⟩

Carvel: Manx (the Isle of
Man) ⟨a song⟩

Casimir: Slavic ⟨he
proclaims peace⟩

Cedric: Celtic ⟨chieftain⟩

Chalmer (Chalmers):
Teutonic ⟨head of a
household, chamberlain⟩

Chandler: English
⟨candlemaker, he
provides light⟩

Charlton (Carleton, Carlton,
Charleton): Anglo-Saxon
⟨from Charles's
homestead⟩

Clay: Teutonic ⟨of the
earth, mortal⟩

Clement (Clemence): Latin
⟨merciful, kind⟩

Clive (Cleve): From an
English surname; also
Teutonic ⟨cliff⟩

Clovis: from a medieval
French ruler, from whose
name Louis is also
derived; also Teutonic
⟨famous warrior⟩

Colin (Cole): sometimes
shortened from Nicholas;
also Celtic ⟨young and
virile⟩

Conroy: Celtic ⟨persistent⟩

Corbin: Latin ⟨the raven⟩

Coryell: Greek ⟨helmeted,
ready for battle⟩

Crispian (Crispin): Latin
⟨curly-haired⟩

Crispus: from Crispus
Attucks, first man killed
in American Revolution

Culver: English ⟨dove,
peace-loving⟩

Dag (DAHG): Scandinavian
⟨day, brightness⟩

Dallas: Celtic, from a
Scottish place

Damek (DAHM-ek): Czech
form of Adam ⟨man of
the red earth⟩

Damian (Damien): Greek
⟨taming, he makes people
gentle⟩

Dana (Dane): Scandinavian
⟨a Dane⟩; also short for
Hebrew Daniel ⟨judged
by God⟩

Dante (DAHN-tee or
DAHN-tay; sometimes
anglicized to DAN-tee):
from the name of the
medieval Italian poet;
Latin ⟨lasting⟩

Delmar (Delmer): Latin ⟨of
the sea⟩

Desmond: French ⟨of the
world, sophisticated⟩; also
an Irish surname ⟨one
from South Munster⟩

Dexter: Latin ⟨right-
handed, dexterous⟩

Donovan: Celtic ⟨dark
warrior⟩

Doran: Greek ⟨a gift⟩; Celtic
⟨a stranger⟩

Dorian: Greek, uncertain
meaning

Dougal (Doyle, Dugald):
Celtic ⟨dark stranger⟩

Drew: English shortening of
Hebrew Andrew ⟨manly⟩

Drummond: Celtic ⟨he lives
on the hilltop⟩
Duncan: Celtic ⟨swarthy
chief⟩
Durward: Teutonic
⟨unfailing guard⟩

Edson (Edison): English
⟨son of Ed⟩
Einar (I-nar; Danish Ejnar):
Scandinavian
⟨nonconformist, he thinks
for himself⟩
Eldred (Eldrid): Teutonic
⟨battle counselor⟩
Ellery: Teutonic ⟨the alder
tree⟩
Ellsworth (Elsworth): Anglo-
Saxon place name ⟨Elli's
place⟩
Elmo: Latin, from Greek
⟨friendly, lovable⟩
Elwin (Elwyn, Wynn):
Anglo-Saxon ⟨Godly
friend⟩
Emlyn: Welsh ⟨waterfall⟩
Emory (Emery, Italian
Amerigo—for whom
America was named):
Teutonic ⟨work, rule⟩
Errol: usually a variant of
English Earl ⟨nobleman⟩;
sometimes Latin
⟨wandering⟩
Esmond: English ⟨protected
by God's grace⟩
Ethan: Hebrew ⟨steadfast,
strong and reliable⟩
Eustace (YOO-stus): Greek
⟨productive⟩
Evan (EE-vuhn or EH-
vuhn): Welsh form of

John ⟨God is gracious⟩
Everard: Teutonic ⟨always
true; strong as a wild
boar⟩

Fabian (Fabiano): Latin
from Fabius, a dilatory
general; hence implies
⟨procrastinating,
indecisive⟩; original
meaning ⟨bean grower⟩
Fairfax: English ⟨light-
haired⟩
Felipe (feh-LEE-peh):
Spanish for Greek Phillip
⟨lover of horses⟩
Fergus: Gaelic ⟨strong man⟩
Flavian: Latin Flavius
⟨yellow-haired⟩
Fletcher: English surname
⟨arrow-maker⟩
Florian: Latin ⟨flowering⟩
Fulton: English place name
⟨poultry farm⟩

Gabriel: Hebrew ⟨hero of
God, God gives him
strength⟩
Garrick: Teutonic (English)
place name and surname
(a leading eighteenth-
century actor) ⟨Gara's
place⟩
Gaspar (Caspar, Casper,
Gaspard, Jasper, Kaspar,
Kasper): Spanish from
Persian ⟨master of
treasure⟩
Gavin (Galvin): variant of
Celtic Gawain ⟨white
hawk⟩
Giles: Greek, Latin ⟨shield-

bearer; young goat⟩

Glendon: Celtic ⟨from the shady valley⟩

Godfrey: Teutonic ⟨divinely peaceful⟩

Goodwin (Godwin): English ⟨good friend, God's friend⟩

Graham: Celtic ⟨from the gray home⟩

Granville: French ⟨large estate⟩

Gregor (Gregorio, Gregory, Grigor): Greek ⟨vigilant⟩

Griffith (Griffin): Welsh ⟨fierce lord; red-haired, ruddy⟩

Grover: English surname ⟨one who lives in or near a grove⟩

Gunnar (GOO-nahr) (Gunther): Scandinavian ⟨warrior⟩

Gustave (Gustaf, Gustavus): Scandinavian ⟨noble staff, God's staff⟩

Guthrie: Celtic ⟨war hero⟩, or Celtic place name ⟨where the wind blows free⟩

Hale: Anglo-Saxon ⟨in good health⟩; also an English place name and surname ⟨nook, corner⟩; also Hawaiian (pronounced HAH-lee) for Harold ⟨army ruler⟩

Hamilton: English place name and surname (sometimes spelled Hambleton) ⟨grassy hill⟩

Hanley: English place name and surname ⟨high meadow⟩; Irish ⟨warrior⟩

Hartwell: English place name ⟨deer's spring, where the deer drink⟩

Hassan: Arabic ⟨handsome⟩

Hendrik (Enrico, Hendrick, Henri): Dutch variant of Henry ⟨ruler of the home⟩

Heywood: English place name ⟨high or enclosed wood⟩

Hilliard: Teutonic ⟨war guard⟩; most often from the English surname ⟨enclosure on a hill⟩

Holbrook: English surname ⟨stream in the valley⟩

Houston: Scottish surname ⟨Hugh's town⟩

Igor (Inge, Ingmar): Scandinavian, Slavic ⟨hero⟩

Ingmar (Ingemar): Scandinavian ⟨well-known son⟩

Ingram (Ingraham): from the English surname based on Scandinavian Ing, a mythical hero ⟨Ing's raven⟩

Ivar (EE-vahr) (Ives, Ivor, Yves): Scandinavian ⟨archer with a yew bow⟩

Jacinto (hah-SEEN-toh): Spanish from Greek ⟨purple, hyacinth⟩

Jared: Hebrew ⟨descendant, the inheritor⟩

Jasper (Casper, Gaspar, Kasper): English from Persian ⟨master of treasure⟩

Javier (hahv-ee-AIR; Xavier): Arabic ⟨bright⟩; Spanish (Basque) ⟨he has a new home⟩

Jens (JENZ; or Scandinavian YENS): Scandinavian form of John ⟨God is gracious⟩

Jeremy (Jeremiah, Jerry): Hebrew ⟨exalted by God⟩

Joel: Hebrew ⟨the Lord is God⟩

Jonas: Hebrew ⟨the dove, peace⟩; Lithuanian form of John ⟨God is gracious⟩

Jorge (HOHR-heh): Spanish equivalent of George ⟨farmer⟩

Julian (JOO-lee-uhn; or Spanish HOO-lee-AHN): from Latin Julius ⟨youthful, downy-cheeked⟩

Junius: Latin ⟨forever young⟩

Justin (Justus): English from Latin ⟨the just⟩

Kendall: English place name ⟨valley of the Kent River⟩

Kendrick: Anglo-Saxon ⟨royal rule⟩

Kenyon: English place name ⟨Einion's mound⟩; also from Celtic Fingin ⟨light-haired⟩

Kerry: Celtic ⟨dark⟩; English ⟨ship captain⟩

Kester: Dutch place name; sometimes a form of Greek Christopher ⟨Christ-bearer⟩

Kimball: English place name ⟨royal hill⟩

Konane (ko-NAH-nee): Hawaiian ⟨bright moonlight⟩

Kyle: English, Scottish ⟨strait, firth, narrow waterway⟩

Lambert: Teutonic ⟨his country's light⟩

Lance: Short for Latin Lancelot (Launcelot) ⟨he who serves⟩

Landon: Anglo-Saxon ⟨from the long hill⟩

Langley: Anglo-Saxon ⟨from the long meadow or wood⟩

Lars: Scandinavian form of Lawrence ⟨laurel, victory⟩

Leander: Greek ⟨like a lion⟩

Lionel: French ⟨little lion⟩

Llewellyn: Welsh ⟨lionlike, lightning⟩

Lorant (LOH-rawnt): Hungarian, from Latin ⟨laurel, victory⟩

Lucien (Lucian): French, from Latin Lucius ⟨light⟩ (A name sometimes given to a child born at dawn)

Madison: English from Hebrew Matthew ⟨God's

light⟩ (In U.S. sometimes from President James Madison)

Malcolm: Scottish ⟨follower of St. Columba "dove"⟩

Manfred: Teutonic ⟨man of peace⟩

Manuel (mah-noo-EL) (Emmanuel): Spanish ⟨God be with us⟩

Mayer (Meyer, Myer): Teutonic ⟨farmer⟩

Maynard: Teutonic ⟨strong and steady⟩

Merton: Anglo-Saxon ⟨from the place by the sea⟩

Merwyn (Mervin, Merwin): Celtic ⟨friend of the sea⟩

Morgan: Welsh ⟨sea-dweller⟩

Morley: English place name ⟨wood by a marsh⟩

Murray: Scottish ⟨one from the sea⟩, or the place Moray ⟨beside the sea⟩

Neville: French place name ⟨new town⟩

Newton: English and Scottish place name and surname ⟨new town⟩

Nigel (NIGH-jul): Greek, Latin ⟨dark⟩

Noel: French from Latin ⟨Christmas, Christmas carol⟩

Nolan: Celtic ⟨famous, noble⟩

Norbert: Teutonic ⟨brightness of the north⟩

Oakley: Anglo-Saxon ⟨oak tree grove⟩

Odell: Teutonic ⟨prosperous⟩; English place name ⟨woad hill⟩

Ogden (Ogdon): Anglo-Saxon ⟨oak valley⟩

Olaf: name of several Scandinavian kings ⟨ancestral relic⟩

Orlando (Roland, Spanish Roldan): Italian, Spanish ⟨from the famous land⟩

Ormond (Ormand): Irish place name; also Teutonic ⟨protector⟩

Osmond (Osmont, Osmund): Teutonic ⟨divine protector⟩

Palmer: English ⟨palm-carrying crusader⟩

Parker: English surname ⟨keeper of a park, gamekeeper⟩

Pavel (PAH-vyel): Slavic for Paul ⟨small⟩

Pembroke: Welsh place name ⟨headland⟩

Porter: English from Latin ⟨gatekeeper, one who carries goods⟩

Prentice (Prentiss): English and French, from Latin ⟨learner, apprentice⟩

Prescott: English place name ⟨priest's cottage⟩

Preston: English place name and surname ⟨priest's place⟩

Raoul: French form of
Teutonic Ralph,
Randolph ⟨protection,
wolf⟩

Raphael: Hebrew ⟨God
heals⟩

Redmond: Teutonic
⟨adviser, protector⟩

Rico (REE-coh): Spanish,
Italian shortening of
Enrico; Teutonic
Heinrich or Henry ⟨ruler
of the home⟩

Roald (ROO-ahld):
Scandinavian ⟨famous
ruler⟩

Roderick (Roderic, Spanish
and Portuguese Rodrigo):
Teutonic ⟨rich in fame⟩

Roscoe: Teutonic ⟨from the
deer forest⟩; also an
English place name

Rupert (Ruppert; variant of
Robert): Teutonic ⟨bright
fame⟩

Sandor (Sander, Sanders):
Slavic, Hungarian form
of Greek Alexander ⟨he
helps people⟩

Schuyler: Dutch ⟨scholar,
teacher⟩

Sean (SHAWN) (Shane,
Shawn): Celtic form of
John ⟨God is gracious⟩

Selby (Shelby): English
place name and surname
⟨place of willows or copse⟩

Sherman: English surname
⟨shearer of wool⟩

Sherwin: Teutonic ⟨swift

runner⟩ (literally "cutting
the wind"); Anglo-Saxon
⟨bright friend⟩

Sherwood: English place
name ⟨shire forest⟩

(Siegfried (SEEG-freed)
(Siegfrid, Sigfrid,
Sigvard): Teutonic
⟨glorious peace⟩

Sigurd (SEE-gerd):
Scandinavian ⟨victorious
guardian⟩

Sinclair (St. Clair): Scottish,
English from French
place name ⟨bright, clear⟩

Slade: English ⟨child of the
valley⟩

Stanford (Stafford): English
place name ⟨stony ford⟩

Sumner: English, French
⟨summoner (a minor
official who summoned
people to appear in
court)⟩

Sylvester (Silas, Silvan,
Silvester, Sylvan,
Sylvander): English from
Latin ⟨forest dweller⟩

Terrill (Terrell): Teutonic
⟨descended from Thor
the powerful⟩

Thor: Scandinavian king of
the gods

Thoreau (thuh-ROH):
usually from the nature
writer and pacifist Henry
David Thoreau, based on
a French form of
Theodore ⟨gift of God⟩

Thornton: English place

name ⟨thorny place⟩

Tomas (Spanish: toh-MAHS; Slavic: TOH-mahs) (Thom, Thomas): Greek, Aramaic ⟨a twin⟩

Townsend: English surname ⟨from the edge of the town⟩

Travis (Travers): English surname ⟨crossroads⟩

Tristram (Tristan): Celtic, Latin ⟨sad face, sorrowful⟩

Tyrone: Celtic, meaning uncertain

Upton: English place name ⟨town or village on the hill⟩

Vaughn (VAWN) (Vaughan): Celtic ⟨little⟩

Veryl (Verald, Verrill): Teutonic ⟨manly⟩

Walden (Waldo): English place name ⟨forested valley⟩; Teutonic Wald ⟨forest⟩

Welby: English place name ⟨farm by a spring⟩

Whitney: Teutonic ⟨from the white island⟩; English place name and surname ⟨white island⟩

Wilfred (Wilfrid): Teutonic ⟨determined peacemaker⟩

Winfield: Teutonic ⟨friend of the soil⟩; English place name, Wingfield ⟨place for grazing⟩

Winston: English place name and surname ⟨Winec's or Wine's home⟩

Winthrop: English place name and surname ⟨Wina's farm, (possibly) friendly village⟩

Woodburn: English place name and surname ⟨stream in the forest⟩

Woodley: English place name ⟨wooded meadow, wooded flat area⟩

Wylie (Wiley): English place name with various meanings, including that of the Wiley River ⟨tricky⟩ (As a personal name, may be interpreted as ⟨clever, resourceful⟩)

Xavier: Arabic ⟨bright⟩

Yale: English ⟨from a secluded place⟩

York: English place name ⟨where the yew trees grow⟩

Zale: Greek ⟨power of the sea⟩

Zane: Rare English form of John ⟨God is gracious⟩

3

FADS
AND FANCIES
IN BESTOWING
(OR INFLICTING)
NAMES

READY FOR CHIPS
OFF THE OLD BLOCK

According to Arlene Gregory of Delaware, Ohio, a man from that place, named Douglas Fir Trees, married Jane Wood.

Ms. Gregory reports that other members of the Trees family are also named for tree varieties. With the aid of a tree manual, the family could come up with some fine names indeed.

One of the most beautiful for a girl might be Carolina Silver Bell Trees, although Carolina also goes with Water Ash, Cherry, Red Maple, and Poplar.

Georgia wouldn't be bad, either, with Georgia Oak Trees as one possibility, followed naturally in the Buckeye state by Georgia Buckeye Trees. Georgia Hackberry Trees leaves something to be desired.

The pine family offers some good ones: Rosemary Pine Trees, Virginia Pine Trees, Walter Pine Trees, and Jack Pine Trees.

Myrtle is also good—maybe just Myrtle Trees—or possibly Myrtle Holly Trees or Myrtle Oak Trees, but certainly not Wax Myrtle Trees. Holly Trees, minus Myrtle, would be especially suitable for a Christmastime baby.

Laurel Trees would be attractive, as would Magnolia Trees, and Laurel Magnolia Trees has a good rhythm.

Maybe we should be dubious about Honey Locust Trees, Juneberry Trees, and Mimosa Trees, and Tupelo Gum Trees sounds a little messy.

The Trees family can eliminate most tree-names with no more than a glance. No Big-toothed Aspen Trees, for example. Hairy Balm-of-Gilead Trees would have to be spelled Harry. Slippery Elm sounds like a poor choice, too, and so do some of the hickories such as Pignut, Mockernut, and Kingnut. Hoary Basswood and Bastard White Oak haven't a chance.

Some of the oaks have rather unpleasant names: Cow Oak, Possum Oak, Turkey Oak, and Scrub Chestnut Oak. The Hog Plum isn't much better.

Nobody would name a baby Pawpaw Trees. There's a comic-strip character named Lolly, but Loblolly Bay Trees would be ridiculous. Believe it or not, there's a Farkleberry tree, also known as Sparkleberry or Tree Huckleberry. Huckleberry did all right for Mark Twain's leading boy, but that name hasn't caught on outside of Hannibal, Missouri.

NUMBERING ONE'S CHILDREN

In some families of ancient Rome at least some of the sons might be given numbers to indicate the order of birth. The fifth son, Quintus, was often given a number, perhaps because it was at that point when some families had exhausted their supply of favorite names. Sextus, Septimus, and Octavius may have been based on paternal boastfulness.

If the Romans had been consistent, they could have named ten sons Primus, Secundus, Tertius, Quartus, Quintus, Sextus, Septimus, Octavius, Novus, and Decimus.

In modern times there is much less numbering, especially

when birthrates fall. However, a former heavyweight boxing champion, the Italian Primo ⟨first⟩ Carnera, had a younger brother named Secondo. In English, Quentin, derived from Quintus, is the most likely choice, and some parents who don't know Latin have used it even for a firstborn. There's a rather rare feminine version of it, Quintilla. Octavius and the feminine Octavia are now rare, but were still fairly common a hundred years or so ago. Primus, Secundus, and Septimus are listed in some books of forenames, but are rarely used.

THE WILD POPPY

Asked why she had named her twins Morphine and Opium, a young mother explained: "Well, I read in a paper that morphine and opium is products of a wild poppy. The poppy of these younguns was jist about as wild a man as I've ever knowed."

In another community a girl who was one family's great hope and joy went away to college, promising that she would come back with a diploma. Instead she came back pregnant. When a baby girl was born, of course she was named Diploma.

That was perhaps a better name than the two bestowed on the offspring of another girl who had gone astray and then gone back home. She called her twins Saffilis and Gonora. (Sodom and Gomora were the choices of still another young woman.)

And who knows what was in the minds of the couple who called *their* twins Max and Climax?

NEWS AFFECTS NAMING

In the years after William the Conqueror and his Norman followers defeated the English at the Battle of Hastings in 1066, William became one of the most popular names for infant boys.

The tendency to choose names related to current or recent events has existed ever since. Bill Schemmel of Decatur, Georgia, wrote a brief article for *Harper's* about names chosen in the 1960s and 1970s for children born in a large Atlanta hospital.

The presidency of John F. Kennedy, Schemmel reported, led not unexpectedly to many John Fitzgeralds and also to a

Gerald Fitzgerald and a Joan F. Kennedy, and Jacqueline's name was somewhat echoed by Jacka Lyon and Jackalette. The Kennedy assassination had unfortunate onomastic results such as Lee Harvey, Ozzwald Fitzgerald, Rotunda Cortege, and Flame Eternal. The marriage of the former Mrs. Kennedy to Aristotle Onassis led to many Aristotles, Athenas, and Olympias, as well as to an Airy Onassa and Jackie Canasta.

A 1967 peace discussion between President Lyndon Baines Johnson of the U.S. and Aleksei Kosygin of the USSR brought a flurry of peace-hopeful names, including Linden Alex, Banes Alexander, and Alexi Banes, as well as Alexa for some girls.

The hurricane Camille, in 1968, caused a temporary run on that name, according to Schemmel. And Watergate aroused so much interest in everyone involved that such combinations as Rodino Talmadge (for two prominent participants in the hearings) were made up. Perhaps the strangest name was in recollection of presidential adviser John Ehrlichmann. A little Atlanta girl was named Earlic Ann Mann.

YOU MEAN THERE'S MORE THAN ONE BARBARA WALTERS?

A relative of the author of this book is named Ann Landers. Unlike the more famous Ann, she doesn't like to answer letters or to give advice. She says that except for an occasional surprised eyebrow, doubting look, or chuckling inquiry, her name has caused her little trouble.

But sharing a name with a celebrity sometimes does present very special problems.

For example, consider John Hancock, from northern Indiana. A salesman said to him, "Just put your John Hancock on this line." So John wrote "John Hancock," and the salesman almost hit him. "Smart guy!" the salesman exclaimed. "I need *your* signature, not that of the fella that signed the Declaration of Independence. Or—was it the Constitution?"

John's new wife happened to have a policy that she had taken out earlier with the John Hancock insurance company.

She called the company concerning a change she wanted to make. When she said, "This is Mrs. John Hancock," the company representative hung up.

The John Kennedys, some of them lifelong Republicans, are numerous—eleven of them in a Manhattan phonebook, for instance, including one John F. Imagine the situations that must have arisen for some of them when a different John Kennedy was president.

During the Watergate hearings, Richard Nixons from coast to coast reportedly received occasional crank calls, most often from drunks in the middle of the night.

Lynell Mickelson, writing in the Knight-Ridder Newspapers, quotes from an elderly Warren Harding of Duluth: "I'm no relation to that fellow. My middle name is Lloyd, not Gamaliel. I was president of my eighth grade class before he ever became president, and I was named after my uncle in Nebraska."

Ronald Reagan, a Minneapolis Democrat, got uncounted congratulatory phone calls on election night in 1980, including some from people who tried not very successfully to fake the voice of loser Jimmy Carter. (Maybe one of them really *was* a Jimmy Carter.) Mr. Reagan later had to list his phone under his wife's first initial, remarking thankfully that her name doesn't start with *N*.

Mickelson also tells of a Roman Catholic priest, the Reverend William Graham, who finds the Southern Baptist Reverend Billy Graham "immensely tedious," but who jokes, "I'm thinking of changing my name to Karol Wojtyla"—the pre-papal name of Pope John Paul II.

Barbara Walters, a Minneapolitan, wasn't born with that name. She was Barbara Ryberg before she married a Walters in 1977, when the TV news anchorwoman and her million-dollar contract were much in the news. "Suddenly," says Mickelson, "simple things, like withdrawing money from the bank, drew wisecracks. Cashing checks in stores inspired Baba Wawa imitations from total strangers." One compensation: other strangers told her she looked much younger than she did on TV.

Divorced now, Barbara will make sure that her next husband isn't named Mandrell or Streisand.

WHAT EVER HAPPENED TO
SIX-TOED PETE?

Bob Riedy, an Arizonan who does radio broadcasts about the old days, bemoans the passing of picturesque nicknames, especially those that focused on physical imperfections. "When the scene was young," he says, "we had robust monickers like 'Big Nose Kate,' 'Johnny behind the Deuce,' 'Three-finger Brown,' 'Six-toed Pete,' and 'Peg-leg Smith.'" Now we settle for a commonplace substitute like "Tex."

"'Cherry Creek Red,'" says Riedy, "would no more have answered to his given name, Bernard, than admit to drinking sarsaparilla. 'The Cuban Queen' would have scratched the eyes out of anyone who addressed her as Amelia, and 'Lefty' Hankins would have killed to protect the secret of his given name, Buford."

Riedy moralizes, "We have lost some vital ingredients of Americana during the process of civilization."

NAMES BRIGHTEN HIS DAY

An Associated Press reporter interviewed Everett Williams about the collection of unusual names he had made during his thirty-four years with the Florida Bureau of Vital Statistics. On Mr. Williams' list, the reporter found, are some that may brighten almost any vital statistician's day. For example:

Mac Aroni	Pansy Flowers Greenwood
Betty Burp	Sports Model Higginbotham
Curlee Bush	Strange Odor
Full Dress Coat	Sky Rocket
Emancipation Proclamation Cogshell	Cigar Stubbs
	Starlight Cauliflower Shaw
Cherry Daiquiri	Tootsie Roll

Names chosen for twins include Early and Curly, A. C. and D. C. (perhaps the father was an electrician), Bigamy and Larceny, and Pete and Repeat (but apparently no Kate and Duplicate).

Mr. Williams' most unusual find? ⅝ Johnson, with a fraction instead of a first name!

NOT EVERYBODY PRONOUNCES
ENROUGHTY AS DARBY
(OR, AIN'T GENEALOGY FUN?)

After H.L. Mencken's *The American Language* appeared in 1919, his office received many letters adding to its store of information. One F. W. Sydnor told of the confusion caused in Henrico County, Virginia, by a duplication of names. Mencken incorporated the story in his *American Language: Supplement II* in 1948.

> The records show one *Darby Enroughty* (pronounced En-ruff-tee) to have been living near Four-Mile creek in 1690. He had a son named *John* and one named *Darby*. Later there were two *John Enroughtys* living in the same locality, cousins, whose name was frequently found in the records. Double Christian names were rarely used in those days, and it became necessary to distinguish between the two *Johns*. *John Enroughty*, the son of *John*, was known by his Christian name, but *John*, the son of *Darby Enroughty*, was designated *John Enroughty the son of Darby*, *John Enroughty of Darby*, and at least once as *John Darby*. The *Enroughtys* of Henrico and those known as *Darby* (real name *Enroughty*) are all descendants of *Darby Enroughty*. Those bearing the name *Enroughty* are the descendants of his son *John*, and those bearing the name of *Darby* are the descendants of his son *Darby*.

All clear?

HEADACHES FOR A
GENEALOGIST

In the Middle Ages sometimes two brothers or other near relatives had exactly the same name. Genealogists have sometimes run into a wall in attempting to determine which of two thirteenth-century Fulk fitz Wains was really the ancestor they sought, or which Robert Helias de Say, or which John le Strange. Then there was John Matravers, who by different wives had sons named John, and the younger of those had two sons named John.

In France such a problem was usually avoided. A younger brother of Jehan ⟨John⟩ was sometimes named Jehannot ⟨little John⟩, and sometimes a second Guillaume ⟨William⟩ was named Guillot ⟨little William⟩.

The duplication of names occasionally extended to girls. The will of a sixteenth-century Englishman, Thomas Reade, refers to "my daughter Katheryn the younger" and "my eldest daughter Katheryn."

HOW MANY JOHNS AREN'T NAMED JOHN?

A publication of the U.S. Immigration and Naturalization Service, *Foreign Versions, Variations, and Diminutives of English Names*, lists about one hundred twenty-five variants of *John* used in eighteen languages. Among the possibly unexpected ones are Zane, Janko or Janicko or Janeczek or Jankielek, Ioannis, Giannes, Juhani, Hannu, Ansis, Ivashka and Ivasenko, Vanechka and Vanyushko, Jovan, Yochanan, and Juanitocho.

Better known are Evan, Jan, Johann(es), Jean, Hans, Janos, Giovanni, Jonas, Juan, Vanya, and Ivan. Note that the Russian Ivan Ivanov has a name with exactly the same meaning as John Johnson.

There are close to ninety or one hundred variations of Joseph, and about as many of Alexander, Andrew, Anton, August, Basil, Francis or Frank, George, Gregory, Jacob, Michael, Paul, Peter, Stephen, Walter, or William.

Among women's given names, Mary or its equivalent Maria is apparently the champion, with over two hundred versions and diminutives, but Ann and Anna and their alternatives come close. Other multiform feminine names include Anastasia, Barbara, Catherine or Katherine, Dorothy, Eleanor and Ellen and Helen, Elizabeth, Irene, Jane or Joan or Jeanne (among the feminine equivalents of John), Josephine, Lillian, Margaret, Rosa or Rose, Sophia, Stephanie, and Theresa, all of which appear in well over sixty versions.

DID ANYBODY CONFUSE HIM WITH GENERAL ELECTRIC?

"My grandmother hated nicknames. When my father, whom

she had named Leslie, began to be called 'Les' by his boyhood friends, she was greatly upset. She thought she was safe in naming the next boy Guernsey Eliphalet Luther.

"Her strategy didn't work. His friends gave him a nickname, too—'Doc.' And since he intensely disliked being Guernsey Eliphalet, he always used just his initials, G. E., in signing checks and other papers."

YA GOTTA HAVE A
MIDDLE NAME, SEE

In the U.S. armed forces everyone is assumed to have no fewer than three names. If there is no middle name or initial, that fact is noted in parentheses (NMI). Sometimes rookies, seeing NMI as part of another man's name, may say, "You gotta helluva funny middle name. Dya call it Nummy, or what?"

When an initial is shown on one's birth certificate instead of a name, the word (*only*) is placed after it by the armed forces. So Captain Harry S. Truman was officially Harry S. (only) Truman.

COMRADE CHEVROLETOVICH

Russian babies—not just Americans—are sometimes given unusual names, such as Chevrolet, Telephone, and Napoleon Bonapartovich. One couple called their twins Ping and Pong. Other names were those of "mechanisms, animals, kitchen appliances, and sociopolitical formations," according to a Russian writer, G. Kotoyan. Perhaps the most patriotic given name is one that would be translated "Fullfill-the-Five-Year-Plan-in-Four-Years."

HOW DO YOU PRONOUNCE
PURCELL, MAURICE, AND DORAN?

In England and Ireland the first syllable of names like the following is usually stressed, but American usage moves the stress to the end.

	British	**American**
Bernard	BUR-nerd	ber-NARD
Burnett	BUR-nut	ber-NET

Costello	COS-tuh-lo	cos-TEL-o
Gerard	JURD	juh-RARD
Jacoby	JAC-uh-bee	juh-KO-bee
Mahony	MAY-uh-nee	muh-HO-nee
Maurice	MOR-us	muh-REES
Moran	MOR-un	mo-RAN
Savile	SAV-ul	suh-VILL
Waddell	WAD-ul	wuh-DELL

THINK OF A PRESIDENT
WHOSE INITIALS WERE H.U.G.

Hiram Ulysses Grant was the baptismal name of the infant who would grow up to be the victorious Civil War general and the eighteenth president of the United States.

The young Hiram feared that his initials would lead to much teasing by his West Point fellows, but the appointing congressman inadvertently did him a favor. Hiram's mother's maiden name was Simpson, and the congressman nominated Ulysses Simpson Grant to the military academy.

Question: Which initials would be better vote-getters, U.S.G. or H.U.G.?

THIS HOPENS THE DOOR TO
HOTHER POSSIBILITIES

An early onomatist, the British Charles Bardsley, enjoyed telling this story:

> A child was brought to the font for baptism. "What name?" asked the parson. "John" was the reply. "Anything else?" "John *honly*," said the godparent, putting in an "h" where it was not needed. "John Honly, I baptize thee..." continued the clergyman.

The child was entered with the double name.

NAMING AMONG
PRIMITIVE TRIBES

Pliny, an ancient Roman naturalist, said that in the Atlas mountains of northwest Africa there were tribes of *anonymi* (people without names). As late as the early twentieth century other tribes of *anonymi* were reported in relatively isolated parts of the world. In sparsely settled areas where customs of naming had not developed and where everyone knew everyone else intimately, there was perhaps no feeling that one had to address anyone in a particular way. (Similarly, it is said, some husbands and wives even in socially advanced countries never use each others' names in dialogue. In many an Irish play of this century the head of the family is referred to only as "himself," or when appropriate as "herself" or "yourself.")

The naming practices of primitive tribes in the nineteenth and twentieth centuries have varied greatly. In some tribes, as in civilized societies, names are bestowed at birth, but in others there may be delays until puberty or some other significant milestone, or perhaps until a time when signs seem especially propitious. Up to a century ago some African tribes apparently called each newborn son "gun," each girl "hoe," and delayed attaching more specific names for several years. In some places a child might be named for circumstances existing at the time of birth—names perhaps equivalent to Big Rain, Dry Weather, Hungry Time, or Victory Dance. Thus the names of several children could constitute an abbreviated history of the family unit or the tribe.

According to British onomatist C. L. Ewen, it was not always the parents who chose a child's name. The tribal chief might have that privilege, or possibly a medicine man or his equivalent, or maybe a council of elders.

The most general custom among the savage tribes was to give a child the name of a deceased ancestor, but any descriptive word which might indicate sex, order of birth, race, office, physical feature, god, historical fact, or a more fanciful concept, served the purpose of a distinguishing label.

Practices in naming were often intertwined with superstition. Some names were never to be spoken, or were not made known (even to the bearer) until adulthood. Some names, if used properly, might be regarded as protection against injury or witchcraft. In certain tribes a name could not be knowingly reused. The Ojibway Indians, it is said, considered it dangerous to speak the names of their own husbands and wives.

Instead of being relatively permanent, the name of some primitives changed. Ewen gives as examples Waiyau boys whose names changed at puberty, Wangata men whose names changed when their first child was born (a proof of potency), and the Kwakiutl Indians of British Columbia, whose names changed with the coming of winter or summer. Some Eskimos on becoming old would take new names, hoping that the change would result in renewed strength. Other Indians would take over the name of a dead person to assure that person's immortality. In some places each significant event in one's life would bring a new name, so that an old and honored person might have eight or ten names.

Slaves imported to the Americas came from many tribes, and what seems to be the same name might have a different meaning in each language. Ordinarily the African names appeared to be one, two, or three syllables, and to refer to common things in the people's lives—articles of clothing, trees or smaller plants, places, parts of the body, or tribal customs—or to abstractions such as friendship or surprise. (A 120-page "Dictionary of African Origins" is included in N.N. Puckett and M. Heller's *Black Names in America*.)

Most noteworthy is that with possibly a few exceptions the primitive names were not hereditary and were therefore not family names. Each individual was given his or her own name, which only rarely would be passed on to a son or daughter. So there was no equivalent of, say, the Hunter family or the Fisher family.

Some ancient personal names, not necessarily from primitive tribes, were very long and might consist of elements that made the word equal to a complete sentence. Ewen gives a Babylonian example that would be translated "O Ashur, the Lord of heaven and earth, give him life," an early Japanese name consisting of fifty-four "letters," and a Basque name that meant ⟨the lower field of the high hill of Azpicuelha⟩, as well as a seemingly pessimistic Sanskrit name that meant ⟨disease, pain, grief, and misfortune⟩ —perhaps an attempt to ward off such calamities.

THEN THERE WAS THIS GUY NAMED SMOKED SALMON

In the late eighteenth century a ship was wrecked on the New Jersey coast. A baby boy, name unknown, was the only person found alive in the wreckage. The person who found him said that God had preserved him, and opined further that the infant must have been able to swim like a fish. So the child was called Preserved Fish—Preserved being a not-uncommon name among Puritans and their descendants. He spent a long adult life in New York City, where his name was often commented upon by strangers as a great curiosity.

HOW ABOUT LIBERTY, EQUALITY, AND FRATERNITY?

In England in the mid-nineteenth century a boy was christened And Charity. Why? He had two sisters, named Faith, Hope.

RHODE ISLAND DE LAFAYETTE?

Benjamin Franklin, on learning that a child had been born to the Marquis and Marquise de Lafayette, wrote a letter of congratulation. He suggested that they plan to have thirteen children in all, to be named for the thirteen American colonies. He said, "Miss Virginia, Miss Carolina, and Miss Georgia will sound prettily enough for the Girls, but Massachusetts and Connecticut are too harsh for the Boys, unless they were to be Savages."

Some of the others—Delaware, New Hampshire, New Jersey, New York, and Rhode Island—might be a little awkward, too.

THE TROUBLES OF JOB

In the church register of St. Helen, Bishopsgate (England), dated September 1611, this touching little story is told:

> Job rakt-out-of-the-asshes, being borne the last of August in the lane going to Sir John Spencer's backgate, and there laide in a heape of sea-cole asshes, was baptized the ffirst day of September following, and dyed the next day after.

(See Job 2:8: "...and he [Job] sat down among the ashes.")

ANDROGYNOUS NAMES

In a *New Yorker* story by Elizabeth Tallent, the major character, an elderly scientist, is thinking about his daughter-in-law, with whom he has a love-hate relationship. Her given name is Ashley. "Even her name, he sometimes thinks, is simply one more aspect of the androgyny in which young women camouflage themselves nowadays."

Androgyny means ⟨having both female and male characteristics in the same body⟩. Hermaphrodites are androgynous, and Sunday supplements and even the sports pages sometimes carry stories about transsexuals, whose external sexual characteristics have been altered by surgery. Physiologists tell us that qualities of both sexes are present in every living being, so that to a greater or lesser extent every person is androgynous.

It is doubtful, however, that any deep awareness of androgyny is in the minds of parents who name an infant Ashley, Beryl, Gerry, or the like. A conversation like this may take place:

Parent 1: If it's a girl, I sorta like the name Ashley. It's a little unusual though.

Parent 2: Yeah, that's not bad. And your cousin Ashley would be pleased, wouldn't she?

Parent 1: I suppose so, although she once told me that people can't tell from the name whether she's a man or a woman. Some men do have that name, she said. She mentioned a famous professor, Ashley Montagu.

Parent 2: Oh, well, professors!

Parent 1: I think it's kinda cute for a girl, myself.

Parent 2: OK with me. What's a good middle name to go with it?

Whatever the reason, names that do not clearly indicate a child's sex seem to be much more common in America today than ever before. The feminist movement may be part of the explanation, abetted by approaches toward equality in the workplace, athletics, and the home. The trend toward reduced emphasis on gender differences shows up also in such things as increased feminine initiatives in dating and its follow-ups, in unisex hair-cuts, and in the wearing of slacks by both sexes. Today we may not be able to tell on sight whether an approaching stranger is male or female, and after we hear the given name we still may not be sure.

Things were different in the old days. Think, for example, of our early presidents and their first ladies: George and Martha, John and Abigail, Thomas and Martha, James and Dolley, James and Elizabeth. Only one in each pair wore the pants, and the names left no doubt about which it was. Maybe in the future we'll have presidential couples named Gerry and Kerry, or Beryl and Shelley, even Frankie and Johnny, and who can be sure which one will be the male?

But maybe not. Some people assert that individuals with equivocating names seldom reach high positions in any profession—not even in entertainment, although one rock music man who calls himself Alice Cooper has gone both far and far out.

Today's birth announcement lists have many names similar to those given below, with indistinguishable or at least uncertain gender. Usually, it is true, Frances still signifies a girl, Francis a boy. Marian used to be a girl, Marion a boy, but today both names are used for both sexes. Terry is probably but not assuredly a boy, and a "cute" spelling such as Terri, Terrie, and Teri is more likely to represent a girl.

Ashley (-ly)	Jackie (-y)	Lyle
Bert (-i, -y)	Jan	Lynn(e)
Beryl	Joe, Jo	Marian, Marion
Billie (-y)	Joyce	Marty (-ie)
Bobbie (-y)	Karen (-in)	Merl(e), Myrl(e)
Brook (e, -s)	Kelly (-ey)	Nick (-ie), Nikki
Carol(e), Carrol(1)	Kerry (-i, -ie)	Paige, Page
Cary (-ey)	Kim	Pat
Chris, Kris	Kit	Shelley (-y)
Evelyn	Lavern(e)	Shirley
Frankie (-y)	Lee, Lea, Leigh	Stacey (-y, -ie)
Gale, Gail	Leslie, Lesley	Terry (-i, -ie), Teri
Gerry (-ie), Jerry		Tracy (-ie)

CHANGING YOUR NAME
IS ALMOST LIKE
CHANGING YOUR LIFE

When the St. Louis Cardinals won the World Series in 1982, one of the stars was a rookie outfielder, Willie Dean McGee.

Willie liked to be called Willie. He didn't like to be called "E. T."

E. T., which stands for ⟨extra-terrestrial⟩, was the name of a lovable but odd-looking being from outer space featured in one of the most popular movies of the year. Like E. T., Willie McGee has dark skin and a pinched-looking face. Lanky, easy-going Willie, one of the speediest players in baseball despite a wobbling style of covering the outfield, was nicknamed E. T. by opposing players who imagined a resemblance in both appearance and movement. Then announcer Howard Cosell also began calling him E. T.

"I appreciate people calling me by *my* name," Willie said in his polite way in the locker room. "Nobody should be able to change your name. It's almost like changing your life."

The nickname didn't hurt Willie's World Series play, however. He made at least three sensational catches, and he was only the third rookie ever to hit two home runs in one Series game.

NO MO' CHILDREN

A married couple, according to an old joke, had three children, named Eeny, Meeny, and Miney. They explained, "There ain't gonna be no Moe."

4

CHOOSING A NAME FOR *YOUR* BABY:

Most parents give careful thought to choosing the first and middle name that will accompany their newborn child through infancy, childhood, and adulthood, perhaps into the graying, experience-wrinkled years that Robert Browning called "The last of life, for which the first was made." (The preceding lines are "Grow old along with me/The best is yet to be.") The names chosen should not just be suitable for the small bundle but also for the future business man or career woman, the future adult who may someday need, in turn, to choose names for still another generation.

In the list of questions that follow, not all will seem equally important to everyone. All, however, are questions that many parents take seriously.

1.   *Should the baby be named for a relative? a good friend? a celebrity?*   Fewer names today than in the past are chosen on these bases. When relatives' or friends' names *are* chosen, they often are middle rather than first names.

If Uncle Wilbur or Aunt Paula is very dear, naming an infant for him or her may be a deserved tribute. But consider this anecdote related by Audrey K. Duchert in the magazine *Names*:

> In 1884, a daughter was born to the Charles Hemenways of North Leverett, Massachusetts, and was named Ruby Marion. A neighbor inquired, "Charles, why didn't you name her Hepsabeth, after your mother?" He replied, "I loved my mother, but I love my daughter, too, and I wouldn't wish such a name on her."

Remember, too, that if you name the child for Aunt Paula, Aunt Corinne may feel hurt. And if you name her or him for your best friend—well, friendships have been known to break up.

Some babies are named for movie stars or other well-known people. There's nothing wrong with that, although the star's name and fame may fade quickly and the use of the name may prove only a fad.

2.   *Should you choose a name that is now "in"?*   Fads do exist in naming. In one decade, for example, David and Kevin for boys, and Karen and Jennifer for girls, may be "in," but a decade or so later, both may be largely replaced by new favorites.

Do you want your child five or six years from now to be one of the four Davids or the five Jennifers in a class, or do you prefer a name that, while not necessarily unique, does distinguish your child from most of the others? Or, on the contrary, do you consider a name better if it suggests that the child really "belongs" with the others, even to the extent of an identical given name?

3.   *Should you choose a name that is highly unusual?*   Maybe somewhere you encounter the name Girisa (gee-REE-shuh), originally Hindi as an alternative name for the god Siva, meaning ⟨mountain lord⟩, and used in parts of India for boys as well as girls. You like its exoticism and the grandeur of its lordly denotation.

Ask yourself whether most people could pronounce it and spell it, and whether it matters that they probably couldn't. The name has the advantage that it certainly would be a conversational icebreaker. How important is that? If your little girl grows up to be a staid, conventional person, will Girisa be a suitable name?

4.   *How may the name affect the child's future?*   No definitive studies have been made of the effect a name may have on a person's life, but on page 39 of this book you will find reports on two studies, one saying that boys christened Jack, Bud, and the like usually grow up to be outdoorsy, he-man types, and the other saying that men with names such as Rodman Carew Michaelson have a better than average chance of becoming business tycoons.

5.   *Is the name in conformity with your religious preferences?*   Many Jewish families like to honor a well-liked but deceased family member. Roman Catholic families are expected to use the name of a canonized saint as either the first or middle name; since the number of saints is large, there are seldom problems.

A Catholic is unlikely to name a son Luther, Calvin, or Wesley, and non-ecumenical Protestants may avoid a name that suggests a denomination other than their own. Many biblical names are appropriate for both the Jewish faith and the various Christian faiths. (See the lists on pages 149 to 153.) Parents who adhere to none of the organized religions may want to avoid names that suggest anything pertaining to specific faiths.

6.   *Is the name suitable for both a child and an older person?*   Tina may sound fine for a six-pound bundle of joy, but less appropriate for the 160-pound woman she may become. Stacy and Tracy have a young, ungrandmotherly sound.

On the other hand, some names sound too old for a little child. Some people say that no one under forty should be called

Edna or Maud, and some say that Nathaniel is a name befitting only an old man (although its meaning is ⟨gift of God⟩).

Such classification of names as "young" or "old," it must be admitted, is a highly personal, subjective matter and may depend largely on people we know who have a particular name.

7. *Is the name merely "cute"?* Names like Ima and Iva are generally to be avoided, as in Ima Rose and Iva Thorn. Also unsound is any name that combines cutely with the surname— Ruby Redd or Roxie Stone, for instance.

8. *If the surname is simple and common, are the other names also rather simple and common?* This does not mean that if the surname is Brown the child's first name must be William or Mary, but some people hear a jarring or anticlimactic note in Throckmorton McAllister Brown or Hilary Ermentrude Brown. Some, however, argue that something rather spectacular is needed to offset the plainness of Brown. Still others prefer moderately uncommon names with the ordinary surname—maybe Roger Edmund Brown or Marilyn Lucille Brown.

9. *Is the name appropriate to the ancestry?* Some Polish people, for instance, like to choose names that bear at least a hint of the child's Polish heritage—not necessarily Stanislas but perhaps Stanley. Some folks wear their heritage very proudly and want it to be reflected in their children's names, as was true of an Illinois Irish family whose children were Terence, Deirdre, Colleen, and Patrick, and who at last report were expecting either a Michael or a Kathleen.

If the first and second names seem to indicate a heritage different from that of the surname, some people may be confused by the mixed signals: Giovanni Domingo Schmidt, for instance. On the other hand, parents with differing ancestral backgrounds may want to select given names that at least suggest the mother's background. Often the middle name may serve that purpose: William Antonio Schmidt, possibly.

10. *Is the name too alliterative?* Richard *R*eed *R*athburn and *K*atherine *K*elda *K*eefe? Most people wouldn't want so much repetition of the same sound.

11. *Is the meaning of the name one that you believe appropriate?* Several books available in most libraries give definitions of names, as do supplements to some dictionaries; a few hundred are given here on pages 25 and 42. Although many people are barely aware that names *have* meanings, choices may be affected when the definitions become known. For example, one strongly feminist couple decided against Henry when they found that it means ⟨ruler of the home⟩, and some pacifist parents ruled out a few dozen boys' names that had military connotations. And if two couples who named their daughters Lesbia and Gomora had been better informed, they might not have made those choices. Dolores, a beautiful name, has been rejected by some couples who found it means ⟨lady of sorrows⟩.

A bookish couple decided in favor of Cuthbert when they found it means ⟨brilliant wisdom⟩, and another couple, wishful for their daughter's success in life, chose Eunice because its meaning is ⟨joyously triumphant⟩.

12. *Are the first and middle names sufficiently different?* One couple named their daughter Helen Elaine—very pretty; but Helen and Elaine are really the same name, and others of the sixty or more in the Helen group include Eleanor, Ellen, Alena, Lena, Leonora, and (hard to believe) the Russian Olenko and Galinochka. Obviously there is no law against such duplication, but carried to an extreme it could lead to a name such as Robert Roberto Roberti.

13. *Does the rhythm of the three names (and of the first and last name alone) please you?* Some people dislike two names of one syllable each, like Kent Clark (although Superman Clark Kent did all right). Samuel Taylor Coleridge's poetic ears were offended by a two-syllable name with the accent on the second syllable, like Adele or Eugene. "Never take an iambus as a Christian name," he advised in recommending Edith and Rotha as the two best names for girls. Actually, it is two iambics in succession that would displease many people: Maureen Malone, for example.

There's no complete agreement about which onomastic rhythms are most attractive, and it is certainly true that euphonious vowel and consonant combinations can often overcome possibly unpleasant rhythms. In general, people who compile books about given names recommend unequal numbers of syllables in the names. For instance, with a one-syllable surname a two- or three-syllable given name may be best: Conrad Lake, Roberta Mead; with a two-syllable surname a one- or three-syllable given name: Grace Keller, Rosamund Leclaire; with a surname of three or more syllables, a one- or two-syllable given name: Ray Gallagher, Nancy Rutherford. But attractive exceptions to these principles do exist.

14. *Does the middle name have a function?* The middle name may have a family or religious connection, as suggested previously. Often it may be the mother's maiden name or some other name associated with her family.

It can become a future alternative to the first name, which the child may in later years want to use instead of the first name. For example, a boy named Robert Leighton Correll, after being known to teachers and fellow students as Robert or Bob for over twenty years, decided that for the purposes of his profession R. Leighton Correll would provide an air of distinction that was not present in Robert L. Correll.

15. *What is the nickname likely to be? Do you like it?* Although it is impossible to predict for certain what nickname other children will give a boy or girl, the odds are that it will be one of the conventional ones: Ed for Edward or Edgar, Liz or Betty for Elizabeth, and so on. To some extent, then, parents control what the nickname will be. Ideally it should be a nickname that will sound attractive in conjunction with the last name. One unfortunate boy, whose last name was Dick, was christened Richard, for which Dick is a nickname. He was thus Dick Dick, which became Tick Tick, Tick Tock, and other variants. His elementary schoolmates' fun became even greater when one of them went to a zoo and discovered a small African antelope called a dik-dik.

One of Dick's classmates was a girl named Ariadne, who was first nicknamed Airy, then Windy.

16. *Does the name indicate gender clearly?* A television actress named Michael Learned has had to insist that *Miss* be placed before her name in the list of credits. When one sees such names as Marion, Jan, Merl(e), Beryl, Shirley, or Leslie, one cannot be sure whether the bearer is female or male.

Maybe in an age in which many people are working for a leveling-off of sex differentiation, everybody should be named Marion, Jan, etc. But if parents decide to give a child such a name, the choice should be a carefully reasoned one.

17. *Is the name easy enough to pronounce and to spell?* A girl named Ursula had to tell people repeatedly that her name was to be pronounced UR-suh-luh, not ur-SOO-luh. And our friend Ariadne found that almost none of her classmates and not all of her teachers could spell her name.

18. *If you believe in numerology, are you satisfied with what the numbers tell you?* The author of this book happens not to be a believer, partly because numerologists contradict one another. They have widely different methods of equating letters and numbers and no less different interpretations of the results. But if you are a believer, apply your favorite formula and see whether you like what it says about the numerological vibrations of the name you are considering.

19. *Are both parents happy or at least satisfied with the name?* The man and the woman cooperated in conception and will (hopefully) cooperate in the child's nurture and upbringing. In a good marriage a child can be an added cohesive force. As far as possible, nothing about the child, including the name by which he or she is called every day, should be divisive of the family.

20. *Some years in the future, when the child asks, "Why did you name me _____?" will you be able to give a good, clear answer?*

PART II

THE NAMES WE INHERIT

5

THE NAMES THAT MOST OF US ANSWER TO

THE ONE HUNDRED MOST COMMON AMERICAN SURNAMES

In 1974 the Social Security Administration (SSA) compiled a list of American surnames for which they had 10,000 or more files each. At that time the bureau found it had 3,169 names on the list—presumably the most common American surnames. The top one hundred are given here.

Because the SSA's computer recorded only the first six letters of each name on the list, letters given here in parentheses have been added to indicate the most common additional letters.

Rank	Surname	No. of SSA Records, 1974
1	Smith	2,382,509
2	Johnso(n)	1,807,263

3	Willia(ms) (mson)	1,568,939
4	Brown	1,362,910
5	Jones	1,331,205
6	Miller	1,131,205
7	Davis	1,047,848
8	Martin(ez) (son)	1,046,297
9	Anders(on) (en)	825,648
10	Wilson	787,825
11	Harris(on)	754,083
12	Taylor	696,046
13	Moore	693,304
14	Thomas	688,054
15	White	636,185
16	Thomps(on)	635,426
17	Jackso(n)	630,003
18	Clark	549,107
19	Robert(s) (son)	524,688
20	Lewis	495,026
21	Walker	486,498
22	Robins(on)	484,991
23	Peters(on)	479,249
24	Hall	471,479
25	Allen	458,375
26	Young	455,416
27	Morris(on)	455,179
28	King	434,791
29	Wright	431,157
30	Nelson	421,638
31	Rodrig(uez)	416,178
32	Hill	414,646
33	Baker	412,676
34	Richar(ds) (dson)	409,262
35	Lee	409,068
36	Scott	408,439
37	Green	406,989
38	Adams	406,841
39	Mitche(ll)	371,434
40	Philli(ps)	362,013
41	Campbe(ll)	361,958
42	Gonzal(ez) (es)	360,994
43	Carter	349,950

44	Garcia	346,175
45	Evans	343,897
46	Turner	329,752
47	Stewar(t) (d) (dson)	329,581
48	Collin(s)	324,680
49	Parker	322,482
50	Edward(s)	317,197
51	Murphy	311,337
52	Cook	298,396
53	Rogers	298,288
54	Griffi(n) (th) (ths)	291,862
55	Christ(ian) (opher) (ianson) (enson) (ensen)	281,525
56	Morgan	273,267
57	Cooper	269,560
58	Reed	267,589
59	Bell	267,026
60	Bailey	263,908
61	Kelly	262,701
62	Wood	258,422
63	Ward	257,686
64	Cox	256,842
65	Lopez	254,535
66	Steven(s) (son)	254,165
67	Howard	248,065
68	Sander(s) (son)	245,440
69	Bennet(t)	243,553
70	Brooks	242,491
71	Watson	240,219
72	Gray	239,604
73	Rivera	238,457
74	Nichol(s) (son)	237,129
75	Hernan(dez) (des)	235,498
76	Hughes	231,754
77	Ross	231,054
78	Myers	230,561
79	Sulliv(an)	239,839
80	Long	229,615
81	Price	225,893
82	Russel(l)	220,676

83	Foster	220,156
84	Daniel(s) (son)	219,156
85	Hender(son)	218,715
86	Perez	217,801
87	Fisher	216,884
88	Powell	212,681
89	James	212,201
90	Perry	211,478
91	Butler	210,515
92	Jenkin(s) (son)	208,325
93	Barnes	206,776
94	Reynol(ds)	198,326
95	Patter(son)	198,205
96	Colema(n)	197,123
97	Simmon(s)	196,506
98	Graham	194,096
99	Wallac(e)	194,067
100	Stephe(ns) (nson)	192,023

Those one hundred names account for about one-sixth of the total of all Americans.

THE FOUR CHIEF KINDS
OF SURNAMES

Until late in the Middle Ages—say 600 to 800 years ago—few people had more than one name. Because the names chosen for children were usually repetitious, with maybe a dozen Williams or Emmas in a single village, there must often have been confusion about which William or Emma was meant.

To reduce the confusion, people would add some words for further identification:

William from the dale (the place where he lived)
William who is the son of John (the father's name)
William the cooper (the occupation)
William the short (a description)

These were natural, almost inevitable, ways of identifying, and they turned eventually into the four classifications into which nearly all European—and hence American—surnames now fall. (Asian and African names developed various patterns of their own.)

The unimportant words in the English identifications would tend to be slurred over and then omitted in speaking:

William dale
William John's son
William cooper
William short

The capital letters now used in writing names were added later.

These were not yet family names—not until the custom arose of passing down the second name from father to children. When William Cooper's son Robert was called Robert Cooper even though he was a tailor or a fletcher, a family name came into being. When William Johnson's son Bertram was Bertram Johnson rather than Bertram Williamson, there was a family name. The son of William Dale might live on a hill instead of down in a dale, but he had a real family name if people called him, say, Peter Dale. William Short, even with that family name, might be six feet tall.

The word *surname* has become equated with *family name*— a name that can be inherited. *Sur-* means ⟨additional⟩ or ⟨extra⟩. The surname is the additional name which identifies the family of the person whose name is Bertram or Bertha or whatever.

In modern America, surnames based on place names (Hill, Winchester, etc.) are the most frequent, accounting for over 40 percent of the total. Patronyms, which are usually fathers' names or other ancestral names but may be names of famous people such as Alexander or Bartholomew, make up about 30 percent. About 16 percent of our surnames are occupational (Carpenter, Mason), and about 11 or 12 percent are descriptive (Swift, Armstrong). Only 1 or 2 percent fall into other categories, and those are most often Asian names (Song, Tanaka) or Middle Eastern names (Ibrahim, Mustafa) that are simply transliterated from the original language.

FIFTY MOST COMMON
AMERICAN SURNAMES
BASED ON OCCUPATIONS

About one-sixth of American surnames are derived from the names of occupations that were common during the name-giving period, about 600 to 800 years ago.

This list gives the top fifty most common names, in order of frequency, together with brief explanations of most.

1. *Smith*
2. *Miller*
3. *Taylor* (an old spelling of *tailor*)
4. *Clark* ⟨scholar, scribe, clergyman⟩ (The British pronounce *clerk* as "clark")
5. *Walker* ⟨cleaner of cloth⟩ (Clothmaking was a leading cottage industry in the Middle Ages. See also Webb, Fuller, and Tucker, following.)
6. *Wright* ⟨carpenter or metalworker⟩
7. *Baker*
8. *Carter* ⟨driver of a cart⟩
9. *Stewart* ⟨person in charge of a household, estate, or farm⟩
10. *Turner* ⟨worker with a lathe⟩
11. *Parker* ⟨gamekeeper; person in charge of a park or hunting area⟩
12. *Cook*
13. *Cooper* ⟨maker of tubs, barrels, casks, wooden pails⟩ (Metal, then plastics, later supplanted wood and largely eliminated coopers.)
14. *Bailey* (several spellings) ⟨administrative officer, estate manager⟩
15. *Ward* ⟨watchman, guard, keeper⟩
16. *Howard* (originally Heyward) ⟨person in charge of hedges or fences, boundary-watcher, guard against straying livestock; (sometimes ewe-herder)⟩ (About one third of today's American Howards are black, because of the popularity of Oliver Howard, Civil War Commissioner of the Freedmen's Bureau.)
17. *Myer(s)* (from German; equivalent to Meyer, Meier, Mayer, etc.) ⟨chief servant or overseer; a farmer⟩
18. *Foster* (= Forester) ⟨warden of a forest; gamekeeper⟩

19. *Fisher* ⟨person who caught fish or sold them⟩
20. *Butler* ⟨person in charge of bottled goods or wine casks; maker of bottles⟩
21. *Hayes* ⟨person in charge of hedges or fences; = Hayward, Howard; (sometimes) one who lived in a hedged area or near it⟩
22. *Schmidt* (German for Smith)
23. *Snyder* (Dutch for Taylor. Many a German Schneider changed the spelling to Snyder or Snider after coming to America.)
24. *Porter* ⟨gatekeeper; one who carried things⟩
25. *Spencer* ⟨dispenser, custodian of a storage room⟩ (A sort of civilian quartermaster of the Middle Ages.)
26. *Hoffman* (from German; several other spellings) ⟨owner or manager of a farm; a farm worker⟩
27. *Webb* (= Weaver and German or English Web(b)er; Webster was a female weaver) ⟨weaver of cloth⟩
28. *Tucker* ⟨person who cleaned cloth or thickened it⟩
29. *Wagner* (also Wag(g)oner) ⟨one who built or drove wagons; cartwright⟩
30. *Mason*
31. *Meyer* (See No. 17)
32. *Hunter* ⟨a person who hunted game⟩
33. *Hunt* (= Hunter)
34. *Warren* ⟨keeper of a game preserve⟩ (Also sometimes a place name for one who lived near a game preserve or near a rabbit hutch; sometimes a patronym for ⟨descendant of Warin "protection).")
35. *Gardner* (also Gardiner) ⟨gardener⟩
36. *Schultz* (German; many spellings) ⟨magistrate, administrator, foreman, overseer⟩
37. *Knight*
38. *Weaver* (See No. 27)
39. *Berry* ⟨servant in a manor⟩ (Also a place name for one who lived in or near a fortified place or on a hill.)
40. *Chambers* (also Chamberl(a)in) ⟨person in charge of a royal or noble reception chamber or of the household⟩
41. *Carpenter* (French Carpentier) ⟨worker with wood⟩

42. *Chapman* ⟨peddler, tradesman⟩
43. *Harper* ⟨person who played a harp for a nobleman or at fairs, etc.⟩
44. *Cohen* (Hebrew; several spellings) ⟨rabbi or priest (especially one said to be descended from Aaron)⟩
45. *Fuller* ⟨person who cleaned cloth or thickened it⟩
46. *Schneider* (See No. 23)

47. *Franklin* ⟨a substantial landholder of medieval times, a freeholder⟩
48. *Zimmerman*(n) (German for Carpenter)
49. *Weber* (See No. 27)
50. *Keller* (German) ⟨one who worked in a place for storing food; one who made women's caps or hairnets⟩ (Also a place name for ⟨one who came from Keller "wine cellar"⟩)

FIFTY MOST COMMON AMERICAN SURNAMES THAT ARE PATRONYMS

Almost one-third of American surnames are patronyms, which are of two types: a name that indicates who one's father or other ancestor was, or the name of a famous person such as a biblical or historical figure.

The fifty most common American patronyms, in order, are listed here. Those with more than six letters may have alternative forms besides those given here.

1. *Johnson* ⟨son of John⟩
2. *Williams, Williamson* ⟨son of William⟩
3. *Jones* ⟨son of John⟩
4. *Davis* ⟨son of Davie (a pet form of David)⟩
5. *Martin, Martinez, Martinson* ⟨son of Martin (from the god Mars)⟩
6. *Anderson, Andersen* ⟨son of Andrew⟩
7. *Wilson* ⟨son of Will⟩

8. *Harris, Harrison* ⟨son of Harry⟩
9. *Thomas* ⟨son of Thomas⟩
10. *Thompson* ⟨son of Thomas⟩
11. *Jackson* ⟨son of Jack (a pet form of John or sometimes Jacob)⟩
12. *Roberts, Robertson* ⟨son of Robert⟩
13. *Lewis* ⟨descendant of Lewis⟩

14. *Robinson* ⟨little son of Rob (a pet form of Robert)⟩
15. *Peterson, Petersen* ⟨son of Peter⟩
16. *Allen* ⟨descendant of Alan⟩ (May also be a place name, from any one of several British rivers.)
17. *Morris, Morrison* ⟨son of Morris⟩
18. *Rodriguez, Rodrigues* (Spanish or Portuguese) ⟨son of Rodrigo⟩
19. *Richards, Richardson* ⟨son of Richard⟩
20. *Adams* (numerous variants) ⟨descendant of Adam⟩
21. *Mitchell* ⟨descendant of Michael⟩
22. *Phillips* (numerous variants) ⟨descendant of Phillip⟩
23. *Gonzalez, Gonzales* (Spanish or Portuguese) ⟨son of Gonzalo⟩
24. *Garcia* (Spanish or Portuguese) ⟨descendant of Garcia (= Gerald)⟩ (May also be a place name)
25. *Evans* (Welsh) ⟨son of John⟩
26. *Collins* ⟨little son of Cole (a pet form of Nicholas)⟩
27. *Edwards* ⟨son of Edward⟩
28. *Murphy* (Irish) ⟨descendant of Murchadh (= sea warrior)⟩
29. *Rogers* ⟨son of Roger⟩
30. *Griffin, Griffith, Griffiths* (Welsh) ⟨descendant of Griffith⟩
31. *Christian, Christianson, Christenson* (several variants) ⟨son of Christian (= follower of Christ)⟩
32. *Morgan* (Welsh) ⟨descendant of Morgan⟩
33. *Kelly* (Irish) ⟨grandson of Ceallach (= contentious)⟩ (Is usually a place name if English or Scottish)
34. *Lopez* (Spanish) ⟨son of Lope or Lupe (= wolf)⟩
35. *Stevens, Stevenson* ⟨son of Stephen⟩
36. *Sanders, Sanderson* ⟨son of Sander (= Alexander)⟩
37. *Bennett* ⟨little descendant of Benne (a pet form of Benedict)⟩
38. *Watson* ⟨son of Wat (a pet form of Walter)⟩
39. *Nichol, Nichols, Nicholson* ⟨descendant of Nicholas⟩
40. *Hernandez, Hernandes* (Spanish or Portuguese) ⟨son of Hernando⟩
41. *Hughes* (Welsh or English) ⟨son of Hugh⟩

42. *Sullivan* (Irish)
⟨grandson of Suilebhan
(dark-eyed)⟩
43. *Price* (Welsh) ⟨son of
Rhys⟩ (An earlier form
was ap Rhys = son of
Rhys, but the *a* was
dropped)
44. *Daniel, Daniels,
Danielson* ⟨son of
Daniel⟩
45. *Henderson* ⟨son of
Henry⟩
46. *Perez, Peres* (Spanish or
Portuguese) ⟨son of
Pero (= Pedro = Peter)⟩
47. *Powell* (Welsh) ⟨son of
Howell⟩ (An earlier form
was ap Howell; see 43)
48. *James* (Welsh or
English) ⟨descendant of
James⟩
49. *Perry* (Welsh) ⟨son of
Harry⟩ (Earlier ap
Harry; see 43)
50. *Jenkins, Jenkinson* ⟨little
son of Jen (pet form of
John)⟩

TWENTY-FIVE MOST COMMON
AMERICAN SURNAMES
DESCRIBING PEOPLE

About one-tenth of American surnames describe the appearance
of some especially notable characteristic of an ancestor who
lived several hundred years ago. Most of these relate to obvious
physical qualities, but a few indicate traits of mind, personality,
or character.

In some instances a person may have been thought to
resemble an animal, such as a fox, and may have been called
by that name. In this book, however, names derived from
animals, birds, and fish are given in separate lists.

The top twenty-five descriptive names are listed here along
with their most common meanings.

1. *Brown* ⟨brown-haired⟩
2. *White* ⟨light-
complexioned;
(sometimes) white-
haired⟩
3. *Young* ⟨a younger
brother, or anyone
younger than another
in the family or other
group; young-looking⟩
4. *Gray* ⟨gray-haired⟩
5. *Long* ⟨tall⟩
6. *Russell* ⟨small and red-
haired⟩
7. *Black* (also Blake)
⟨(usually) dark,
swarthy, dark-haired;
(sometimes the
opposite) light-
complexioned, blond,

pale⟩ (Two similar Old English words, *blaec* and *blāc*, had these opposite meanings, and a name might come from either.)

8. *Little* ⟨short, small⟩
9. *Reid* (Scottish variant of Reed) ⟨red-haired, ruddy⟩
10. *Curtis* ⟨courtly, courteous, well-bred, elegant⟩
11. *Powers* ⟨poor man; (sometimes) one who has taken a vow of poverty; (sometimes) a respelling of a Welsh place name, Powis or Powys⟩
12. *Klein* (German; also Kline, Cline) ⟨short, little⟩
13. *Gross* (German) ⟨large, heavy⟩
14. *Sharp* ⟨keen-witted, intelligent, fast-thinking⟩
15. *Blake* (See No. 7)
16. *Wise* ⟨learned, experienced, sage⟩
17. *Weiss* (German for White)
18. *Moody* ⟨brave, bold, impetuous, proud, headstrong⟩ (The modern meaning of *moody* was not applied until Shakespeare's time.)
19. *Lang* (German for Long)
20. *Lloyd* (also Loyd, Lloyds; Welsh) ⟨brown-haired or gray-haired or brownish in complexion⟩
21. *Short* ⟨small in stature⟩
22. *Moreno* (Spanish, Italian) ⟨dark-complexioned⟩ (In its rare use as a Hebrew name, it comes from a title meaning ⟨Master⟩)
23. *Bass* ⟨short, fat⟩
24. *Golden* ⟨one with golden hair⟩ (May also be derived from Golduin ⟨gold, friend⟩)
25. *Savage* ⟨wild, fierce, uncouth⟩

THE TWENTY MOST COMMON NAMES IN NINE AMERICAN CITIES

These rankings are based on counts in telephone directories of the early 1980s. Since low-income families are somewhat less likely to have telephones, names of such families may be underrepresented. In other words, it is possible that in some places Spanish names rank higher than shown here.

Note how ranks vary between cities. Although Smith is the leader in six, it is badly beaten by Johnson in Chicago, edged out by both Williams and Johnson in Los Angeles, and is preceded by six Hispanic names in Greater Miami (where Rodriguez outscores Smith two to one).

Note also that if you check future directories you may find that some names have moved up or down in rank, although seldom more than one or two places in a single year.

Greater Atlanta

Atlanta names conform in general to the national pattern.

1. Smith	8. Wilson	15. Miller
2. Johnson	9. Thomas	16. Anderson
3. Williams	10. Thompson	17. Taylor
4. Brown	11. White	18. Walker
5. Jones	12. Harris	19. Clark
6. Davis	13. Martin	20. Robinson
7. Jackson	14. Moore	

Boston

In Boston, Cohen, Murphy, and Kelly rank higher than in most places.

1. Smith	8. Jones	15. Wilson
2. Brown	9. Murphy	16. Lewis
3. Johnson	10. Davis	17. Taylor
4. Williams	11. Kelly	18. Moore
5. Miller	12. Anderson	19. Robinson
6. Cohen	13. Thomas	20. King
7. White	14. Harris	

Indianapolis

Indianapolis, like Atlanta, is similar to the national pattern.

1. Smith	8. Wilson	15. Martin
2. Johnson	9. Thompson	16. Anderson
3. Miller	10. Taylor	17. Jackson
4. Jones	11. White	18. Young
5. Williams	12. Clark	19. Scott
6. Brown	13. Moore	20. Walker
7. Davis	14. Thomas	

Denver

The rank of Martinez reflects Denver's growing Hispanic population, although other Spanish names are as yet comparatively few there.

1. Smith	8. Davis	15. Clark
2. Johnson	9. Wilson	16. White
3. Miller	10. Martinez	17. Thomas
4. Brown	11. Martin	18. Lewis
5. Williams	12. Thompson	19. Allen
6. Jones	13. Taylor	20. Young
7. Anderson	14. Moore	

Los Angeles

Williams, in a close race, defeats both Johnson and Smith in Los Angeles. The rank of Lee reflects in part the Oriental presence. Note that seven of the top twenty names are Hispanic.

1. Williams	8. Rodriguez	15. Miller
2. Johnson	9. Hernandez	16. Thomas
3. Smith	10. Martinez	17. Harris
4. Jones	11. Lopez	18. Anderson
5. Brown	12. Davis	19. Wilson
6. Lee	13. Jackson	20. Perez
7. Garcia	14. Gonzalez	

New York
(Manhattan)

Not unexpected in Manhattan's list are the high ranks of Lee (partly because of a big Chinatown) and of several names that are generally Jewish. The big news is that in recent years Rodriguez has moved in front of Schwartz.

1. Smith	8. Jones	15. Green
2. Brown	9. Davis	16. Martin
3. Miller	10. Rodriguez	17. Lewis
4. Johnson	11. Schwartz	18. Thomas
5. Cohen	12. Harris	19. Robinson
6. Williams	13. Friedman	20. Wilson
7. Lee	14. Levine	

Chicago

Johnson beats Smith in Chicago. Jones and Brown have been switching places in a battle for fourth.

1. Johnson	8. Jackson	15. Moore
2. Smith	9. Anderson	16. White
3. Williams	10. Wilson	17. Martin
4. Jones	11. Harris	18. Lewis
5. Brown	12. Thomas	19. Thompson
6. Davis	13. Taylor	20. Walker
7. Miller	14. Robinson	

Greater Memphis

Memphis departs only slightly from the national pattern.

1. Smith	8. Moore	15. Walker
2. Jones	9. Jackson	16. Martin
3. Johnson	10. Harris	17. Thompson
4. Williams	11. Wilson	18. Anderson
5. Brown	12. White	19. Robinson
6. Davis	13. Thomas	20. Young
7. Taylor	14. Miller	

Greater Miami

Smith not only loses to six Hispanics in Miami but is pursued by six more among the top twenty. And look where Jones is.

1. Rodriguez	8. Martinez	15. Sanchez
2. Gonzalez	9. Perez	16. Jones
3. Garcia	10. Diaz	17. Davis
4. Lopez	11. Johnson	18. Martin
5. Hernandez	12. Williams	19. Gomez
6. Fernandez	13. Brown	20. Jackson
7. Smith	14. Alvarez	

ALL IN THE FAMILY

Judge: Defendant, nobody on this jury is kin o' yern, is they?
Defendant: Cain't rightly say how many of 'em is kin till I count 'em up, Uncle Bill.

6

CHANGING
NAMES

ELEVEN REASONS WHY SOME AMERICANS
HAVE CHANGED THEIR NAMES

Many thousands of Americans have surnames that they or their ancestors did not bring to these shores. The changes have been made for varied and sometimes individual reasons, often involving such considerations as those listed here.

1.   *Necessity*   Toy Chan's name didn't look like Toy Chan in China, where it consisted of two rather elaborately drawn characters (logographs) that were utterly meaningless in America and obviously couldn't be printed in one of our phone books. So here it was written with Roman letters that can be sounded somewhat like the original. Toy Chan does not accurately reflect the Chinese pronunciation, but it presumably comes as close as our alphabet allows. Similarly, names written originally in Hebrew, Cyrillic, Arabic, and a number of other alphabets had to be transliterated into the one used in the United States.

Less dramatically, because most American typewriters and typesetting machinery cannot cope with the diacritical markings used above or below certain letters in several European languages, those marks usually disappeared shortly after the boat stopped at Ellis Island.

2. *Inability to spell.* Sometimes an immigrant could not spell his or her name. When a name was told to an immigration official, the official had to write it as it sounded to him—perhaps something very different from the real spelling. The new spelling often became the official one. Similarly, an employer might misspell a name but an illiterate immigrant would not know the difference.

3. *Carelessness.* An immigration or other official might through carelessness spell a name incorrectly or illegibly, and a timid immigrant might not object.

4. *Difficulty in pronouncing or spelling a name.* Some names, perhaps Polish more than any other, are difficult for most Americans to spell or pronounce. Czajkowski means ⟨where the gulls are⟩, so one Mr. Czajkowski changed his name to Gull. A Mr. Dzeckaeiar simplified his to Decker. Paul Revere's father, whose name was Rivoire, changed it to Revere "so the bumpkins can pronounce it easier."

5. *Disagreements with relatives.* A member of a family might change his or her name—considerably or slightly—to avoid being associated with a disliked relative.

6. *Desire to break with the past.* America represented a new beginning, and some newcomers had no desire to retain anything that reminded them of an unhappy past.

Some criminals choose aliases to dissociate themselves from crimes they have committed, as well as to avoid detection for crimes they may commit.

7. *Desire for material success.* There was a widespread feeling, sometimes justified, that a "wrong" or "bad" name could prevent one from getting a job or becoming prosperous. Second or third generation Americans in particular might change their names to others that supposedly lacked any stigma. In a largely French-speaking part of Louisiana a German König translated his name to Roy, a Weiss to LeBlanc, but also in Louisiana a French Roy translated his name to King. A number of Jewish actors changed to noncommittal names before going far in show business. (See page 103.)

8. *Fear of bad treatment.* Some newcomers had fled from lands where they were mistreated and they believed, rightly or

wrongly, that a change of name might avert further mistreatment here. In World War I, many German-Americans changed their names because they feared abuse and were indeed sometimes cruelly treated. (See page 96.)

9. *Holding the coattails of earlier arrivals.* Knowing that the French Lafayette was regarded as an American hero, some French-Americans changed their names to Lafayette.

10. *Getting rid of a semantic objection.* Gelbfisch ⟨goldfish⟩ for no good reason seemed humorous to many Americans. Frankenstein reminded them of the creator of the monster. Some Americans blushed when they had to try to pronounce Fuchs or Lipschitz. Such names were often changed.

11. *Dislike of the original name.* Many Jewish people, in particular, disliked the names that may have been forced on them in Germany, Russia, or elsewhere, and eagerly altered them to something more appealing. A Mr. Ochsenschwantz ⟨ox tail⟩ happily became a Mr. Freedman.

It is impossible to say which of these reasons was the most likely cause of change, but the fourth (difficulty of pronunciation or spelling) was certainly high on the list. Immigrants in general were eager to conform to what they found in their new homeland, and their children and grandchildren even more so. If a name was so unlike others that teachers, for instance, had trouble with it, it was often simplified. One teacher, who couldn't pronounce a complicated name ending in *-witch*, told two little brothers that in her class their last name would be Holz. Their father came to see her one day and introduced himself as Mr. Holz.

ZBIGNIEW BRZEZINSKI

The Polish-American Zbigniew Brzezinski was an important shaper of foreign policy in Jimmy Carter's presidential administration. Said a contemporary wiseacre, "Where but in America could a man named Zbigniew Brzezinski make a name for himself without changing it?"

SHAKING OFF THE BAD LUCK

Some Indonesians, after recovering from serious illness or other severe misfortune, change their names. Presumably the evil spirit that was responsible will be confused and become unable to recognize and pursue the former victim.

AMERICA ENTERED THE WAR, AND THE MUELLERS BECAME MILLERS

To blend in more easily with other Americans, many relative newcomers—usually in their first, second, or third generation here—have changed their names. For many Germans the process accelerated in the early years of World War I, when Germany was perceived as the enemy. And then when, in April 1917, the United States actually entered the war, name-changing speeded up still more.

One reason for changing was that German-Americans increasingly considered themselves ordinary Americans with no or few remaining close ties to their former homeland. Like everybody else they were attending war rallies, buying Liberty Bonds, talking about a war to end war, castigating Kaiser Bill, and watching their own sons march off to be gassed in muddy trenches or pierced by jagged shrapnel.

With misguided patriotism, some other Americans—usually the relatively uneducated—began to express distrust of German-Americans, to call them Kraut and Heinie, to throw eggs at their houses, to beat up their children on the schoolground, to accuse them of spying or at least of sending money to help the Kaiser. In chauvinistic zeal they changed the name of sauerkraut to Liberty cabbage, hamburger to Salisbury steak, weiners to hot dogs (a term first reported a few years earlier in the *Saturday Evening Post*).

Under such pressures, many Muellers or Müllers, perhaps after clinging to their name for several American generations, translated it to the cognate Miller. Schmidt translated to Smith, Weiss to White, Lang to Long. Other translation changes are illustrated by these names:

Braun to Brown	Jaeger to Hunter	Klein to Small
Koch to Cook	Koenig to King	or Little
Metzger to	Schneider to	Krafft to Strong
Butcher	Taylor	Schwartz to Black
Weber to	Ziegler to Mason	Zimmerman
Weaver		to Carpenter

Sometimes, instead of translating, these Americans merely changed a letter or two. Schneider, for instance, might become Snyder (a Dutch spelling); Bauer became Bower; Schaffer, Shafer; Fischer, Fisher; Stauffer, Stover; Bloch, Block; Schoen, Shane.

Occasionally a much more drastic shift would be made, especially with a long, conspicuously German name such as Meisenheimer, which might become any "American" name that struck the family's fancy. It is doubtful that name changes made any German-Americans any more or any less patriotic. And not all of them changed. The Mueller boy, the newly named Miller, and the Miller with English ancestors all died together in the bloody mud along with Carey, Scarlatti, Svensson, Jones, Latowski—and all the rest.

By World War II the distrust of German-Americans had largely disappeared, and name changes among them were comparatively few. Most Japanese-Americans were hidden away in internment camps, so they didn't have to think about name changes, and anyhow their Oriental features would have made a name such as Green or Johnson seem ridiculous. Otherwise, Mizukami might have imitated some of the Muellers and modified his name to Mize or partially translated it to Waters.

THE RABBIT
WHO BECAME AN IRISHMAN

A Czech family named Zajíc, which means ⟨rabbit⟩, came to the United States and found that no one in the largely Irish community could pronounce their name in the good old Czech way. They thought about translating the name to Rabbit, but others laughed at that. Someone suggested Hare, but an Irish neighbor recommended O'Hare as having definite advantages. So the Zajíc children, renamed O'Hare, quickly blended in with their Irish schoolmates.

The irony is that O'Hare has no connection with rabbits. It's an Irish patronym meaning ⟨grandson of Ir⟩ or ⟨grandson of Aichear "embittered"⟩.

The Irish won another victory with the Sýr family, whose Czech name means ⟨cheese⟩. They decided that they would like the German equivalent, Käse, but Irish acquaintances said that Käse didn't seem very American and persuaded them to choose the somewhat similar-sounding Casey. No relation to cheese, of course: Casey means ⟨descendant of Cattasach "watchful"⟩.

HOW TO CHANGE YOUR NAME

Law does not require any set procedure for name change. The chances are that a large majority of changes in the United States have been made without any legal action whatever. The person or persons simply decided what name they wanted and then began using it.

The complexities of modern life, however, make it desirable to have a name change approved by a court. Information about a person may now be kept in literally hundreds of places such as credit files, armed forces files, government offices, and a host of others. Changing a name without having an official record made may greatly increase the difficulty of keeping all these records straight, or of appealing when a seeming injustice has been done. Questions concerning wills and inheritance may be almost impossible to answer without adequate records. If a faraway uncle, for instance, bequeaths a million dollars to Lucy Rable, and if she has changed her name to Melinda Orwell without having an official record made, she may have to spend a large part of the inheritance just to prove that she is Lucy Rable and the niece of the dead man.

Official change of name is simple and normally entails low court costs or none at all, although if for any reason the petitioner wants assistance from a lawyer, the costs may climb. Normally you will simply make an appointment with a local circuit

judge and will take along evidence—preferably a birth certificate—to show who you are. In all likelihood the judge will do
no more than ascertain your present name and the desired
name, and then sign a legal form endorsing the change. A
talkative or curious judge who is less harried and hurried than
most may also ask the reasons for change. The request will
almost certainly be approved, although (especially with persons
whose knowledge of the English language and of American
customs is slight) the judge may recommend further consid-
eration. One immigrant family, for instance, thought that Siffle
would be close to the sound of the name they brought from
the old country, but the judge, knowing that the similarity to
syphilis might later cause embarrassment, suggested that Seffle,
Siffer, or Safford might be a better choice.

Whether or not a change of name is recorded officially,
certain agencies need to be notified. The post office, obviously.
The phone company, the landlord, credit card companies, and
anyone else to whom payments must be made regularly. The
agency that issues drivers' licenses and the one that keeps track
of voter registration. In some cases the armed forces, a draft
board, immigration officers, a parole board or parole officer,
or any other official body to whom one has a legal obligation.
The Social Security Administration requires notification, although it does not assign a new number.

TEN TYPES
OF ALTERATION IN SURNAMES

A person changing a name in America usually has an unlimited
range of selection. He or she may choose any name that has
ever existed if it can be written or at least approximated in the
Roman alphabet and if it does not break the current code concerning obscenity. The name may even be an invented one that
perhaps no other person has ever used.

Ordinarily, though, name-changers do not go to extremes,
if for no other reason than the desirability that the name be
pronounceable, reasonably short, and not embarrassing to its
holders or the people they may meet.

Most names are changed in one of these ways:

1.   *Transliteration from another alphabet.*   A Pole named Ruc-
zynski need not change the name, because Poles use the Roman
alphabet, as Americans do. But a Russian with essentially the
same name must transliterate it from the Cyrillic. It will probably come out Ruczynsky, but it may not, since there is not an
exact letter-for-letter correlation between Cyrillic and Roman.
For example, Russian has letters pronounced like our blends
zh, ts, ch, sh, shch; its E is pronounced *yē*, Ë is *yo*; and X is about
like *kh*. It is because of such differences that one may find the
same name (Tschaikovsky, for instance) spelled in two or more
ways.

Oriental and Arabic names obviously must be transliterated. So to some extent must names in Roman alphabets that
use various diacritical marks with certain letters, although usually the only changes made in those is the dropping of the
marks. Composer Antonin Dvorak's surname, for instance, is
written Dvořák in his native Czechoslovakia (which explains why
it is pronounced duh-VOR-zhock).

2.   *Shortening.*   This is probably one of the two most frequent
types of change. Sometimes only a letter is dropped, as when
Meyer decides he wants to be Myer. Sometimes the loss is considerable, as when four Greeks, each named Pappageorge,
changed their names to Papp, Pappa, Pappas, and George. A
Polish Kolodziejchuk cut back to Kolodi. Feuchtwanger became
Wanger, and Dingfelder became Feld.

The surgery can occur at either end, or both: Koenigs-
berger may become Konig, Berger, or Berg. Rarely, the cut
may be in the middle: a Kasminski became Kaski.

3.   *Getting rid of unusual letter combinations.*   In central and
eastern Europe, as well as in some other countries, some letter
combinations occur that are seldom if ever found in English.
These include, for instance, *cz, sz, dz, fj, hj, hl, hn,* and *tk* (at the
start of a syllable). These are often reduced in the United States
to a single letter, so that Swedish Hjelmstrom, for example, may
be changed to Helmstrom. Or the change may be greater: one
Tkach became Thatcher.

4.   *Making a name seem more "American."*   This overlaps number 3, but does not necessarily include unusual letter combi-

nations. Hordy switches to Hardy, Hoit to Hoyt. Adamowski changes to an unquestionably American Adams.

5. *Substituting.*   A German shopkeeper named Meier switched to Meyer because he found that was how most of his customers and suppliers thought his name was spelled. Because a Mr. Mass didn't like Roman Catholics, he became Moss, but a worshiper in the Catholic faith got even by a complete change of name, from Parsons to Priest.

6. *Lengthening.*   This is rare, but for personal reasons it sometimes occurs. A Syrian-American named Hadad, for example, changed to the more conventional spelling, Haddad. And a number of Poles who liked the *-ski* ending so frequently found in Poland, added it when they came here, although perhaps an even larger number dropped it. Some Polish Rybaks switch to Ryback. Some Czech Hrubys lengthen the name to Horuby, but probably more shorten it to Ruby.

7. *Transposition of letters.*   A family named Borert transposed the *b* and the first *r* to become Robert.

8. *Translation.*   This and shortening are the two most frequent types of change. German Freund becomes Friend; French Meunier, Miller; Italian Piccolo, Small; Slavic Svec, Shoemaker; German Blumenthal, Bloomingdale.

9. *Shift in pronunciation.*   This happens very frequently and usually without being intended. A Latino name, Perez, for instance, in the homeland is normally pronounced PER-ez, but in the United States most people call it Per-EZ. Ivan J. Kramoris had said that he prefers the accent on Kra-, as it would be in most Slavic languages, but that Americans automatically say Kra-MOR-is. Louis Adamic liked Ah-DAH-mitch, but Americans wavered between AD-um-ik and Uh-DAM-ik. A person named Pitz lost the battle to retain the pronunciation PEETZ.

10. *Substitution of an entirely different name.*   Some people, including some whose ancestors came to America long ago, simply do not like their names and switch them to something else. Ernest Maass compiled a long list of names to which Cohen was changed: Brunswick, Cane, Carlton, Carsen, Clark, Cole, Collins, Cone, Cowan, Cunard, Gerard, Kelly, Kennedy, and others.

7

PROFESSIONALS WHO CHANGED THEIR NAMES

ONE HUNDRED AND SIXTY-FOUR ACTORS AND ACTRESSES: ORIGINAL NAMES

Tell me, I pray thee, thy name.—Genesis 32:29

Walter Matuschanskayasky obviously had a good reason for changing his name before becoming an actor. He is known today as Walter Matthau.

You may want to decide for yourself whether each of these other actors and actresses—past and present—gained or lost by change of name.

Eddie Albert—Edward Albert Heimberger

Fred Allen—John Florence Sullivan

Woody Allen—Allen Stewart Konigsberg

June Allyson—Ella Geisman

Julie Andrews—Julia Wells

Ann-Margret—Ann-Margret Olsson

George Arliss—George Augustus Andrews

James Arness—James Aurness

Beatrice Arthur—Bernice Frankel

Fred Astaire—Frederick
Austerlitz
Lauren Bacall—Betty Joan
Perske
Lucille Ball—Dianne
Belmont
Anne Bancroft—Anne-
marie Italiano
Ethel Barrymore—Ethel
Blythe
Lionel Barrymore—Lionel
Blythe
Rex Bell—George F.
Beldam
Jack Benny—Benjamin
Kubelsky
Milton Berle—Milton
Berlinger
Sarah Bernhardt—
Henriette-Rosine Bernard
Vivian Blaine—Vivienne
Stapleton
Amanda Blake—Beverly
Louise Neill
Robert Blake—Michael
Gubitosi
Shirley Booth—Thelma
Booth Ford
George Brent—George
Brendan Nolan
Fannie Brice—Fanny
Borach
Charles Bronson—Charles
Buchinsky
George Burns—Nathan
Birnbaum
Raymond Burr—William
Stacey Burr
Ellen Burstyn—Edna Rae
Gillooly

Richard Burton—Richard
Jenkins
Red Buttons—Aaron
Chwatt
Judy Carne—Joyce Botterill
Diahann Carroll—Carol
Diahann Johnson
Irene and Vernon Castle
(dancers)—Irene Foote
and Vernon Blythe
Lon Chaney, Jr.—Creighton
Chaney
Cyd Charisse—Tula Finklea
Chubby Checkers—Ernest
Evans
Claudette Colbert—Lily
Claudette Chauchoin
Mike Connors—Kreker
Ohanian
Gary Cooper—Frank James
Cooper
Joan Crawford—Lucille Le
Sueur, then Billie Cassin
Tony Curtis—Bernard
Schwartz
Yvonne de Carlo—Peggy
Yvonne Middleton
Ruby Dee—Ruby Ann
Wallace
Angie Dickinson—Angeline
Brown
Marlene Dietrich—Maria
Magdalene Dietrich
Phyllis Diller—Phyllis
Driver
Troy Donahue—Merle
Johnson
Diana Dors—Diana Fluck
Kirk Douglas—Issur
Danielovitch Demsky

Patty Duke—Anna Marie Duke

Dale Evans—Frances Octavia Smith

Nanette Fabray—Ruby Bernadette Nanette Fabarés

Barry Fitzgerald—William Shields

Joan Fontaine—Joan de Havilland

Dame Margot Fonteyn (ballet)—Peggy Hookham

Redd Foxx—John Elroy Sanford

Arlene Francis—Arlene Francis Kazanjian

Zsa Zsa Gabor—Sari Gabor

Greta Garbo—Greta Gustafsson

Ava Gardner—Lucy Johnson

John Garfield—Julius Garfinkle

Judy Garland—Frances Gumm

James Garner—James Baumgarner

Mitzi Gaynor—Francesca Mitzi Marlene de Czanyi von Gerber

Ben Gazzara—Biago Anthony Gazzara

Lillian Gish—Lillian de Guiche

Ruth Gordon—Ruth Jones

Elliot Gould—Elliott Goldstein

Cary Grant—Archibald Alexander Leach

Peter Graves—Peter Aurness

Buddy Hackett—Leonard Hacker

Jean Harlow—Harlean Carpentier

Rex Harrison—Reginald Carey

June Havoc—Ellen Evangeline Hovick

Sterling Hayden—John Hamilton

Helen Hayes—Helen Hayes Brown

Susan Hayward—Edythe Marrener

Rita Hayworth—Margarita Cansino

William Holden—William Beedle

Judy Holliday—Judith Tuvim

Bob Hope—Leslie Townes Hope

Hedda Hopper (columnist)—Elda Furry

John Houseman—Jacques Haussmann

Rock Hudson—b. Roy Scherer; took Roy Fitzgerald as legal name

Tab Hunter—Arthur Gelien

Walter Huston—Walter Houghston

Betty Hutton—Betty Thornburg

Burl Ives—Burl Icle Ivanhoe

Al Jolson—Asa Yoelson

Jennifer Jones—Phyllis
Isley

Boris Karloff—William
Henry Pratt

Danny Kaye—David Daniel
Kaminski

Buster Keaton—Joseph
Francis Keaton

Dorothy Lamour—Mary
Leta Dorothy Kaumeyer

Lassie—Pal

Sir Harry Lauder—Harry
MacLennan

Stan Laurel—Arthur
Stanley Jefferson

Vivien Leigh—Vivian
Hartley

Jerry Lewis—Joseph
Levitch

Carole Lombard—Jane
Alice Peters

Sophia Loren—Sofia
Scicolone

Myrna Loy—Myrna
Williams

Shirley MacLaine—Shirley
MacLean Beaty

Guy Madison—Robert
Moseley

Jayne Mansfield—Vera
Jayne Palmer

Fredric March—Frederick
Bickel

Julia Marlowe—Sarah
Frances Frost

Dean Martin—Dino
Crocetti

Walter Matthau—Walter
Matuschanskayasky

Steve McQueen—Terrence
Steven McQueen

Ray Milland—Reginald
Truscott-Jones

Ann Miller—Lucille Ann
Collier

Liza Minnelli—Lisa Minelli

Carmen Miranda—Maria
do Carmo Miranda da
Cunha

Marilyn Monroe—Norma
Jean Mortenson

Yves Montand—Ivo Livi

George Montgomery—
George Montgomery Letz

Zero Mostel—Samuel Joel
Mostel

Paul Muni—Muni
Weisenfreund

Pola Negri—Appollonia
Chalupiec

Mabel Normand—Mabel
Fortescue

Kim Novak—Marilyn
Novak

Merle Oberon—Estelle
Merle O'Brien Thompson

Margaret O'Brien—Angela
Maxine O'Brien

Maureen O'Hara—Maureen
FitzSimons

Jack Palance—Walter
Palahnuik

Mary Pickford—Gladys
Mary Smith

Jane Powell—Suzanne
Burce

Paula Prentiss—Paula
Ragusa

Martha Raye—Margaret
Tersa Yvonne O'Reed

Debbie Reynolds—Mary
Frances Reynolds

Ginger Rogers—Virginia McMath

Roy Rogers—Leonard Slye

Mickey Rooney—Joe Yule, Jr.

Telly Savalas—Aristotle Savalas

Romy Schneider— Rosemarie Albach-Retty

Lizabeth Scott—Emma Matzo

Randolph Scott—Randolph Crane

Mack Sennett (producer)— Michael Sinnott

Ann Shirley—Dawn Evelyeen Paris, then Dawn O'Day

Dinah Shore—Frances Rose Shore

Phil Silvers—Philip Silversmith

Red Skelton—Richard Skelton

Elke Sommer—Elke Schletz

Sissy Spacek—Mary Elizabeth Spacek

Kim Stanley—Patricia Kimberly Reid

Meryl Streep—Mary Louise Streep

Barry Sullivan—Patrick Barry

Max von Sydow—Carl Adolf von Sydow

Robert Taylor—Spangler Arlington Brugh

Danny Thomas—Amos Jacobs

Rip Torn—Elmore Rual Torn, Jr.

Lana Turner—Julia Jean Mildred Frances Turner

Twiggy—Lesley Hornby

Rudolph Valentino— Rodolpho Alfonzo Raffaelo Pierre Filibert Guglielmo di Valentina D'Antonguolla

Nancy Walker—Ann Myrtle Swoyer

Warner brothers (producers) —Albert, Harry, Jack, and Samuel Eichelbaum

John Wayne—Marion Michael Morrison

Gene Wilder—Jerry Silberman

Shelly Winters—Shirley Schrift

Natalie Wood—Natasha Gurdin

Jane Wyman—Sarah Jane Fulks

Loretta Young—Gretchen Young

FORTY-SEVEN
MUSICIANS AND MUSICAL ENTERTAINERS:
ORIGINAL NAMES

Tony Bennett—Anthony
  Benedetto
Irving Berlin—Israel Baline
Eubie Blake—James Hubert
Maria Callas—Maria
  Kalogeropolos
Ray Charles—Ray Charles
  Robinson
Alice Cooper—Vincent
  Furnier
Bobby Darin—Robert
  Cassotto
Johnny Desmond—
  Giovanni de Simone
Dion—Dion Di Mucci
Bob Dylan—Robert
  Zimmerman
Duke Ellington—Edward
  Kennedy Ellington
"Mama" Cass Elliott—Ellen
  Naomi Cohen
Fabian—Fabian Anthony
  Forte
Freddie Fender—Baldemar
  Huerta
Connie Francis—Concetta
  Franconero
Crystal Gayle—Brenda
  Gayle Webb
Bobbie Gentry—Roberta
  Streeter
Dizzy Gillespie—John Birks
  Gillespie
Skitch Henderson—Lyle
  Russell Cedric Henderson
Hildegarde—Hildegarde
  Loretta Sell

Billie Holiday—Eleonora
  Fagan
Engelbert Humperdinck—
  Arnold Dorsey
Elton John—Reginald
  Kenneth Dwight
Tom Jones—Thomas Jones
  Woodward
Gypsy Rose Lee—Rose
  Louise Hovick
Liberace—Wladziu Liberace
Julie London—Julie Peck
Tony Martin—Alvin
  Morris
Dame Nellie Melba—Helen
  Porter Mitchell
Lauritz Melchior—Lebrecht
  Hommel
Joni Mitchell—Roberta Joan
  Anderson
*Jacques Offenbach—Jacob
  Eberst
Patti Page—Clara Ann
  Fowler
Minnie Pearl—Sarah
  Ophelia Colley Cannon
Roberta Peters—Roberta
  Peterman
Edith Piaf—Edith Gassion
Della Reese—Deloreese
  Patricia Early
Artie Shaw—Abraham Isaac
  Arshawsky
Nina Simone—Eunice
  Kathleen Waymon
Ringo Starr—Richard
  Starkey

Cat Stevens—Steven
  Georgion
Connie Stevens—Concetta
  Ingolia
Franz von Suppé—
  Francisco Ezechiele
  Eermeegildo Suppé
  Demelli

Conway Twitty—Harold
  Lloyd Jenkins
Bruno Walter—Bruno
  Walter Schlesinger
Muddy Waters—McKinley
  Morganfield
Hank Williams, Sr.—Hiram
  King Williams

---

*The Encyclopaedia Britannica *explains, "He was the son of a cantor at the Cologne Synagogue, Isaac Juda Eberst, who had been born at Offenbach am Main. The father was known as 'Der Offenbacher' (i.e., the man from Offenbach), and the composer was known only by his assumed name."*

FIFTY-NINE SPORTS FIGURES:
FAMILIAR NAMES AND "REAL" NAMES

Common nicknames such as Tom, Dick, and Hank are not included in this list.

Sparky Anderson—George
  Anderson
The Bambino—George
  Herman "Babe" Ruth
Sal the Barber—Salvatore
  Maglie
Bear Bryant—Paul Bryant
Rick Barry—Richard Barry
The Big O—Oscar
  Robertson
Big Poison—Paul Waner
Big Train—Walter Johnson
Yogi Berra—Lawrence
  Berra
Ty Cobb—Tyrus Cobb
Crazy Legs—Elroy Hirsch
Daffy Dean—Paul Dean
Dizzy Dean—Jay Hanna
  Dean
Joltin' Joe Dimaggio—
  Joseph Dimaggio

El Cordobés—Manuel
  Benitez Perez
The Galloping Ghost—
  Harold "Red" Grange
The Gipper—George Gipp
Lefty (Goofy) Gomez—
  Vernon Gomez
Lefty Grove—Robert Grove
Rocky Graziano—Rocco
  Barbella
The Greatest—Cassius Clay
  (later Muhammad Ali)
Gabby Hartnett—Charles
  Hartnett
The Horse—Alan Ameche
Catfish Hunter—Jim Hunter
Iron Man—Henry Louis
  (Lou) Gehrig (also Joseph
  Jerome McGinnity)
Sandy Koufax—Sanford
  Koufax

The Lip—Leo Durocher
Little Mo—Maureen
Connolly
Little Poison—Lloyd Waner
Joe Louis—Joe Louis
Barrow
Connie Mack—Cornelius
Alexander McGillicuddy
The Man—Stanley (Stan)
Musial
Rocky Marciano—Rocco
Francis Marchegiano
Pistol Pete Maravich—Peter
Maravich
Nellie—Jacob Nelson Fox
Satchel Paige—Leroy Paige
Papa Bear—George Halas
Pelé—Edson Arantes do
Nascimento
Boog Powell—John Powell
Betsy Rawls—Elizabeth
Earle Rawls
Pee Wee Reese—Harold
Reese
Branch Rickey—Wesley
Branch Rickey
Sugar Ray Robinson—Ray
Robinson (b. Walker
Smith)

Pete Rozelle—Alvin Ray
Rozelle
Bubba Smith—Charles
Aaron Smith
Duke Snider—Edwin Snider
Willie Stargell—Wilver
Dornell Stargell
Casey Stengel—Charles
Dillon Stengel
The Stilt—Wilton (Wilt)
Chamberlain
Sunny Jim—James
Bottomley
Birdie Tebbetts—George R.
Tebbetts
Y. A. Tittle—Yelberton
Abraham Tittle
Rube Waddell—George
Edward Waddell
Rube Walberg—George
Elvin Walberg
Jersey Joe Walcott—Arnold
Raymond Cream
The Whip—Ewell Blackwell
Hack Wilson—Lewis Robert
Wilson
Cale Yarborough—William
Caleb Yarborough
Yaz—Carl Yastrzemski

8

A CHAPTER FOR
THE SMITHS

SMITH 2,382,509;
THATCH(ER) 10,001

Only 3,169 surnames represent over half of the American people. In fact, over 56 percent of all Americans will answer to one of those names.

Smith, as everyone knows, heads the list. When the Social Security Administration last counted, it had in its files the earnings' records of 2,382,509 Smiths. The actual number of living Smiths may be somewhat smaller or somewhat larger than that, since the records of dead Smiths are in the files, but they are compensated for by children and others who do not yet have Social Security numbers.

After Smith, the next 3,168 names all had 10,000 or more of their records in the SSA files. At the bottom of this group stood Thatch, which also includes such names as Thatcher, with 10,001.

The rest of the 1,286,556 SSA names are divided up among the other 44 percent of the population—about 186 persons per name.

MORE FACTS
ABOUT SMITHS

1.   Smith County, Kansas, is the geographic center of the United States, and Smith Center is its county seat.

2.   The first colonial American Smith family (not the first individual) was that of John Smith—the one who founded Barnstable and Sandwich, Massachusetts, early in the seventeenth century. His wife bore him thirteen children. (So that's why there are so many Smiths!)

3.   In England eleven baronets and twenty-eight knights are named Smith, although that name is usually hidden behind some more high-sounding facade.

4.   Five American colleges have Smith as part of their name.

5.   Five Smiths are in the College Football Hall of Fame. Browns and Millers come in second, with four each.

6.   Three first ladies were Smiths: Abigail Smith Adams, Margaret McKall Smith Taylor, and Rosalynn Smith Carter.

7.   Unusual given names of Smiths:
    Five Eighths Smith
    William McKinley Louisiana Levee Bust Smith (born during a flood)
    Major Smith
    Minor Smith
    Bright Smith
    Orange Smith
    Icycle Smith
    Loyal Lodge No. 296 Knights of Pythias Ponca City Oklahoma Smith
    Omega Smith (the end)

8.   One John Smith has boasted that when still a bachelor, he had a fan club that girls and women of his community formed. It was, of course, called the Pocahontas Club.

9.   A Jim Smith Society meets in Las Vegas. (Guess what the criterion for membership is.)

10.   In 1978, according to Elsdon Smith (who else?), 1.0144 percent of Americans were named Smith. He estimated a total

of 2,180,960 of them. Add in variants such as Smythe or Smid and the total rises to 2,378,440. Add to that the names such as Kowal and Haddad which are equivalent to Smith, and the total becomes (conservatively) 4,736,350.

11. Let's translate Elsdon Smith's figures into visual terms.

Imagine that all 2,180,960 "real" Smiths join hands and form a circle with its center in Smith County, Kansas. The circle will reach central Nebraska on the north and the Oklahoma line on the south. To the west the Smiths walk not far from the streets of Denver, and to the east they are near Topeka.

Next, imagine the center of the human circle to be in Albany, New York. The line of Smiths now encompasses Philadelphia, New York City, Boston, Rochester, and Harrisburg, all of Connecticut, Rhode Island, Massachusetts, and New Jersey, and most of New Hampshire, Vermont, and New York, and about a third of Pennsylvania. A couple of hundred thousand other Smiths in the circle have to let go of their neighbors' hands and paddle around in the Atlantic.

A similar Johnson circle would have a radius about three fourths as long, and one composed of Williamses and Williamsons would be a little over five eighths as long, with the Brown and Jones radii somewhat shorter than that.

WHAT DOES A SEXSMITH
DO WITH A SEXAUER?

Sexsmith sounds like a urologist or a gynecologist, but that origin appears unlikely. A variant is Sixsmith, which suggests that this smith must have come from Sixte, a place in France. Elsdon Smith, however, suggests that the original Sixsmith may have made small (six-inch?) daggers or swords. A guess that Sexsmith made sextants and other navigational instruments is dubious, for the word *sextant* was invented after the name-giving period.

Sexauer (variant Sexaur) is easier. He or she came from Sexau, a place in Germany.

(Inevitably, such names lend themselves to jokes. "Do you have a Sexauer in this office?" "No but we get long coffee breaks.")

SOME HOG FARMERS
YELL "HOOEY"

William Sooy Smith, a contracting engineer, got tired of being a Smith. He wanted a name that would be not only uncommon but even unique.

One day he had a burst of inspiration. He decided to combine his middle and last names. He became William Sooysmith.

H. Allen Smith, who told the story in *People Named Smith*, says that the change didn't improve things a great deal, because "Sooy is a cry used in calling hogs."

LEGITIMATIZING
ACCIDENTAL SMITHS

Abraham Lincoln used to tell a story about an Illinois justice of the peace whose commission and seal had not yet arrived. He married one impatient couple anyway and gave them this receipt:

> State of Illinois
> Peoria County

> To all the world Greeting. Know ye that John Smith and Peggy Myres is hereby certified to go together and do as all folks does, anywhere inside coperas precinct, and when my commission comes I am to marry em good and date em back to kivver accidents.

COULD THERE BE A
JONES SPINOFF?

TNSDUNSPHI. Maybe that set of letters doesn't look very exciting, but it covers a gripe that thousands of persons may echo.

The letters stand for The National Society to Discourage Use of the Name Smith for Purposes of Hypothetical Illustration. You know the sort of thing: "There were these two people, see—we'll call 'em Smith and Jones—and they..."

The organization began in 1942 when Glenn E. Smith, a

graduate student at the University of Minnesota, became annoyed because in many class sessions a professor would say something like, "Now we'll look at a typical taxpayer. Call him John Smith."

So Glenn Smith founded TNSDUNSPHI, raised a few dollars from a few Smiths to publicize it, and soon found himself presiding over a rather flourishing organization.

It is especially appropriate that Glenn E. Smith was the founder. According to H. Allen Smith, Glenn's father was of course a Smith, and his mother's maiden name was Smith, so all four of his grandparents were Smiths, and so were at least four of his great-grandparents, to say nothing of unnumbered uncles, aunts, and cousins.

IMAGINE THAT ALL THE JOHNSONS GATHERED IN MANHATTAN

Only Smiths outnumber Johnsons in the United States.

If all the nominal sons and daughters of John in America and Europe were to assemble on Manhattan island, some of them might either have to get their feet wet in the Hudson or the East River or crowd the bridges to the other boroughs.

To begin with, there would be some 2,000,000 Johnsons from the United States. The British Isles would add a few hundred thousand more. The Johnstons, supplemented by a few Johnstones, would add another couple of hundred thousand.

Jones also means ⟨son of John⟩; about 1,400,000, live in the United States alone. Many of the 600,000 Jacksons trace their ancestry to Jack, a nickname for John, although in some cases for Jacob or James. Evans is a Welsh form of John, and there are over a third of a million Evanses in the United States, plus a few Heavenses. There are also many less common British forms of Johnson, such as John, Johns, Johnikin, Johnigan, Jonson, Ja(y)nes, Jenks, Jenkins(on), Jenner, Jennings, Jennison, and Littlejohn.

So far we haven't ushered in the descendants of John in or from continental Europe. The Scandinavians gave us Hansen and Hanson and their variants, as well as some Jons(s)ons, Johansons, Jensens. Germany has Johann(es) and some forms with Hans such as Hansel or Hanschmidt ⟨the John who is a smith⟩ or Henson, as well as such unlikely looking forms as Gentzen, Geschke, and Ham(m)an(n). The Dutch have Jan(t)sen and some other forms; the Italians, Di Giovanni and various combinations with Gian- such as the Giannini who started the Bank of America, as well as Ianni and diminutives such as Iannello; the Spanish, Ibañez; the Greeks, Gianakakis, Gian(n)op(o)ulos, and Ionnides.

Eastern Europe is overrun with the sons of John. Ivan is a frequent beginning, as in Ivan(ov) (ovic) (ow) (cich) (auskas). Russian Ivan Ivanov is only a disguise for John Johnson, and publisher William Jovanovich, with a Yugoslavian name, is really plain old Bill Johnson. Jan starts maybe a hundred east European variants, such as Polish Janowski or Janiszewski, or Lithuanian Jankauskas, or Hungarian Janosfi. Polish Jasinski goes back to Jas, a nickname for Jan, which means John. The Romanians may spell the name Jonescu or Jonesku, or sometimes Ionescu or Enesco. Lithuanians like Jonynas or Jonnitis, who may turn up as an American pro quarterback named Unitas.

Still other descendants of John, if they convened with the rest in Manhattan, would swell its population even more. By that time some of them would be taking over New Jersey.

THE MOST COMMON NAME
IN THE WORLD

No, it's not Smith, Johnson, or any you're likely to think of immediately.

It's Chang, which according to some estimates is held by some seventy-five million people, as compared to only about three and a half million Smiths.

9

SURNAMES
AND
GENEALOGY

KNOWLEDGE OF NAMES:
A TOOL FOR THE GENEALOGIST

"I was trying to trace my family tree," a young woman we'll call Iris Faulkner said recently, "and I got back as far as my great-great-grandparents, but then I was lost. I just couldn't find anything more about any Faulkners in the area, and I couldn't find out where they came from. Suddenly, like magic, they were just there."

Iris was helped by a friend, Ray, who was better versed in genealogy. He asked her whether she had searched the records of the late eighteenth century for possibly varied spellings of Faulkner.

"Well," Iris said, "I looked for Falkner, and Faukner, and I did find some Faukeners, but they weren't connected to us."

Ray pulled from his shelves a book that listed American surnames of 1790. It showed thirteen spellings of Faulkner in use at that time.

"My guess," Ray said, "is that there may be a clue in one

of these other spellings—most likely Falconer, which is, as you probably know, the meaning of the name. If you can trace it back far enough—and admittedly that can be difficult—you'll probably find that in the Middle Ages, in England, some remote ancestor of yours trained falcons and used them in hunting small game."

Ray proved partly right, partly wrong. The variant that Iris found to be the name of her eighteenth-century forebears was Falkener, not Falconer, but the source and the meaning were what Ray said.

Names are necessarily the focus of much—probably most— of the work of the genealogist, whether amateur or professional. Some newspapers run regular columns of genealogical inquiry, typically consisting of entries requesting help from anyone knowing about the holders of a certain name in the comparatively recent or possibly more remote past. Here are a couple of representative entries:

> Who were parents of Stella HUNTER who m. George CARSON? They were at Heltonville, Lawrence County, in 1876.

> Want parents, marriage date, place, correspondence with descendants of Christely HELLENBURG, HILDENBORG, HILGENBORG, HELLENBORG 1810 Virginia/Tennessee and Mary HOUSHOUR. Known children: Eliza b. about 1851; John b. 1853 m. Lucy A. HANSON Feb. 21, 1872, Monroe County, Ind.; Elizabeth b. about 1860; Mary Catherine b. 1863; Andrew (Jack?) JACKSON, b. about 1843 m. Sarah J. HOUSHOUR Feb. 21, 1867, Lawrence County, Ind.

Information about long-dead people is often hidden in musty records in places such as courthouses and churches, or in research that other genealogists have performed in the past. The Church of Latter Day Saints (Mormons) in Salt Lake City houses the most extensive collection of American genealogical information available anywhere; it is not confined to members of that faith. Canadians have done considerable genealogical work, as have many scholars in all parts of the British Isles and in all of the European nations outside the Communist bloc.

When a search needs to be continued abroad, the various national genealogical societies can often be helpful in supplying leads.

Many public libraries, including some in small towns, also have fairly extensive genealogical collections, usually with emphasis on past residents of the immediate area. An especially good collection is that of the New York Public Library (Fifth Avenue at Forty-second Street), whose librarians, well trained in genealogy, can be very helpful to patrons.

A good source of printed information is the Genealogical Publishing Company, 111 Water Street, Baltimore, MD 21202. It specializes in reprints of books and other materials. A recent catalog has eighty-four pages, with descriptions of about ten books, etc., on each page. From those hundreds of publications, here are some representative titles:

Americans of Royal Descent
Emigrants from England, 1773–1776
Passengers Who Arrived in the United States, Sept., 1821–Dec., 1823 (427 pages)
Southern Families, Vol. XV. (Allred, Anderson, Delafield, Etheridge, Hayes-Hays, Jernigan, Matthews, Rose, Tate, and other families are covered.)
Wallingford, Connecticut, Early Families
Emigrants to Pennsylvania, 1641–1819

Information about marriage notices, baptisms, deaths, and wills is contained in other publications.

The serious tracer of American families must almost always eventually search in foreign sources—whether in person or through printed materials. Again, much guide material is available. One example: two volumes by Margaret D. Falley, *Ancestral Research, Irish and Scotch-Irish*, which give details about the major Irish repositories, dates of coverage of material on specific families, and (in Volume Two) a bibliography of family histories, pedigrees, and source materials published in books and periodicals, and including parish, town, and county histories, church records, and summaries of family data.

Names! The more the genealogist knows about names, the more successful the investigation may be. Always the search is based on names, but glimpses of the people whom the names represent are not infrequent. In almost everyone's family there are likely to be found civic leaders and highwaymen, women who brought up large families after losing husbands, maiden ladies or prostitutes, workers in occupations now almost vanished, soldiers or sailors who died young or became colonels or sea captains, illegitimate as well as legitimate children—each person (except possibly infants) with a name, a life, a story that transcends the brief notice in an old church or on a hard-to-decipher tombstone.

In Thomas Gray's still-familiar words, written in the eighteenth century,

> Beneath those rugged elms, the yew-tree's shade,
>   Where heaves the turf in many a mouldering heap,
> Each in his narrow cell forever laid,
>   The rude forefathers of the hamlet sleep.
>   Their name, their years, spelt by the unlettered Muse,
>   The place of fame and elegy supply.

The modern genealogist sometimes provides the missing elegy.

HOW TO FIND THE MEANING OF A SURNAME

The best source of surnominal meanings is Elsdon C. Smith, *New Dictionary of American Family Names.* (New York: Harper & Row, 1973). Smith briefly defines and gives the nationality of some 20,000 names, including all the most common names and many that are unusual. However, even that book can include fewer than 2 percent of the more than a million American surnames; a treatment of all the names would require many volumes and would be prohibitively expensive.

If Smith does not appear to list the name you are interested in, look to see whether he may have placed it under any possible variant spelling. Next, check a dictionary of the language that the name probably comes from. If it is an occupational name, a descriptive, or a general place name such as the equivalent of Lake, the dictionary should help.

If you think it may be the name of a specific place, consult a detailed map of the country—if possible, one that includes the names of rather small towns, as a good road map does. Many uncommon German names, for instance, are taken from town names or names of specific mountains or other physical features. If you suspect that the name is a patronym, you may find (especially among Slavic names) that it is a variant spelling of the name of a saint or other famous person. Saint Basil, for instance, shows up in such varied forms as Vasely, Wasielawski, and Vasilevich; Alexander, as Lesko, Olcksandrenko, Sandor.

With Italian and Slavic names, watch especially for nicknames and shortened forms. For instance, among Italian names, although the equivalent of Anthony may be Antonelli or a variant, it may also be Tonelli or a variant of that; Francisco sometimes appears as Cisco, Ciscolo, or Ciccone; Jacob is almost unrecognizable as Giacomo, Chiapetta, Como, and Mazzucci; Nicholas may show up as Colonna, and Thomas as Massi or a variant.

Further hints may be found in this book—e.g., the information about diminutives (page 123) or about affixes that mean ⟨son of⟩ (page 121). Two other sources are Elsdon Smith's *American Surnames* (Philadelphia: Chilton Book Company, 1969), and J. N. Hook's *Family Names* (New York: Macmillan Publishing Company, 1980).

HOW TO RECOGNIZE
EVERYBODY'S LITTLE BOY

Over 30 percent of American surnames have the meaning of ⟨son of⟩, ⟨grandson of⟩, or ⟨descendant of⟩, and very frequently such patronyms are signaled by a prefix or a suffix. Often the ancestral background of a name can easily be determined from the affix. The following clues are generally accurate indicators, although the fact that people have sometimes changed their names to those representative of other nationalities creates some exceptions.

acs, as in Lukacs, Hungarian for ⟨descendant of Luke⟩
aitis, *onis*, as in Petraitis or Petronis, Lithuanian for ⟨son of Peter⟩
ak, as in Michalak, Polish for ⟨descendant of Michael⟩. Sometimes spelled *ack* in the U.S.

akis, *akos*, as in Petrakis, Petrakos, Greek for ⟨descendant of Peter⟩

ap or *Up*, as in ap Richard or Upjohn, Welsh for ⟨son of Richard⟩, ⟨son of John⟩. Now rare, having been reduced to *P*, as in Powell, or *B*, as in Bowen.

chuk as in Klemchuk, Ukrainian for ⟨descendant of Clement⟩

czyk, *czak*, as in Rybarczyk, Polish for ⟨son of the fisherman⟩, Matczak ⟨son of Matthew⟩

D', *De*, *Di*, as in Italian D'Angelo ⟨son of the angel⟩, De Stefano ⟨son of Stephen⟩, Di Bernardo ⟨son of Bernard⟩. In French or Spanish names, *De* usually indicates a place rather than a person.

ek, *ik*, as in Polish Janicek, Janik ⟨descendant of John⟩

enko, *inko*, as in Pavlenko, Paolinko, Ukrainian ⟨son of Paul⟩

es, as in Lopes, Portuguese ⟨son of Lope or Lupe⟩. Sometimes may be Spanish.

escu, as in Antonescu, Romanian ⟨descendant of Anthony⟩. Sometimes spelled *esco*.

ez, as in Martinez, Spanish ⟨son of Martin⟩. Occasionally *az* or *es* is a variant.

Fitz, as in Irish or English Fitzsimmons ⟨son of Simon⟩

Mac, *Mc*, *M'*, *Me*, as in MacNeil, McNeil, M'Neely, Meneely, Scottish or Irish ⟨son of Neil or of Conghal⟩. See also page 143.

O', as in O'Dea, Irish ⟨grandson of Deoghadh⟩

off, *ov*, as in Petroff or Petrov, Russian ⟨son of Peter⟩. Sometimes Bulgarian.

ovic, as in Jankovic, Yugoslavian ⟨son of John⟩. Often dropped or changed to *ovich* in the U.S. The *o* may be missing or substituted for.

ovich, as in Grigorovich, Russian ⟨son of Gregory⟩. Sometimes Yugoslavian. The *o* may be another vowel, or missing.

ovici, as in Grigorovici, Yugoslavian (Serbian) ⟨son of Gregory⟩

poulos, as in Antonopoulos, Greek ⟨descendant of Anthony⟩. Often appears as a variant or *os*.

s, as in Evans, Welsh ⟨son of John⟩. Appears often in English names, too.

sen, as in Norwegian or Danish Svensen ⟨son of Sven⟩

son, as in Swedish Swanson ⟨son of Swan⟩, Swedish or Norwegian Olson (also Olsen in Norway) ⟨son of Ole or Olaf⟩, English Williamson ⟨son of William⟩. Sometimes shortened to *s*.

vicius, as in Lithuanian Matulevicius ⟨descendant of Matthew⟩
wiak, *wicz*, as in Polish Bartowiak ⟨son of Bartholomew⟩,
Adamowicz ⟨son of Adam⟩. Often respelled as *vits* or *witz*.
Diminutives also often carry the suggestion of ⟨little son of⟩.

See the following article.

THANK HEAVEN
FOR LITTLE ONES

A young Italian mother was caressing her infant. "Ah, Pietro
mio," she cooed. "Piccolo Pietro. Petri mio. Petrelli mio. Te
amo, Petrelli."

It was probably in such a way that diminutives began—
pet names that mean ⟨little⟩. They are often based on the father's name; perhaps little Pietro's father was also Pietro. But
sometimes the source is a pet form of the name, as Petri is of
Pietro, or sometimes it is merely the infant's name with a diminutive ending.

In English, Jenkinson, Jenkins, and Jenks are interesting
examples of diminutives. Jen is a nickname for John; *-kin* is an
English (originally Low German) diminutive ending; and *-son*
or the *-s* in Jenkins and Jenks means ⟨son of⟩. So each of the
three names means ⟨little son of John⟩. Wilkinson, Wilkins, and
Wilks are parallel names: ⟨little son of Will⟩. The diminutive
-kin appears in many other names, such as Watkins ⟨little son
of Walter⟩, Elkin ⟨little Elie or Elias⟩, and Larkin ⟨little Law-
rence⟩.

Another English diminutive is *-cock*, as in the name of
Gordon Johncock ⟨little John⟩, a prominent auto race driver;
Hitchcock or Hedgecock is ⟨little Hitch (a nickname for Richard)⟩. In the form *-cocks* or *-cox* the meaning ⟨son of⟩ is added,
so Wilcox is ⟨little son of Will.⟩.

The endings *-ie*, *-y*, and *-ey* are sometimes diminutives, as
in Willie or Will(e)y, but are not reliable indicators, since often
they mean ⟨island⟩, as in Hardie or Hardy, or (with *l*) ⟨a meadow⟩,
as in Fairlie or Fairley.

Many English surnames were borrowed from the French
after the Norman Conquest. If you see an English name ending
in *-eau*, *-el(le)*, *-et(te)*, *ot(te)*, or *-on*, or in the double diminutive
-elin, *-elet*, *-inet*, or *-elot*, the odds are that it was originally a

French name. Examples of some of these, from either English or French, are Watteau, Mallet(t)(te), Marriott, Hamon, Michelet or Michelin, and Philpott, referring respectively to little Vatier, Mal, Mary, home, Michel, and Philip.

The most distinctive of the several Irish diminutives are -*an* and especially -*gan*. Ryan and Nolan, for example, go back to Celtic words meaning ⟨little king⟩ and ⟨little noble one⟩. The ending -*gan* appears in scores of names such as Finnegan ⟨little fair one⟩ and Milligan ⟨little bald one⟩.

The Germans most often use -*ke* (to which the English -*kin* is related): Gehrke ⟨little spear-wielder⟩, Lemke ⟨little Lem or Lampo⟩. Less frequent is -*lein* as in Heinlein ⟨little Heinrich⟩; the ending may be written as -*len*. Sometimes -*isch* appears: Janisch ⟨little John⟩.

The Dutch may use -*ke*, too, as well as -*je*: Lutje ⟨little folk⟩ and Henke ⟨little hedged place⟩.

Lithuanian diminutives include -*ikas*, -*ulis*, and -*kus*, as in Jonikas and Janulis, both of which mean ⟨little John⟩, and Butkus ⟨little Butkintas⟩. Onomatists who saw the gigantic all-pro Dick Butkus playing defense for the Chicago Bears doubted the appropriateness of the name.

The Italians are the greatest lovers of diminutives. All these endings appear again and again: -*etti* and -*etto*; -*ello*, -*ella*, -*elli*, and the Neapolitan -*illo*; -*ini* and -*ino*; -*occo*, -*ucci*, and -*uzzo*. A few examples: Marinelli ⟨little Martin⟩, Morello or Moretti ⟨little Amore⟩ or ⟨little dark one⟩, Parillo ⟨little treasure⟩, Paolino or Paolini ⟨little Paul⟩, Piccini ⟨little man⟩, Masucci ⟨little Thomas⟩.

The opposite of a diminutive is an augmentative—much more rare. In Italian, -*one* is often an augmentative. For example, Petrone or Petroni(o) is ⟨big Pietro⟩, and Capone supposedly has a big head.

10

SOME
JEWISH FAMILY
NAMES

ZVONKO RODE'S FIFTEEN
SOURCES OF JEWISH FAMILY NAMES

1. Biblical names: Abraham, Aaron, etc.

2. Derivation from biblical names: Sacks (from Isaac), Lewin (from Levi)

3. Translations of biblical names: Baruch ⟨blessed⟩ sometimes becomes Benedict or Selig. Ephraim (associated with fish) might become Fisch(el), Rybowitz, Karp, Hecht ⟨pike⟩, Heilbut ⟨halibut⟩, Lax or Lox.

4. Hebrew names with German or Yiddish endings: David could become Tevele, and Simon might become Schimmel or Suskind. (Elsdon Smith, however, mentions no Jewish connection with the last two names.)

5. Equivalents of Hebrew names: Gabriel might become Gebert or Gebhardt; Jacob could be Koppelmann.

6. Names indicating place (especially numerous): Bachrach

(a town), Bing (from Bingen), Birnbaum (a town), Halpern (Heilbronn), Hirschberg (town), Schoenfeld (town), Steinberg (town), Tannhauser ⟨one who lived in a forest house⟩.

7.   Countries: Schwab (from Schwaben, Swabia), Hess (German), Österreicher (Austrian), Welish, Reuss(er) (Russian), Turk

8.   House signs: Adler ⟨eagle⟩, Blum ⟨flower⟩, Engel ⟨angel⟩, Nussbaum ⟨nut tree⟩

9.   Patronyms: Bendavid ⟨son of David⟩, Isaacson, Mendelsohn, Abramowicz, Jacobovitz

10.   Trades and occupations: Cantor, Goldschmidt, Koch ⟨cook⟩, Steiner ⟨mason⟩, Ta(e)nzer ⟨dancer, juggler⟩

11.   Descriptions: Kraus ⟨curly⟩, Rothbard ⟨red beard⟩, Jaffe ⟨beautiful⟩, Zadik ⟨just⟩

12.   Nicknames: Graf, Kaiser, Koenig

13.   Arbitrary (probably imposed): Kanarienvogel ⟨canary bird⟩, Mausehund ⟨mouse dog⟩, Raubvogel ⟨predatory bird⟩, Regenbogen ⟨rainbow⟩, Cohnreich ⟨rich Cohen "priest"⟩

14.   Acronyms: Zak (from zera kedoshim ⟨the seed of martyrs⟩). See below.

15.   Changed names: Silver from Silberberg ⟨silver mountain⟩, Wilson from Weichselbaum ⟨cherry tree⟩, Winston from Weinstein (a mountain's name), Wolf from Wolkowicz ⟨son of Wolf⟩

Rode gives many additional examples. Note that Jews and Gentiles use many of the same names.

NAMES THAT ARE
ACRONYMS

Some 170 Jewish names, according to an article by Joshua H. Neumann, are acronyms—names based on the initial letters of two or more words. Names in Hebrew are written without vowels, but with dots below or above consonants to show where vowels must be inserted. (For non-Jewish readers the vowels are supplied in transcriptions.)

Two   illustrations   of   acronyms: *ben   Rabbi   Nach-*

man → *Baran*; zera *Kedoshim* ⟨the ancestor of martyrs⟩ → *Zak*.

Here are other examples, but it must be remembered that some of these names (Bach, for instance) more frequently come from other sources.

Beth Chadash (a book title) → Bach
ben Reb Tzabok → Baratz
ben Reb David → Bard, Barth, Bradt, Bardowicz
ben Reb Moshe Shmuel → Barmash
ben Shimson → Basch
Chatan [hatan] *Reb Pinkhas* ⟨son-in-law of Pinkhas⟩ → Charap
dayan umelitz ⟨judge and defender⟩ → Dym
kohen tzedek ⟨priest of righteousness⟩ → Katz
moreh tzedek ⟨teacher of righteousness⟩ → Metz
Rabbi Moshe ben Maimon → Rambam
Shabbetai Cohen → Schach
sheyibye leorekh yamin tovim ⟨may he live long and good days⟩ → Schalit

UNUSUAL WAYS
TO SELECT SURNAMES

Instead of being named for a place, a person, an occupation, personal appearance or other characteristics, some people get their surnames in ways that seem odd.

During the late eighteenth and early nineteenth centuries, in parts of what is now Germany, laws were passed requiring all Jews without surnames to adopt them. France's Napoleon and Russia's Tsar Alexander issued edicts to the same effect. Some Jews were unwilling and suspicious of the rulers' motives, but governments insisted. For a fee, a Jew could buy an attractive name such as Diamant, Saphire, Rosenthal ⟨rose valley⟩, or Grünberg ⟨green mountain⟩. Those who refused to pay, or could not, might be told that their names were to be Eselkopf ⟨donkey head⟩, Verderber ⟨wrecker⟩, Schmalz ⟨grease⟩, Drachenblutt ⟨dragon blood⟩, Saumagen ⟨sow belly⟩, or Wanzenknicker ⟨louse cracker⟩. Needless to say, most such names have been changed since that time.

Biblical names were often forbidden, but many Jews dared

to adopt them anyway. For that reason thousands of Jews are named Abraham, Abram, Abramowicz, and the like. Some Jews opened their Bibles randomly and picked the first name they saw. Benzion Kaganoff tells of a rabbi who opened the prayer book and assigned the first word on a page as the name of one family in his congregation, the second word to a second family, and so on, until all had surnames. In some German-controlled parts of Hungary, Jews were arbitrarily assigned one of four names: Weiss, Schwartz, Gross, or Klein. A few Jews chose names popular in the literature of the time; Kaganoff gives Sternberg and Morgenthau as examples.

Some American Indians, too, were forced to choose surnames. Ordinarily they or an Indian agent translated a nickname; in that way came Running Deer, Lone Wolf, Red Cloud, and similar names, but also some derisive names such as Fool Head, Crooked Nose, or Cowardly Fox. H. L. Mencken says that one agent mistranslated Young Man Whose Very Horses Are Feared into Young Man Afraid of His Horse. Other names referred to bodily functions or parts not mentioned in most American names.

Chinese legend says that all Chinese names—there seem to be no more than a thousand of them—are derived from an ancient poem, "The Families of a Hundred Houses." As a result, literally millions of unrelated people may be named Chang, Chin, Li, or other common names.

Similarly, Korea has but few names. Gary Jennings tells a story of an American officer, who during the Korean war said to his Korean friend, "Let's get the hell out of here, Kim," and two thirds of the company started to run away.

Jennings asserts more seriously that the few Chickahominy Indians surviving in Virginia are all named Bradley. "The name commemorates either the popularity or the fecundity of an early English colonial, a runaway indentured servant, who joined and married into the tribe."

NAMES
OF
BLACKS

NAMES OF SLAVES

Black slaves were each given, as a rule, a very common English name. Among 972 names recorded between 1619 and 1799, Newbell Niles Puckett, a black scholar, found these to be the leaders:

Jack (57)   Caesar (21)   Frank (16)
Tom (47)   Dick (20)   Charles (15)
Harry (34)   John (18)   Joe (14)
Sam (30)   Robin (18)   Prince (14)
Will (23)

Much further down the list came names surviving from Africa, most often with only one or two representatives among the 972 in the sample. These included, for instance, Anque, Bumbo, Jobah, Quamana, Taynay, and Yearie.

The names of women slaves followed a similar pattern. Here are the most common of their names in a sample of 603:

Bet (38)	Betty (15)	Nan (13)
Mary (22)	Sarah (15)	Peg (12)
Jane (18)	Phillis (14)	Sary (12)
Hanna (16)		

Some of the women, too, were still called by African names such as Abah, Bilah, Comba, Dibb, Juba, Kauchee, Mima, Sena.

In both sexes a higher proportion of African names might have survived if Africans had all spoken essentially the same language. But there are hundreds of African languages; the 100 million people in the Bantu group alone, for instance, speak more than 300 different languages. The slaves were not all brought from the same part of Africa, and consequently often could not understand one another. They were likely to accept as the "right" name whatever a white owner or foreman called the slave who had just been brought in.

In French-speaking Louisiana, slave names reflected the dominant language and so were generally different from those in the English colonies. There the names were often François, Jean, Pierre, and Leon for men, and Manon, Delphine, Marie Louise, Celeste, and Eugenie for women. Spanish areas had male slaves with names such as Francisco, Pedro, and Antonio, and females named Maria, Isabella, and Juana.

NAMES ADOPTED
BY FREE BLACKS

Slaves almost always had but one name, but when they became free they immediately chose surnames while usually (not always) keeping the given names they had been accustomed to. When retained, a given name was generally changed to its full form: Thomas, not Tom; Elizabeth, not Bet. Jack was no longer among the leaders.

Hundreds of free blacks fought in the American Revolution. They included, in the Fourth Connecticut Regiment, these surnames, among others:

Freeman (the
   most popular)
Johnson
Brown
Greene

Rogers
Ball
Caesar
Jackson

Liberty
Phillips
Rhodes
Vassall

After the Civil War a few slaves took the name of a former master—possibly sometimes out of affection, other times because of indifference or a lack of any better idea. In general, though, they tried to conform to the customs of the land in which they were then (at least on paper) completely free men and women. One of the customs, it seemed, was for most people to have one of 200 to 300 especially common names. The extent to which the former slaves chose these common "white" names for themselves is shown in this list of the top fifteen names among blacks of Augusta, Georgia, in 1877:

1. Williams (2)
2. Jones (4)
3. Johnson (3)
4. Smith (1)
5. Jackson —

6. Thomas —
7. Brown (5)
8. Walker (11)
9. Davis (6)
10. Green —

11. Robinson —
12. Scott —
13. Harris —
14. Turner—
15. Anderson —

(The number in parentheses shows the rank of the same name, when available, among Augusta's whites in the same year.)

EIGHT STEMS FROM *ROOTS*

Alex Haley's famous *Roots* detailed the tracing of his ancestry back to Africa. The following events are among those that occurred during its amazing reception after publication and again after episodes based on it were presented on TV—one of the most successful series in television history.

1.   On February 18, 1977, "Kunta Kinte Reid, a 7-pound, 11-ounce baby boy, was born to John and Nefhertiti Reid in Harlem Hospital." His mother was quoted as saying, "Like Kunta Kinte [the main character in *Roots*], he should be free, and he should be somebody and know that he is somebody."

2.   In that same month, nineteen other babies born in New York City were named Kunta Kinte or Kizzy (Kunta Kinte's daughter). There were also fifteen such names reported from Los Angeles, ten from Detroit, and eight from Atlanta, as well as a male and female pair of twins in Cleveland.

3.   Travel agencies in March 1977, reported "a virtual explosion of American interest in travel to Africa," especially via Air Afrique. Some agencies started special "Roots" tours that went to Senegal and included time in Jaffure, Gambia, where Kunta Kinte was born.

4.   Although Doubleday published *Roots*, other houses moved to share the wealth. Random House, for instance, reissued *Generations*, concerning family histories, and published a book of selections related to the theme of *Roots*, with Haley as a consultant. Random House and Miami-Dade Junior College co-operated in a *Roots*-based project with tapes, films, books, and courses—bought immediately by 150 institutions.

5.   Scholars conducted interviews with slaves' descendants who still lived in the relatively isolated Sea Islands off the coast of South Carolina and Georgia.

6.   The Carnegie Foundation underwrote a Madison High School (Brooklyn) program to fight ethnic tensions, and other schools and colleges started programs similar in purpose, with or without foundation support.

7.   David Duke, director of the Knights of the Ku Klux Klan, asked the ABC-TV network, which put on the televised *Roots*, for equal time to respond to its "vicious malignment of whites." His request was denied.

8.   Usually in the Genealogy Room of the New York Public Library most of the chairs had been vacant, but on some occasions A.R. (After *Roots*) a seat was hard to find.

FOR COLORED GIRLS [AND BOYS] WHO HAVE CONSIDERED SUICIDE: When the Rainbow is Enuf

In the 1970s a play opened in New York with the above title (minus the bracketed words). It was written—and acted in—

by an unknown young black woman named Ntozake Shange, which everybody wondered how to pronounce (and still may not be sure).

The *New Yorker* referred to "stunned audiences" and said the play was "made up of poetry, music, dancing, and light. ...Ntozake Shange's poetry is mordantly witty, unpredictable, and disciplined. It has to do with love and death and the deepest feelings of young women—in particular, black young women." The play had a long run, was exported to other cities, was made into a TV movie, and was followed by another play by the same author.

Who is Ntozake Shange? A young woman who spent much of her growing-up time in St. Louis, "the place from which runaway slaves might reach freedom and Canada via the Underground Railroad." An intense young woman who resented needing three locks on her Harlem apartment door. "I wanted to be a Mississippi River gambler like Tyrone Power, done up with his fancy frock coat and his ruffled sleeves and his big hat," she told the *New Yorker*.

She studied at Barnard and at the University of Southern California, and she used to read her poems aloud in San Francisco bars and bookstores. She absorbed Simone de Beauvoir, Herman Melville, Carson McCullers, Edna St. Vincent Millay, Jean Genet. "I guess I've been in every black nationalist movement in the country, and I found that the flaw in the nationalists' dream was that they didn't treat women right."

Her grandmother, she says, would understand the use of "Colored Girls" in the title. "I was a regular colored girl, with a family that was good to me." But "I write about pain."

"Five years ago I took an African name."

Her natal name: Paulette Williams, which she says is a "slave name."

Her father is Dr. Paul T. Williams, a surgeon—no slave—who plays drums and knew Charlie Parker.

Her mother was a psychiatric social worker; she switched to teaching early childhood development at Trenton State College.

Changes by blacks to African (or often Middle Eastern) names were fairly frequent, especially after boxer Cassius Clay became Muhammad Ali. Boastful, "I'm the greatest," but often able to live up to his boasts. Colorful, spouting his "poetry" before and after many of his fights. In the words of an old commercial for motor oil, "Tough—but oh so gentle."

Lew Alcindor, the basketball giant who once led UCLA's national championship teams, now, as Kareem Abdul-Jabbar, continues to lead as a professional player with the Los Angeles Lakers.

Here and there, other athletes and non-athletes followed Cassius and Lew and Paulette in name changes, and no doubt many more debated the possible emotional advantages and the uncertain disadvantages of taking such a step. Those who made a change seem to have been thoughtful, sometimes intellectual, often bitter about past hurts, and understandably unwilling to move at the slow pace of time—"I want it all, and I want it now." Protesters, but not violent—protesters seeking a way to show their resentment against whites and their pride in blackness by adopting names more appropriate to their black heritage.

On most of the streets of Harlem, though, on the South Side of Chicago, and in Watts, and in predominantly black areas of the other major cities, and through the small towns and in the tobacco and cotton and rice fields of the south, the names are still generally Smith, Johnson, Williams, Brown, and the like. Most blacks haven't followed Paulette and Cassius and Lew, certainly not all the athletes, by any means, as a glance at the rosters of any professional sport will show. And not all the authors—not, for instance, Alex Haley, which means ⟨one who lives along the way to the manor house or great hall⟩. Of course Haley is no longer just along the way.

FROM ENGLAND

THOSE GOOD
OLD ENGLISH NAMES

In searching through records kept by English courts and other
official bodies—records mainly from the thirteenth and fourteenth centuries—C. L'Estrange Ewen found many surnames
he considered amusing. He reported these and more serious
stuff, in his *History of Surnames in the British Isles.*

We may wonder whether W. Cockesbrayn of Sussex was
very smart. Geoffrey Drinkedregges of Lincolnshire must have
been very thirsty. J. Fivepeni was apparently less lucky than
Hugh Findesilver.

Perhaps Hackewude's axe was dull. We can rejoice with
Edward Havejoy, and perhaps with Richard Hotgo, but we must
be sorry for J. Rotenhering of Yorkshire and George Shotbolte
of Essex. We've probably all known someone like C. Smartknave
and Thom. Swetemouth.

Here are others from Ewen's list to pique interest and
curiosity:

W. Barlicorn	Maudlyn Brickbatt	Rich. Catskin
Hy. Blancfrunt	J. Bullimore	Rich. Cokeye
J. Brasskettle	Rob. Buttermouth	Hugh Doggetail

J. Domesoft
Thom. Drinkmilk
J. Drunken
Mary Eightacres
Alan Evilchild
Anne Godhelpe
(or Godhelpe
Anne)
Serle Gotokirke
Rob. Hanging
W. Harepyn
Sarra Hopshort
Mary Isbroke
Rich. Lateboy
Harvey Leaping-
well

Geoff. Lickefinger
Rob. Litelbodi
J. Litelskill
Maud Lusshefish
Rog. Milksoppe
Rich. Nettelbed
W. Oldflessh
J. Onehand
Alice Peckechese
Rich. Pitchfork
Grace Pluckrose
J. Pokepot
J. Ratellebagge
Rich. Ringgebelle
Geo. Sawhell
Hen. Scrapetrough

J. Shepewassh
Rob. Silverspon
W. Smalwryter
Ann Speerpoint
Aug'tine Spurne-
water
W. Strokelady
W. Stykkefyshe
— Sweatinbed
Jacob Tiplady
Hen. Tukbacon
J. Underdonne
Walt. Wanderbug
J. Waytelove
Rob. Witheskirtes

Ewen says, "No attempt will be made by the writer to determine origin, meaning, or classification of these examples, which will be left entirely to the reader." A wise decision!

CAN YOU READ
THIS MAN'S NAME?

We don't know how the world's greatest dramatist spelled his name. All of his surviving signatures are shown here, and not one is any more decipherable than the signatures appended by many modern businessmen to their letters.

One thing that those signatures do seem to show is that he didn't spell his name Shakespeare.

His contemporaries often did, though. That's what printers put on the title pages of most of his plays that were issued singly (the quartos), and also on the famous posthumous collection known as the First Folio. And his friend Ben Jonson wrote "Shakespeare" at least once and "Shake-Speare" another time.

Other sources, including various business and legal records, show these spellings.

Shagspere	Shackespere	Shaxspere
Shakspere	Shakespere	Shackespeare
Shake-speare	Shakspeare	Shakspere
Shackspere	Shakespear	

In 1930 a scholar found a total of ninety-three early and late variants of the name. Why so many variations? Mainly because in the Elizabethan age, spelling was not yet standardized. People still spelled almost as they chose; the same person might sometimes spell the same word in different ways, and there were no adequate dictionaries by which one could check a spelling.

What, then, is the "right" spelling of the dramatist's name? "Shakespeare" has the support of tradition as well as wide usage when the writer was still alive. But some handwriting experts say that his signatures—at least some of them—probably say "Shakspere." Both Shakespeare and Shakspere can be found in modern scholarly writing.

BRITISH
HYPHENATED NAMES

The British custom of using hyphenated names, observed mainly by prominent, estate-owning families, has never really caught on in the United States, although some years ago H. L. Mencken did discover a Congressman named Horace Seely-Brown. Some married women have retained their maiden names, as when Louise Rae Clark became Louise Rae Clark-Simmons. Much more often, however, a modern American woman who wishes to retain her former name for business, professional, or other reasons, simply does not adopt her husband's name. Mrs. Simmons may still be known as Ms. Clark. (See also page 268.)

In Britain the heir to money from the female side of a family was sometimes required, by prior consent or by the terms of a will, to adopt the female family name. Sometimes the male family name was then dropped, but in the nineteenth century the custom arose of using both names, with a hyphen between. Winston Churchill, for instance, was really Winston Spencer-Churchill.

The names sometimes became ungainly. A Wellesley-Pole eventually became Pole-Tylney-Long-Wellesley. H. L. Mencken commented on two other names:

> The name of Vice-Admiral the Hon. Sir Reginald Aylmer Ranfurly *Plunkett-Ernie-Erle-Drax*, K.C.B., D.S.O., R.N....would ruin him in the United States. So would that of Walter Thomas James Scrymsoure-Steuart-Fothringham, a Scotch magnate.

Elsdon Smith points out another problem, that of alphabetizing. Librarians, he says, cannot decide whether author Bulwer-Lytton belongs in the B's or the L's.

TITLES OF RESPECT

"These men that you have selected for the grand jury," Judge Doddridge of the Huntingdon, England, Assizes complained to his sheriff, "are not of a rank suitable to serve His Majesty's court in this year of our Lord 1619."

So the sheriff, a man of good humor, picked a new grand jury, headed by Maximilian King. He read his new list aloud to the judge, like this:

Maximilian	KING of Toseland
Henry	PRINCE of Godmanchester
George	DUKE of Domersham
William	MARQUIS of Stukely
Edmund	EARL of Hartford
Richard	BARON of Bythorn
Stephen	POPE of Newton
Humphrey	CARDINAL of Kimbolton
Robert	LORD of Waresley
William	ABBOTT of Stukeley
Robert	BARON of St. Neots
William	DEAN of Old Weston
John	ARCHDEACON of Paxton
Peter	ESQUIRE of Easton
Edward	FRYER of Ellington
Henry	MONK of Stukeley
George	GENTLEMAN of Spaldwick
George	PRIEST of Graffham
Richard	DEACON of Catworth

People with many of these same surnames were still living in or near Huntingdon two centuries later. At least one of them, Maximilian King, had exactly the same name as his distant ancestor.

13

THE
NATIONAL
ORIGINS
OF SOME OF
OUR SURNAMES

FIFTY-FOUR NAME-ENDINGS
THAT MAY REVEAL NATIONAL ORIGIN

This list may help if you sometimes are curious about the nationality or the meaning of a surname. Some of the items are true suffixes, others (especially in German and Scandinavian names) are words that are frequently combined with others.

Additional endings are treated in the articles on *son of* (page 121) and diminutives (page 123).

accio: Italian ⟨bad⟩; Boccaccio ⟨ bad or ugly mouth⟩
bach, *-baugh*: German ⟨brook⟩; Steinbach ⟨stony brook⟩
baum: German ⟨tree⟩; Greenbaum ⟨green tree⟩
beck: Swedish, Norwegian ⟨brook⟩; Harbeck ⟨rabbit brook⟩

berg: German, Scandinavian ⟨mountain⟩; Lundberg ⟨grove, mountain⟩

bert: German, French ⟨bright⟩; Robert ⟨fame, bright⟩

berto, -berti: Italian form of *-bert*; Roberto

brecht: German form of *-bert*; Albrecht, Ruprecht

blad: Swedish, Norwegian ⟨leaf⟩; Lindblad ⟨linden leaf⟩

blatt: German ⟨leaf⟩; Greenblatt ⟨green leaf⟩

bo: Norwegian ⟨farm⟩; Sudbo ⟨south farm⟩

borg: Swedish ⟨castle⟩; Swedenborg ⟨Swedish castle⟩

born: German ⟨stream⟩; Kaltenborn ⟨cold stream⟩

borough, -brough: English ⟨fort⟩; Kimbrough ⟨royal fort⟩

bury, -berry: English ⟨fort⟩; Stanbury or Standberry ⟨stone fort⟩

by: Norwegian, English ⟨farm or village⟩; Ashby ⟨ash tree village⟩

dahl: Swedish ⟨valley⟩; Ekdahl ⟨oak valley⟩

fiore: Italian ⟨flower⟩; Montefiore ⟨flower mountain⟩

ford: English ⟨ford, crossing⟩; Stanford ⟨stony crossing⟩

gard: Norwegian, Danish ⟨farm⟩; Nyga(a)rd ⟨new farm⟩

grave: English ⟨grove⟩; Hargrave (or Hargreaves, Hargrove) ⟨hare's grove⟩

gren: Swedish ⟨branch⟩; Dahlgren ⟨valley branch⟩

hardt, -hard, -hart: German ⟨hard, firm⟩; Gerhart ⟨firm spear⟩

haus: German ⟨house⟩; Neuhaus ⟨new house⟩

heim: German ⟨home⟩; Sonnheim ⟨sunny (or swampy) home⟩

holm: Swedish ⟨river island⟩; Lindholm ⟨linden river island⟩

land: English ⟨land⟩, Scandinavian ⟨farm, part of a farm⟩; Nyland ⟨new or newly cleared farmland⟩

leigh, -lee, -ley, -ly: English ⟨wood, valley, glade, meadow⟩; Ripley ⟨long, narrow meadow or wood⟩

lof, -love: Swedish ⟨leaf, heather⟩; Younglove ⟨young leaf⟩

lund: Swedish ⟨grove⟩; Asplund ⟨aspen grove⟩

man(n): English, German ⟨servant of⟩; Harriman ⟨servant of Harry⟩

mark: Swedish ⟨field⟩; Lundmark ⟨field in a grove⟩

ness: English, Scottish ⟨cape, headland⟩; Harkness ⟨hawk cape⟩

olf, -olfo, -olph: German, Italian, English ⟨wolf⟩; Rudolph, Rudolfo, Rudolf ⟨fame, wolf⟩

one: Italian ⟨large⟩; Capone ⟨large head⟩

ova: Russian ⟨daughter of⟩; Petrova ⟨daughter of Peter⟩

quist: Swedish ⟨twig⟩; Lindquist ⟨linden twig⟩

rop, -rup: English ⟨farm⟩; Northrop, Northrup ⟨north farm⟩

rud: Norwegian ⟨farm⟩; Stensrud ⟨stony farm or clearing⟩

ska: Russian, Czech, or Polish; feminine equivalent of *-sky* or *-ski*

ski, -sky: Russian, Czech, or Polish ⟨ of the nature of; son of; from⟩ (Polish spelling is usually *-ski*)

stad: Danish, Norwegian ⟨farm, place⟩; Flagstad ⟨windy place⟩

stein: German ⟨stone⟩; Finkelstein ⟨little bird stone (pyrites)⟩

strom: Swedish ⟨stream⟩; Engstrom ⟨meadow stream⟩

thal: German ⟨valley⟩; Blumenthal ⟨flower valley⟩

thorp(e):   English ⟨farm⟩; Oglethorpe ⟨one from Odkell's farm⟩

ton: English ⟨settlement, village, town, homestead⟩; Paxton ⟨Pack's homestead⟩

ville: French ⟨estate⟩; Mandeville ⟨one from Mando's estate⟩

wahl, -vall: Swedish ⟨field⟩; Ekwahl, Ekvall ⟨field with oaks⟩

way: English ⟨path, road, way⟩; Greenway ⟨green path⟩

wich: English ⟨dwelling⟩; Greenwich ⟨green dwelling⟩

wiec: Polish ⟨one who (does something)⟩; Mysliwiec ⟨hunter⟩

win: English ⟨friend⟩; Goodwin ⟨good friend, God's friend⟩

worth: English ⟨homestead⟩; Ellingsworth ⟨homestead of the Ellings (Ella's people)⟩

THE TEN MOST COMMON
IRISH-AMERICAN NAMES

1. Murphy	6. Kelley (may be Scottish or English)
2. Kelly (may be Scottish or English)	7. Burke
3. Sullivan	8. Riley
4. Kennedy (often Scottish)	9. O'Brien
5. Bryant	10. McCoy

The great majority of Irish names are patronyms, perhaps signifying loyalty to and affection for one's forebears.

The *O'* in many Irish names means ⟨grandson of⟩ or perhaps more loosely ⟨descendant of⟩; the apostrophe is only a convention followed in writing, although it is sometimes said to represent a supposedly missing *f*. *Mc, Mac,* or *M* means ⟨son of⟩. *Mac* followed by *G* sometimes is written *Ma* as in Maguire. With *M'* a vowel is sometimes substituted for the apostrophe, as when M'Neely becomes Meneely.

THE TEN MOST COMMON
GERMAN-AMERICAN SURNAMES

Many Schmidts have become Smiths, Schneiders are now often Synders or Sniders, and many Fischers are Fishers. The Myer-Myers-Meyer-Meyers-Meier-etc. families have become well mixed. The following, then, is little more than a list of the spellings of German names so great in frequency that they rank high even though many early holders of the name may have changed it.

1. Myers
2. Schmidt
3. Hoffman(n)
4. Wagner (sometimes English)
5. Meyer

6. Schwarz
7. Schneider
8. Zimmerman(n)
9. Keller
10. Klein

IS THAT NAME
SCOTTISH OR IRISH?

A Gordon family in Buffalo always confidently asserted that the name and the ancestral Gordons were Scottish. However, when one of them made a careful genealogical study, she found out that those particular Gordons came from Dublin.

Like Gordon, a number of other names cannot be definitely classified as Scottish or Irish. Campbell and Blair, for instance, are usually thought to be Scottish, but thousands of Americans of Irish ancestry proudly bear those names.

A study that appeared as the "Annual Report of the American Historical Association for 1931" classified forty-five names as follows. (M' here signifies both *Mc* and *Mac*.)

Class I: Practically no Irish use recorded: M'Leod, Munro, M'Pherson, M'Kinnon, M'Laren, Robertson, M'Intosh, Sutherland, M'Kenzie, Bruce, M'Gregor, Cameron, Fraser, Duncan, Ritchie, Ross, Buchanan

Class II. Substantial Irish usage: Christie, M'Donald, Donaldson, Ramsay, Robb, M'Farlane, M'Intyre, Morrison, Murdoch, Tait, Rankin, Baxter, Jamieson, Forsyth

Class III. Names with original numbers in Ireland approaching or exceeding those in Scotland: Ferguson, Campbell, Findlay, Black, Gordon, M'Dougall (with M'Dowell), Moffat, Maxwell, Blair, Craig, Orr, Cummings, Boyd, Cunningham

Incidentally, although some people say that *Mac* always shows Scottish and *Mc* indicates Irish ancestry, the generalization is not correct. Elsdon Smith, one of America's leading onomatists, has written: "The Scots used the Gaelic *Mac* but not the *O.* Both the Irish and the Scots contract the prefix into *Mc* and M'. Such contractions are without special significance, notwithstanding some authorities who have affirmed that *Mac* is Irish and *Mc* is Scottish, and others who have declared just the opposite."

THE TEN MOST COMMON
ITALIAN-AMERICAN SURNAMES

1. Russo
2. Lombardo, Lombardi
3. Romano
4. Marino
5. Lorenzo (may be Spanish)
6. Costa (may be Spanish or Portuguese)
7. Luna
9. Rossi(ni)
9. Esposito
10. Gallo

Although people of Italian descent are numerous in the United States, no Italian name fills much space in directories. The reason is that, like the Irish, the Italians use a large number of surnames, with consequently few appearances of any one name.

CHARACTERISTICS OF
JAPANESE SURNAMES

Most Japanese surnames consist of two parts, with meanings that may or may not seem related. These combinations were made hundreds of years ago, no doubt by people who liked the poetic effect or the connotations of the parts.

As a result, the same component may be found in either first or second position in some names, although one position may be much more common and the other very rare. Matsu ⟨pine⟩, for instance, most often comes first. Here are some examples from the Manhattan and Los Angeles phone books:

Hiramatsu ⟨flat, pine⟩

Matsuda ⟨pine, rice field⟩

Matsuhira ⟨pine, flat⟩

Matsukawa ⟨pine, river⟩

Matsumoto ⟨pine, origin⟩

Matsunaka ⟨pine, middle⟩

Matsuo ⟨pine, little⟩

Matsuoka ⟨pine, hill⟩

Matsushima ⟨pine, island⟩

Matsushita ⟨pine, below⟩

Matsuyama ⟨pine, mountain⟩

Shimatsu ⟨island, pine⟩

Knowing the meanings of even the following few components will enable you to translate hundreds of Japanese names:

are ⟨have⟩

da or ta ⟨rice field⟩

fuji ⟨wisteria⟩

fuku ⟨good fortune⟩

furu ⟨old⟩

gawa ⟨river⟩

guchi or kuchi ⟨mouth⟩

hara or no ⟨field⟩

hashi ⟨bridge⟩

hira ⟨flat⟩

hon ⟨base⟩

hoshi ⟨star⟩

iwa ⟨rock⟩

kami or ue ⟨upper⟩

marui ⟨round⟩

matsu ⟨pine⟩

mori ⟨forest⟩

mura ⟨village⟩

naka ⟨middle⟩

o ⟨little⟩

ō ⟨large⟩

oka ⟨hill⟩

saka ⟨slope⟩

shima ⟨island⟩

shita ⟨below⟩

sugu ⟨bell⟩

toyo ⟨plentiful⟩

wa ⟨peace⟩

yama ⟨mountain⟩

THE TEN MOST COMMON
SCANDINAVIAN-AMERICAN SURNAMES

The spellings of some Scandinavian nationalities are combined in this list, e.g., Anderson, Andersen, Andersson, Anderssen, Andresen, etc. Also, some of these—especially Anderson, Nelson, and the various forms of Christianson—are frequently English.

1. Anderson	6. Hansen
2. Peterson	7. Carlson
3. Nelson	8. Larson
4. Christianson	9. Erickson
5. Olson	10. Swanson

THE TEN MOST COMMON
SPANISH-AMERICAN SURNAMES

1. Rodriguez	6. Martinez
2. Gonzalez	7. Hernandez
3. Garcia	8. Perez
4. Lopez	9. Sanchez
5. Rivera	10. Torres

SIXTEEN NOBLE SPANISH NAMES

Here are some Spanish surnames derived from titles of royalty, nobility, government officials, and members of their entourages. However, in many instances in both Spanish and other languages, a person who today bears the name does not have ancestry of high rank, but one or more of his or her forebears may have served as followers of a noble person, may have acted the role in a play, or may have acted or looked like someone noble.

Baron ⟨baron⟩
Bascompte ⟨viscount⟩
Camerero ⟨chamberlain; monastery worker⟩
Castellan ⟨governor of a castle⟩
Clavero ⟨keeper of the keys⟩
Cocinero ⟨cook⟩
Conde ⟨count⟩
Duque ⟨duke⟩
Escriba ⟨scribe⟩

Hidalgo ⟨lord, nobleman⟩
Infante ⟨younger son or nephew of the king; young monk or nun; foot soldier; baby⟩
Marques ⟨marquis⟩
Montero ⟨huntsman⟩
Portero ⟨royal messenger; gatekeeper⟩
Rey (Reyes) ⟨king⟩
Vasallo ⟨vassal⟩

THE TEN MOST COMMON
WELSH-AMERICAN SURNAMES

Most or all of these names are rather often English, even though Welsh in origin.

1. Williams	6. Evans
2. Jones	7. Rogers
3. Davis	8. Morgan
4. Thomas	9. Hughes
5. Lewis	10. Price

These ten are all among the top one hundred American surnames. The reason why Welsh names appear in such proportionately high numbers is that in Wales comparatively few different names are used, with many holders of the same name. In some towns with several hundred people, maybe only ten or a dozen surnames will be found.

In earlier times many Welsh names were prefixed by *ap* ⟨son of⟩, as in Hugh ap Howell. *Ap* was often contracted to *P* and combined with the last name, as Hugh Powell. The following are among the Welsh names derived in that way:

Parry (ap Harry)	Pritchard (ap Richard)
Penry (ap Henry)	Probert (ap Robert)
Perry (ap Harry)	Prosser, Prowse (ap Rosser)
Pew or Pugh (ap Hugh)	Prynn (ap Rhun)
Ployd (ap Lloyd)	Pulliam (ap William)
Price, Preece (ap Rhys)	Pumphrey (ap Humphrey)

In a few instances, *ap* became *B*: ap Owen → Bowen.

14

SOME OTHER SOURCES OF NAMES

SOME SURNAMES FROM THE BIBLE

Some biblical names appear in dozens of variant forms in the United States. The eponymous children of John are treated in a separate section. Here are abbreviated lists of variants of other popular names from the Old and New Testaments. Forms generally from the British Isles are listed first.

Abraham(s) (son), Abram(s) (son); Polish Abrahamowicz, Abramovitz; Russian Abramovich
Adam(s) (son), Addams, Acheson, Adcock ⟨little Adam⟩, Addison, Aiken, Aitken(s), Akins, Atkin(s) (son), Eason, Keddy, McAdam(s); Czechoslovakian Adamek; Greek Adamopoulos; Italian Adamo, Adduci; Lithuanian Adomaitis; Polish Adamczyk (ovitz) (owski); Russian Adamovich; Spanish Adan
Andrew(s), Anders(on) (en) (sson) (ssen), Andresen, Drew; Polish Andrysiak, etc.; Russian Andreyev; Spanish and Por-

tuguese Andrade; Ukrainian Andrajenko; Yugoslavian Andrejevi

Bartholomew, Bartlett, Barth, Bartel(s), Bates, Battle (sometimes); Czechoslovian Barta; German Bartke, Bart(o)sch; Hungarian Barto(s), Bartok; Italian Bartolini, Bartolomeo; Lithuanian Bartkus; Polish Bartkiewicz, Bartkowski, etc.; Russian Bartkowsky

Christ(ian), (ianson), (ensen), (opher), Christman, C(h)rystel, Crist, Criss, Cris(s)man, Scottish Christie or Christy; Czechoslovakian Kristof; French Christophe; German Christoph, Kris, Krist; Finnish Risto; Greek Christopoulos; Italian (de) Christoforo; Latvian Kriss; Polish Krzysztof, Krzys; Russian Christoff; Spanish Cristobal. (Kristin is a frequent Slavic form.)

Daniel(s) (son); Bulgarian Danilovic; Italian Danielo; Lithuanian Danilevicius; Polish Danielczyk, etc.; Ukrainian Danyluk, Danylenko. (English or French Dana may mean ⟨descendant of Daniel⟩ or ⟨a person from Denmark⟩.)

David(s) (son), Davis, Davie(s), Davison, Davey, Dawson, Dawes, Deakins, Dewey. (Dozens of Slavic variants begin with Dav- or Daw-. Day, when Welsh, usually means ⟨descendant of David⟩ but if English means ⟨dairy worker⟩.)

Elias(on), Eliot, Elliot(t), Ellis(on), Elkins, Welsh Bellis, Ely (sometimes)

Jacob(s) (son) (sen), Cobb(e); Armenian Hagopian; Czechoslovakian K(o)uba; French Jacob or Jacque(s); German Jacobi, Jacoby, Jakob, Jaeckel, Kob(e), Kopp(elmann); Italian Giacomo and other names with Giaco- or Iaco-, Mel(l)one (from Giacomelli), Pucci(ni) (from Iacopucci), Baca (which also may be Slavic); Polish Jakubowski, etc., Polish or Russian Kubik, etc.; Scandinavian Jacobsen, etc., Spanish Diaz or Portuguese Dias (both from Diego = Jacob), Dieguez

James(on), Jami(e)son; Spanish Santiago (from the place Santiago ⟨Saint James⟩)

Jordan, Jorden, Jordon, Jurden, Judd, Judkins, Judson; Italian Giordano

Luke(s) (y), Lukas, Luck, Luck(e)y, Luc(e)y, Lucie, Lukin(s); Bulgarian Luka; French Luce (also from Louis), Lucien; German Luekin(g) (s), Lux; Hungarian Lukacs; Italian (di) Luca, Lucia(no), Lucci, etc.; Polish Lukasz, etc.; Russian

Lukanovich; Spanish Lucero; Ukrainian Luchanko, Lucenko

Mathew(s) (son), Matthew(s) (son), Madison, Mat(ti)son, Macy (sometimes), English or Irish Madden, Scottish or Danish Mathes(on), English or Swedish Mattson, English or French May(s); Czechoslovakian Matousek, Matus (zek) (ow); Finnish Mattinen; German Mathis, Mat(t)hies, Mattheu, Matz(kin), Theis; Italian Maffei, Maffeo, Mattia(ci) (ce); Lithuanian Matul(is) (evicius); Polish Maciejewski, Matuszuski, etc.; Scandinavian Madsen, Madson, Mathies(s)en; Russian Matkovich; Spanish Matias, Mateo(s)

Mark (in England usually refers to boundary markers, but in the forms Marks, Marcus, and Marquis generally is derived from the New Testament Mark. German or English Marx may have either derivation). The biblical origin is apparent in Czechoslovakian Markovitz; French Marceau; Greek Markopoulos; Italian Marco, Marcelli, Marcetti, etc.; Lithuanian Markevicius; Scandinavian or English Martinsen (or -son); Polish Marek, Marcinek, Markiewicz, Markowski; Portuguese or Spanish Marques; Spanish Marquez; Ukrainian Marchik, Marko. Also related by derivation to Martin, from the god Mars.

Michael(s) (son), Mitchell, Mickel(s), Mickens, Micklin, Mickey, Mickie, Mix; Bulgarian Mihailovic; Czechoslovakian Mihalek, Mic(h)al, Miskovic; Finnish Mikkonen; French Michel, Michet, Michaud, Michaux; German Michaelis; Greek Mikalonis, Miklos, Mikos, Mi(c)halopoulos, Mikalaitis; Italian Miceli, Michini, Michelini; Lithuanian Mikus; Polish Michal(ak) (ski) (czewski) (owski); Portuguese or Spanish Miguel; Scandinavian Michaelsen, Michaelson, Mikkelson, Michelsen; Yugoslavian Mikulich

Paul(l) (son) (ey), Scottish M(a)cPhail ⟨son of Paul⟩; Pavel or Paul in several continental languages; Czechoslovakian Pajko, Pav(lik) (ov) (ovic); French Polley; German Paulus, Pavlow; Greek Pavlos, Pavlatis; Italian Paoli, Paulini, Paulino; Lithuanian Pavlauskas; Polish Pawlak, Pawlicki, Pawlowski; Russian Pavlov(ich); Scandinavian Paulsen, Paulson, Poulson; Spanish Paula, Paulo; Ukrainian Pavlik, Pavlenko, Pawluk; Yugoslavian Pavlovich

Peters(on), Pearson, Perkins, Pierce, Peirce, Pearse, Parnell,

Parrot, Parson(s) (sometimes), Person(s), Peary, Peery, Peer(e), Peet(e), Parks (sometimes), Perry (sometimes), Peterkin(s), Peterman, Peterson, Piers, Pierson, Irish Ferrick, Welsh Bearse or Bearce, Perkins(on), Pierce, Piers, Scottish Peete, Perrie, Petry or Petrie, Piri; Bulgarian Petkof, Petroff; Danish Ped(d)ersen, Petersen; Dutch Peet(e), Pieter(s); French Peer(e), Perrau(d) (lt), Perret, Perrin(e), Perron, Peyrot, Pierre, Pierrot; German Peterman(n); Greek Patrakos, Petrakis, Petropolos, Petros; Hungarian Petofi; Icelandic Petersson; Italian Perelli, Pieroni, Perillo, Per(r)one, Petrelli, Petri, Petrone, Petrucci, Pieroni, Pierro, Pietro; Lithuanian Petkus, Petraitis, Petronis; Norwegian Ped(d)ersen, Peterson, Pettersen; Polish Bieschke, Petrowski, etc.; Portuguese Pires; Romanian Petrescu; Russian Petroff, Petrov(ich), Petruska; Spanish Perez, Pero; Swedish Pers(s)on(s), Peterson, Petterson

Simon(e), Simmons, Simpson, Sim(m)(s), Simeon, Simond(s), Simcock or Simcox ⟨little Simon⟩, Sim(p)kins, Fitzsimmons, Syme(s), Symond(s); Armenian Simonian; French Simeone, Simoneaux; Greek Simonaitis; Italian Simone, Simonini, Simonetti; Lithuanian Shimkus, Simaitis; Polish Sienkiewicz, Simek, Simkowski, Szymanski, Szymczak; Russian Simeone, Sienkiewicz; Scandinavian Simonsen, Simonson; Spanish Jiminez; Yugoslavian Simovic

Stephen(s) (son), Steven(s)(son), Steave(s), Steff(e) (en) (ens), Stim(p)son, Stinson; many continental forms, generally starting with Step- or Stav-, but Spanish Estep or Estevez

Thomas(sen) (son), Thom(p)son, Thom(p)sen, T(h)ompkin(s) (on), Tomblin, Tomlinson, Tomb, Toombs, Massey or Massie (from the second syllable), Scottish McComb, Macomber, McTavish; Czechoslovakian Toman, Tomas(ek) (kovic); French Thomas, Masson, Maslin, Massie; German Thoma(s), Mass; Hungarian Tamas; Italian Masso, Massi, Tomaselli, etc.; Lithuanian Tumas; Polish Tomczak, Tomaszewski, etc.; Spanish Tomas

Some of the other biblical figures whose names survive as surnames in one or more spellings are these:

Aaron	Abner	Augustus
Abel	Amos	Benjamin

Cain	Job	Reuben
Caspar	Joel	Samson
Gabriel	Joseph	Samuel
Gideon	Lazarus	Saul
Isaac	Levi	Solomon
Jeremiah (Jeremy)	Moses	Timothy
Jesus	Noah	Tobias

DIRECTIONS IN SURNAMES

In some surnames the major points of the compass are apparent: East, Eastern, North, Northern, South, Southern, West, Western. They are only a little less visible in many compounds, such as Easterwood, Eastham ⟨eastern homestead⟩, Easton ⟨east village⟩, Northbrook, Northcote or Northcott or Northcutt ⟨north cottage⟩, Northey ⟨north island⟩, Northrop ⟨northern farm⟩, Southcott, Southey, Southworth ⟨southern homestead⟩, Westfield, Westlake, or Weston ⟨west village⟩. Others are less obvious: Escott ⟨east cottage⟩, Essex ⟨east Saxons⟩, Estall ⟨east hall⟩, Esterly ⟨eastern grove⟩, Esterman ⟨one from the east⟩ (but if Jewish, ⟨husband of Esther⟩), Estes ⟨son of East⟩, Estridge ⟨east ridge⟩, Estwick ⟨eastern dairy⟩;

Norberg (Swedish for ⟨north mountain⟩), Norbury ⟨northern fort⟩, Norbert (German for ⟨north, bright⟩), Norcott ⟨north cottage⟩, Norcross ⟨north cross⟩, Nordby (Swedish for ⟨north village⟩), Norden (Scandinavian or Dutch for ⟨one from the north⟩), Norgaard (Norwegian or Danish for ⟨north yard⟩), Norman ⟨northman⟩ or ⟨one from Normandy⟩, Norrington ⟨northern part of the village⟩, Norstrom or Nordstrom (Swedish for ⟨north stream⟩), Norton ⟨north village⟩;

Soder (Swedish for ⟨south⟩, often in compounds such as Soderquist ⟨south twig⟩), Sudbo (Norwegian for ⟨south farm⟩), Sudbury ⟨south fort⟩, Sudlow ⟨south hill⟩, Sussland ⟨southern district⟩, Sutcliff ⟨south cliff⟩, Sutherland ⟨south land⟩, Sutton ⟨south village⟩;

Wester (Dutch for ⟨one from the west⟩), but also in various Scandinavian, German, or English compounds such as Westerberg ⟨western mountain⟩, Westerhausen ⟨western house⟩, Westerveld ⟨western field⟩, or Westerfield, Weston ⟨western village⟩, Wisham ⟨western homestead⟩.

THE HUMAN ZOO

In the Middle Ages, when surnames were generally adopted, few people could read. Signs used simple pictures instead of words to identify a place of business. One might walk down a street and perhaps see pictures of a rooster, a bush, an owl, and a lion, and children might be told, "Go to the Lion and get me some ale."

People who owned one of the businesses or who lived close to the sign often became known by the sign. William near the Lion quite easily was shortened to William Lyon (an old spelling of the word).

Most animal surnames probably arose in that way. Some, however, arose because certain people appeared to share a quality or several qualities of an animal and were thus named. Fox may have been clever and wily, German Baer as strong or as hairy as a bear, and Hare was perhaps unusually fleet. A few surnames arose because a person's occupation involved some kind of animal. Russian Soboleff, for instance, trapped sables.

Wolf, in its several spellings, is the most common name in this group. One reason is that wolves were numerous in Europe, especially in the north, and were feared and admired and often made the subject of tales. Some of these tales involved werewolves—men who could supposedly turn into wolves—an ability now called *lycanthropy*, from the Greek name for the animal.

The following names of wild animals are among those formed in one or more of the three ways mentioned above and still existent, some of them in spellings other than those given here. A few of the terms, such as Cooney for ⟨rabbit⟩, are seldom used now for the animals themselves but survive mainly as proper names.

bear: English, French Bear (sometimes); German Baer, Behr(ens), Behnke; Italian Urso; Ukrainian Vedmedenko
beaver: Czech Bobar
deer: English Deer(e), Hart or Hurt, Pritchett, Doe, Roe, Roebuck; Czech Jelinek; French Cerf; German Hersh, Hirsch; Spanish Reno; Polish Sarna
elephant: English, French Oliphant, Olivant
fox: English Fox, Colfax ⟨black fox⟩; Scottish Guptill; Czech Liska; Finnish Kettunen; German Fuchs; German or Dutch Voss; Italian Volpe; Polish Liss; Russian or Ukrainian Lys(s)

gopher: Russian Suskov.
hare: English Hare, Cooney; Czech Zajicka, Krolik; German or
    Dutch Haas; Polish Krolik; Polish or Ukrainian Zajac; Yu-
    goslavian Kunc
hedgehog: Czech Jeschek
lion: English or Scottish Lyon(s); English Leo; German Lo(e)we,
    Loewy, Lau; Spanish Leon(e)
marmot: Polish Boba(k)
martin: Czechoslovakian Kunka; German Marder; Italian Mar-
    tarano
otter: English Otter; Swedish Utter; Polish Wydra
sable: German Zobel; Polish Sobel, Zabel; Russian Soboleff
squirrel: German Eich(h)orn
unicorn: German Einhorn
walrus: Czechoslovakian Mroz, Mrosek
wildcat: Polish Zbik
wolf: English, German Wolf(f)(e); German Wulf(f); Czech Welk,
    Vlk; Greek Lycos; Hungarian Farkas; Lithuanian Volf;
    Polish Volkow; Russian Volkov; Ukrainian Vovcenko
zebra: Polish Zebrowski

Domestic animals have their namesakes, too, although those
for dog are inexplicably rare, exceptions being Talbot, which
can mean ⟨white hunting dog⟩, Doggett, which can mean ⟨with
a head shaped like a dog's⟩, and Canine.

Horses, goats, and others were often portrayed on business
signs, and some people had characteristics of cats or other animals, but probably most of the following names arose because
of raising or tending the animals.

bull: English Bull(ock), Steer(e), Farr (may also refer to a boar
    or, when Scottish, to a place in Sutherland); German Ochs;
    Polish Bicek; Ukrainian Buhajecko. (Polish Krowa herded
    cows.)
cat: Czech Kocoubek; Italian Gatto(ne), Gatti
goat: English Cheever(s), Haver, Kidd; French Chevrolet,
    Chevrier; German Bock; Italian Capra; Russian Kosloff;
    Ukrainian and Czechoslovakian Kozel(ka)
hog: English Hogg, Pigg(ott), Hogue, Farrow, Purcell, Sugg(s)
horse: English Steed, Stedman, Stott; French Cheval; Italian
    Chevallo, Cavallo; Polish Siwek, Konicki; Polish or Ukrain-
    ian Kolybecki

sheep: English Lamb, Shepherd (various spellings), Withers, Agnew; Bulgarian Beranich; German Scheaffer (various spellings); Polish Beran, Kozlowski (many variants)

Sometimes animal names may be particularly appropriate. A prominent professor of agriculture at the University of Illinois was named Sleeter Bull. His specialty: meats.

BIRDS OF A FEATHER

Pictures of birds were used on many business signs in the name-giving period of the Middle Ages; some people were thought to resemble birds, and others hunted, captured, or trained birds. In these ways the ancestors of an estimated one to two million Americans took their names from the avian part of our world.

The following names are among the many thus derived. Each is held by at least 10,000 Americans, and some, such as Crane and Aguila, by 35,000 or more.

Adler: German ⟨eagle⟩
Aguila: Spanish ⟨eagle⟩
Ahrens: Dutch ⟨eagle⟩
Coe: English ⟨jackdaw⟩
Corbett, Corbin: English ⟨raven⟩ (When Irish, Corbin does not refer to birds.)
Crain, Crane: English ⟨crane⟩
Crow(e): English ⟨crow⟩
Culver, Dove: English ⟨dove⟩
Falco(n) (ne) (ner), Faulkner: Falco or Falcone is Italian for ⟨falcon⟩ or ⟨hawk⟩; English Falconer or Faulkner trained falcons or hunted with them
Finch: English

Fink (several spellings): German ⟨finch⟩
Hawk: English
Ortega: Spanish ⟨grouse⟩
Palumbo Italian ⟨dove⟩
Partridge: English
Poe: English ⟨peacock⟩ (But may also have other derivations.)
Schwann: German ⟨swan⟩
Sparks: English ⟨sparrow hawk⟩
Swan: English
Wren(n): English

In addition, more than a score of other birds have lent us their names, although fewer than 10,000 Americans now use any one of the forms. Note that Slavs in particular seem to like birds' names.

blackbird: Kos, Kosiek
black daw: Kafka
cuckoo: Kukulka
lark: Skowron(ek)
linnet: Konopka
magpie: Pye, Agassiz, Sroka
mallard: Mallard
nightingale: Nightingale, Nachtigall, Slovick, Slowick
owl: Sowa
robin: Cermak (The English surname Robin is usually derived from Robert.)
grosbeak: Ziemba

heron: Her(r)on, Caplenko
lapwing: Czej(k)a
rook: Rook
snipe: Snipe, Kulik
starling: Starling, Szpak
stork: Stork, Capek
teal: Teal(e), Teel(e)
thrush: Drozd
titmouse: Sikora
vulture: Geier, Geyer
wagtail: Pliszka (In 1641 an Elizabeth Wagtail was living in Grimsby, England.)
woodpecker: Speck, Specht

Finally, general names meaning ⟨bird⟩ are not uncommon. Bird itself is the name of over 30,000 Americans, and Byrd even more—about 85,000. German-American Vogel is used by another 30,000, and the Americanized spelling Fogle or Fogel by about 15,000. Finkel ⟨little bird⟩ in combination with Finkelstein ⟨little bird stone⟩ may account for another 15,000. Spanish Garza, which may mean ⟨bird⟩ or more specifically ⟨heron⟩ or ⟨dove⟩, is the name of some 75,000 Americans. Polish Pta(c)k means ⟨bird⟩, and Czechoslovakian Ptacek is a diminutive form ⟨little bird⟩.

MATRONYMS

Matronyms (surnames based on mothers' names) are more often called metronyms or metronymics, but matronym, more clearly based on *mater* ⟨mother⟩ is less confusing.

In naming a daughter, in Iceland or in earlier times in the other Scandinavian countries as well, the equivalent of *daughter* was attached to the father's name. Thus in Iceland the current president, a woman, is named Vigdis Finnbogadottir. If she has a brother, his surname is Finnbogason. The best-known work of Norwegian novelist and Nobel Prize winner Sigrid Undset is the trilogy *Kristin Lavransdatter*, which is set in medieval times when -*datter* was a common ending for girls' surnames.

Those names are less sexist than most European names, because they do not impose -*son* or the equivalent on girls and boys indiscriminately. But they are not matronyms, for they do not memorialize mothers, as Hanson and Sorensen, for example, memorialize fathers. In fact, Finnbogadottir and Lavransdatter honor fathers named Finnboga and Lavran(s).

Not only patronyms but also descriptives and occupational names relate almost exclusively to men rather than women. Descriptive names such as Strong or Long, for example, recall characteristics more often associated with men than with women; few people have the name Buxom or any other that suggests feminine appearance or traits. Few women have been smiths, carters, wheelwrights, and the like, but it is such predominantly male occupations that are the sources of great numbers of names; in contrast, Milkmaids are few.

Some occupations, however, especially those in which many women worked, do have feminine forms beside the masculine ones. Thus Webster is a female Web(b)er or Weaver, Baxter is a female Baker, and Brewster is the feminine equivalent of Brewer. Those names and a few more are occupational names, then, but in a sense are matronyms as well.

The true matronyms, however, are those in which a woman's name appears. They are not numerous, although someone has estimated—probably much too optimistically—that 10 percent of "patronyms" are matronyms.

The most common example of a matronym is Allison, but like the other examples that name may refer to either a female or a male progenitor. It may be derived from Alice, which appeared in various spellings (Allis, Alys, etc.) in the Middle Ages, but it may also be based on the male Ellis or even Allen or Alexander.

Similarly, Emmett and its variants may honor a medieval Emma, but also a male Emery or Emory, or German Emmerich. The rare name Ibbot(son) may be traced to a nickname for Isabel, but the same nickname was apparently used for the masculine Ilbert. Anson is usually ⟨son of Ann⟩.

Till was a nickname for Matilda and also for several rather rare medieval men's names, such as Tilbeohrt. Modern Till(ett) or Tillotson, then, may fairly often be a matronym.

There aren't many more. If it is indeed an honor to have one's name perpetuated in the names of one's descendants, then women have been consistently shortchanged.

Jewish names are not quite so sexist as most. Some husbands in the naming period, which for most Jews was considerably later than for gentiles, took their wives' names. Thus Estermann is ⟨Esther's husband⟩, Dienesmann ⟨Dinah's husband⟩, Hodesmann ⟨Hadassah's husband⟩, and Pearlman ⟨Pearl's husband⟩. Estrin is ⟨descended from Esther⟩, and Esther might also be commemorated as the founder of the Estersons. Rabbi Benzion C. Kaganoff comments, "Often a Jewish family name is associated with the wife's name in cases where she was the breadwinner or where she came from the more distinguished family lineage (*yichus*)." Kaganoff mentions several examples, including Adelman and Edelman, Edelstein (sometimes), Dobkin, Dobrin, and Dus(h)kin.

15

WONDERFUL PEOPLE WITH STRANGE-SOUNDING NAMES

UNCOMMON SURNAMES FROM THE 1790 CENSUS

President George Washington authorized the taking of the first census of the United States in 1790. Many of the surnames recorded in that year have now vanished or become quite rare. These lists and several that follow include a small proportion of those names.

The lists are classified according to their apparent meanings, but in a few instances the names may really mean something else. They may have been misspelled by the census-takers, or the words may have had different meanings two hundred years ago. *Bloomer*, for instance, then meant a flowering plant, not an article of feminine attire. The later meaning is from Amelia Jenks Bloomer, a suffragette not yet born in 1790.

Food

Almond	Goodbread	Onions
Beans	Lard	Redwine
Beets	Milk	Squash
Cheese	Mints	Tart
Custard	Mush	Tongue
Dates	Mustard	Vinegar
Fowl	Olives	

Clothing and Sewing

Beads	Jumpers	Petticoat
Bloomer	Lace	Pin
Boas	Lightcap	Redsleeves
Collar	Mendingall	Scarf
Crape	Mitts	Threadcraft
Frill	Overall	Waistcoat
Frocks	Pattern	

People and Their Characteristics

Barefoot	Humble	Plump
Beeman	Kicker	Rascal
Boney	Knave	Sickman
Councilman	Madsavage	Strut
Fickle	Measley	Toogood
Goodfellow	Older	Toughman
Gump	Peacemaker	Underhand
Hero	Pettyfool	Weedingman
	Pilgrim	

The Body and Its Ills

Blister	Fits	Rickets
Boils	Gout	Salts
Bowels	Gullets	Shoulders
Corns	Lips	Shiver
Cough	Livers	Thumbs
Crampeasy	Nose	Warts
Fatyouwant	Physic	

Houses and Their Furnishings

Brickhouse	Buttery	Cushion
Brickroof	China	Gambrel

Greathouse
Latch
Laughinghouse
Lockkey
Longhouse

Mug
Newbowl
Newhouse
Oldhouse
Porch

Pump
Spoons
Spout
Stonehouse

Merchandise and Commodities

Awl
Barley
Barrels
Boiler
Bomb
Buckhorn
Camphor
Coal
Coop
Coopernail

Coldiron
Combs
Cowhorn
Divans
Fender
Filters
Gouge
Harness
Hogshead
Junk

Ladder
Nipper
Nuthammer
Oven
Screws
Silkrags
Smallcorn
Sulkey
Surrey
Tenpenny

Nature

Birdwhistle
Blizzard
Caraway
Chestnutwood
Coldair
Currants
Flyberry
Hazelgrove

Hornet
Marjoram
Mayberry
Oysterbanks
Parsley
Pheasants
Quince
Rottenberry
Sealion

Slush
Tails
Tallhill
Widedale
Wilderness
Woodsides
Woodyfield
Wormwood

Unusual Combinations

Beersticker
Cathole
Cockledress
Coldflesh
Crackbone
Flybaker
Goodbit
Huntsucker

Liptrot
Livergall
Milkrack
Partneck
Reedhovel
Sharpneck
Shortday
Silvernail
Spitsnoggle

Splitstone
Stophell
Sydensticker
Tallowback
Trueluck
Wallflour
Willibother
Witchwagon

Forenames and Surnames

Unity Bachelor	Sharp Blount	Wanton Bump
Joseph Came	Bachelor Chance	Mourning Chestnut
Comfort Clock	Sermon Coffin	Jemima Crysick
Boston Frog	Snow Frost	Thomas Gabtale
Anguish Lemmon	Thomas Purity	Ruth Shaves
Christian Shelf	Thomas Simmers	Sarah Simpers
Truelove Sparks	Barbary Staggers	Booze Still
Preserved Taft	Peter Wentup	Darling Whiteman

HOW MANY DIFFERENT SURNAMES ARE THERE?

No one knows for sure the number of names by which we call ourselves and one another here in America. Computers for the Social Security Administration in their tally of 1974 found 1,286,556 *different* surnames. But of course that number has changed—changes daily in fact. The last surviving holder of a name may die, and the possessor of a name previously unheard in this country may debark from an airplane.

Besides, the SSA count was itself not complete. The computers were asked to list only the first six letters in each name. So, for example, the names Hernan, Hernand, Hernander, Hernandes, Hernandez, Hernando, and Hernani were counted as a single name (Hernan).

The computer count may have shorted the total by a quarter of a million names—a wild guess. So the total number of different surnames in the U.S. probably exceeds one and a half million.

UNIQUE SURNAMES

"I've never known any other family with a surname just like mine," a man named Kwasimady said. "Is that possible?"

Yes, indeed. The records of the Social Security Administration show a total of 448,663 one-of-a-kind names. An SSA spokesman hypothesizes that most of the oddities are variant spellings. Someone may have misspelled the name, intentionally or not, perhaps changing just one or two letters. So, for example, a Tomlinson may possibly gain uniqueness by writing Tomlansen or perhaps Tomlinsun.

As for Mr. Kwasimady, some of his ancestors may have spelled the name Quasimodo, like that of Victor Hugo's hunchback of Notre Dame or the late Italian poet, Salvatore Quasimodo.

THE SHORTEST
AMERICAN SURNAMES

The X, Y, and Z who perform various actions in high school algebra problems are real people. So are A, B, and C and all the other letters of the alphabet. The files of the Social Security Administration contain the records of these people for whom a single letter serves as the surname:

A—24	H—8	O—16	V—17
B—6	I—12	P—7	W—5
C—16	J—4	Q—2	X—2
D—13	K—4	R—5	Y—5
E—10	L—11	S—8	Z—4
F—3	M—16	T—4	
G—10	N—2	U—7	

One man explained his single-letter name in this way: "I had a five-syllable name starting with D that most people couldn't pronounce. Some of them just called me 'Mr. D.' So I made the change legally."

Since I is the skinniest letter, the people named I may claim the smallest name.

THE LONGEST
AMERICAN SURNAME?

It is not certain whose surname is longest. One unquestionably legitimate candidate is a Greek soldier whose name was recorded by the United States Army as Lambros A. Pappatorianofillosopoulos—twenty-five letters.

Elsdon Smith found a name ten letters longer than that,

in a Philadelphia telephone directory: Wolfeschlegelstein-hausenbergerdorff. Smith called it an "assumed name," perhaps implying that it was made up as a joke or an attention getter. He defined it as "a descendant of Wolfeschlegelstein (one who prepared wool for manufacture on a stone), of the house of Bergerdorf (mountain village)."

However, the *Guinness Book of World Records* (10th Edition) provides more information, saying that the full surname is much longer, totaling 595 letters, but that the holder, who was born in Bergerdorf, Germany, on February 29, 1904, used on printed forms only the 35 letters reported by Smith. In addition the gentleman has twenty-six given names, starting with Adolph Blaine Charles and continuing through the alphabet.

The Guinness authors add that late in life Mr. W shortened the surname to Wolfe + 590, Senior. Whether there is a Junior and, if so, what he calls himself, is not mentioned.

Outside the U.S., one candidate for the longest name is that of a crown prince of Thailand, born July 28, 1952, and reported in *Asia Who's Who* for 1958: Vajiralongkorn Boromachakrayadisornantativongs Devesrdharmrongsuboribal Abhikhunuprakarnmahitaladuldej Bhumibolnaresvarangkura Kittisirisomburanasvangkhavadhna Boromakhattiyarajkumarn. If no one of those names is a record-setter, the seven of them together may come close, especially if the name of Mr. Wolfe + 590 is for any reason ever disqualified. (Maybe he shouldn't be. He was listed as Hubert Blaine Wolfeschlegelsteinhausenbergerdorff, Sr., a dues-paying member of the American Names Society.)

SOME UNUSUAL
BEGINNINGS OF SURNAMES

Theoretically, any two letters could begin a surname, but in actuality some combinations are very rare or even nonexistent. In the current Manhattan phonebook there is only one name listed with the two letters that start each of these names:

Bpgen	Dkada	Fhagen
Bschorr	Dsouza	Fteha
Dfsell	Equinda	Gdanski

Hforoobar	Mzimela	Uosikkinen
Hmura	Nhan	Vhugen
Htain	Nnamdi	Vjesner
Ijams	Nsubaga	Vnuk
Iqbal	Nxumalo	Wcislo
Jn	Pniewski	Wdowka
Kdenovic	Pvar	Wfoulkes
Kgositsile	Pzena	Wg
Ldova	Qvarnstrom	Wsiaki
Mshar	Tfank	Zjawinski
Mwangosi	Ttappalou	Zkhiri

Some of these names come from northern or eastern Europe, others from the Middle East, Africa, or the Orient.

The same directory shows only about a dozen or fewer names beginning with these letter combinations: BZ, CM, DF, DH, DK, DL, DM, DV, DZ, EJ, EO, FF, FJ, GB, GJ, GM, GN, HJ, HL, HN, HR, HV, IU, JH, KJ, KP, KS, KV, LJ, LV, MB, MJ, ML, MN, MP, MR, ND, NK, NT, NW, PT, QA, RZ, SB, SD, SF, SG, SJ, SS, TC, JJ, TK, TL, UI, UY, WL, WN, WS, XH, YZ, ZS, ZD, ZG, ZN, ZR, ZS, and ZV.

Incidentally, the final names in the Manhattan directory are those of Budd Zzzyp and James Zzzzee, which appear to have been made up specifically for that honor.

MISLEADING SURNAMES

Some surnames don't mean what they appear to. We would naturally suppose that the ancestral Moody was a changeable and often gloomy person. But in reality Old English *mōdig*, from which the name comes, meant ⟨bold, brave⟩.

A former college student of the author was a lively young woman who moved and thought rapidly. Her name, Quick, seemed appropriate. Actually, however, when surnames were taken about seven centuries ago, it meant ⟨alive⟩, a meaning that survives in the expression "the quick and the dead."

A medieval Parson wasn't necessarily a preacher. Par was

one of the nicknames for Peter, so Parson is usually the equiv-alent of Peters or Peterson.

The ancestor of Forget, a French name, may not have been forgetful. The name often means ⟨little forge⟩ and refers to a blacksmith.

Philpott has nothing to do with filling or pots. It's a di-minutive of Philip ⟨lover of horses⟩ and so means ⟨little Philip⟩ or ⟨little horse-lover⟩.

Similarly, Coward does not refer to fearfulness or cow-ardice. It refers to the occupation of herding cows and so is comparable to Shepherd or Shep(p)ard.

Many names could also be listed that, although not really misleading, have historical definitions not at all in keeping with the modern image. One of the best examples is Kennedy. Thanks to President John F. Kennedy and many of his relatives, people tend to think of Kennedys as handsome folks. But in Celtic the name could mean either ⟨helmet head⟩ or ⟨he with the ugly or misshapen head⟩.

WHICH NAME IS
THE SURNAME?

In Chinese, Korean, and Hungarian names the surname comes first, so Chin Wu, for instance, is Mr. Chin rather than Mr. Wu, and Nagy István in England or America would be Stephen Nagy. To avoid confusion in the United States, Mr. Chin, too, is likely to sign his name Wu Chin; the listing in the phone book would be Chin, Wu.

Spaniards and Portuguese put the father's surname in the middle, with the mother's surname at the end, sometimes pre-faced by *y* (Spanish) or *e* (Portuguese) to signify ⟨and⟩. So Enrico Garcia y Lopez is Señor Garcia. Garcia, like Chin, will probably list himself under the surname (Garcia), although Pablo Picasso and others have chosen to be known by the matronym.

WHAT'S YOUR LAST
INITIAL?

More American surnames start with S than with any other letter, and X—not unexpectedly—begins the smallest number.

B gets second place, M is third, and K a close fourth. Z surprisingly ranks ahead of Y, and ahead also of I, J, Q, U, and X.

Here are the complete percentages:

Letter	Percent of Names
A	4.8
B	7.0
C	5.5
D	5.9
E	2.5
F	3.3
G	5.2
H	4.4
I	1.2
J	2.0
K	6.4
L	5.0
M	6.5
N	2.7
O	2.6
P	5.5
Q	0.3
R	4.4
S	9.8
T	4.6
U	0.9
V	2.7
W	3.1
X	0.1
Y	1.3
Z	2.2

Some people (usually with names between Aaron and Myles) have claimed that men and women with surnames starting with A through M usually accomplish most in life. They say, for example, that almost two-thirds of our U.S. presidents—twenty-six of forty—have had names in the A to M group.

The journal called *Names* had disputed that. R. V. Dietrich and L. T. Reynolds (impartial, since their last initials are D and R) made a count based on *Who's Who in America* and similar compilations. Their conclusion should comfort people in the

maligned N to Z group: "There is no good basis for any state-
ment to the effect that a discordant relationship exists between
the initial letter of a person's surname and his or her characteristics or achievement."

Another researcher, Gary S. Felton, set out to find whether
low achievers among students tend to cluster in one-half of the
alphabet. He found that poor test scores are spread proportionately, regardless of the alphabet. If, for instance, almost
twice as many S's as L's make low grades, it is because there are
almost twice as many S's in the student body.

IF YOU NEED CREDIT,
GO TO...

This sign was reported on "Real People," NBC-TV, September
22, 1982:

OUR CREDIT MANAGER IS HELEN WAITE.
WHEN YOU NEED CREDIT, GO TO HELEN WAITE.

THEY WERE FUNNY IN THE
FORTIES

For the 1943 movie *The Miracle of Morgan's Creek* two "funny"
names were invented: Ratskynatski and Kockenlocker. At about
the same time, a radio comedian who called himself Parkyak-
arkus was rolling some of his listeners on the living room floor.
He was born Harry Einstein, in show business changed to Harry
Parke, and became moderately famous under the four-syllable
name.

PITY THE POSTMAN IN AMISHLAND

A rural mail carrier in an Amish community in southeastern
Pennsylvania may have unusual problems.

According to an article in *Names* (June 1968) by Elmer E.
Smith, one such postman had on his route 437 people named
Stoltzfus. Ten Stoltzfuses would be fine, even a few dozen would
be bearable, but 437? No way.

Because of the Amish practice of endogamy (marriage only within the sect), for a couple of centuries there has been almost no infusion of new names. As a result, says Smith, "The great majority of Amish [in southeastern Pennsylvania] have only seven different surnames, and twenty surnames constitute 96.7 percent of the total Amish population in that region."

Moreover, "An analysis of 2,611 Amish marriages since 1890 revealed the existence of only forty-two different Amish surnames, and three of those [Stolfzfus 27.2 percent, King (from König) 12.2 percent, and Beiler 10.5 percent] constituted 49.9 percent of that total. Fourteen surnames make up 90 percent of the Amish names."

COULD JOHNNY CARSON
HAVE BEEN WRONG?

Television talk-show host Johnny Carson, in his monologs, has sometimes remarked that the flush toilet was invented in the middle of the nineteenth century by a man named Thomas Crapper.

There really was a Thomas Crapper, rather well-known in his time (1837–1910) as an inventor.

However, *A History of Technology* by Singer *et al* (Oxford University Press, 1958, volume 4, pages 507–508), says that the first such water closet was designed in 1596—three centuries before Crapper—by Sir John Harrington, and that improved models were invented in 1775 and 1778. Singer includes a drawing depicting Harrington's invention. It had a tank several feet above the stool. At the top of the tank was a water inlet and at the bottom a chain or cord to open a valve that permitted water to flow down to the stool. Essentially the same device may be found in some old buildings today.

Obviously, despite Johnny Carson and others, the device slangily called a crapper should be called a harrington or possibly a Sir John.

AND QUACKEN RAISED DUCKS

According to writer Dick Saggio, these are real names and the occupations of the people who hold them: Chief Clayton Crook, police chief, Brunswick, OH; C. Sharp Minor, silent-movie organist, Rochester, NY; Dr. E. Z. Filler (if you said "Dentist," you're right), Roslyn Heights, NY.

THE OWL WITHOUT A VOWEL

From 1949 to 1951 a basketball player named William Mlkvy performed for the Temple University Owls, earning a nearly unanimous All-American rating. The press was understandably delighted by his name, calling him "the Owl without a vowel," overlooking the fact that *y* is sometimes a vowel. The player later became Dr. William P. Mlkvy.

During the Vietnamese war another vowelless name, Ng, was often in print, and some Americans learned to pronounce it as what was described as "a tight *unn*." Columns of Ng's may now be found in some big American city directories.

From Czechoslovakia have come a number of names that appear to have no vowels in their spelling. These ordinarily contain an *r*, which in Czech may serve as a vowel but still gives a vowelless look (in American eyes). Elsdon Smith gives these examples of such odd-seeming names:

Chrt	Srp ⟨sickle⟩
Krc, Krch ⟨cramps⟩	Trc, Trch
Smrt ⟨death⟩	Trft
Smrz	Trh
Srb	Vlk ⟨wolf⟩
Srch	

When immigrants first arrived on these shores, such names were not extremely uncommon, but out of kindness to people who would be baffled by them, immigration officials or the newcomers themselves generally stuck in an obvious vowel.

A Manhattan directory still has Jn and Nj, and many Ng's, and comes close to vowellessness with Brchnel, Brlik, Brztwa, Hrnclar, Hrynklw, and Zmrzlik.

The all-time vowelless champ, however, if we again ignore a *y*, was a fictitious character named Mxyztplk, who came to Earth from the fifth dimension, in one of the first episodes of the comic book version of Superman, who was dreamed up by two teenage boys.

MR. REARDON COULDN'T BE THERE

A prankster invited a number of people, strangers to each other, to dinner. He asked them to introduce themselves and said he would leave it to them to discover during the evening what all of them had in common. They finally figured it out. Two women had the given name Fanny, and the other guests had surnames such as Bottomley, Duff, Pratt, Hinds, Butts, and Botham.

TRENDS IN
AMERICAN SURNAMES

The first United States census was taken in 1790. According to analyses made much later, 83.5 percent of the surnames in that year were English or Welsh; Scots contributed another 6.7 percent and Irish 1.6 percent, making a total of 91.8 percent British. Germans were far behind with 5.6 percent, the Dutch had 2 percent, a few people were unclassifiable, and French and all others made a total of less than 1 percent. The "all others" represented only about five thousand people.

No similar detailed analyses of later census reports have been made, but the predominance of British names was greatly reduced as successive waves of immigration flowed in. English, Welsh, and Scots kept coming, but up until 1860 or so the Irish and Germans were the most numerous newcomers, bringing in hundreds of thousands of people with names such as O'Rourke and Schneider. Scandinavians joined the throngs gradually, and from 1880 to 1914 immigrants from southern, central, and eastern Europe crowded in, sometimes averaging more than a million a year and bringing with them names ending in vowels or in *-vich*, *-wich*, *-ski* or *-sky*, *-opoulos*, and the like.

After World War I, immigration restrictions soon limited the flow, although many German Jews fled here from Hitler's Europe in the 1930s. After World War II, Asian immigrants greatly increased, bringing the one-syllable Chinese and Korean names such as Lee and Kim, the two-part Japanese names such as Yamamoto, the frequently Spanish names of the Philippines, and the Vietnamese names that often had a hard-to-pronounce *Ng-* beginning or other sounds uncustomary in America. As many Asians came in between 1960 and 1975 as had entered during all our earlier history. Especially, though, people with Spanish names came by the hundreds of thousands from Mexico, Cuba, and Puerto Rico.

What of the future? No one can predict with certainty, but probably the Spanish names will continue to outpace most others in growth. Already in 1974 Rodriguez had advanced to thirty-first place, a gain of thirteen notches in ten years, and other Spanish names were increasing somewhat proportionally. Asians, too, are coming in rapidly, having been assisted by a 1965 immigration law that permits more immigrants from the eastern hemisphere than from the western—although quotas have proved very fragile and sometimes impossible to enforce.

World conditions inevitably affect immigration, and thus the names brought to our shores. War, severe depression, or hunger may in the future bring us large numbers of newcomers from some now unlikely part of the world.

WONDERFUL PEOPLE
WITH STRANGE-SOUNDING NAMES

Sometimes a person with a strange-sounding name does well. The late actor Humphrey Bogart achieved fame in his own lifetime, and both Bogart cultists and many in the general public are still happy to see reruns of Bogey movies. W. Atlee Burpee got rich selling seeds (it's not significant that the company now offers "burpless" cucumbers). Mrs. R. O. Backhouse is remembered in a daffodil named for her. Robin Fox and Lionel Tiger made important studies of animal behavior. C. T. Onions (he pronounced it o-NIGH-unz) compiled dictionaries. Bedrich Smetana composed memorable music, even though his surname means ⟨sour cream⟩.

PART

III

WE
NAME
ALMOST
EVERY PLACE
WE KNOW

16

THE CONTINENTS AND THE STATES

HOW THE SEVEN CONTINENTS GOT THEIR NAMES

Some high school graduates and probably most college graduates know how the American continents came to be called America, but it is doubtful that one person in a hundred can say much about the origins of the names of the other continents.

Until less than five hundred years ago the sketchy world maps that existed showed only Europe, Asia, and Africa, along with other undefined areas sometimes labeled Terra Incognita (unknown lands). But in 1507 Martin Waldseemüller, a German geographer and cartographer drew in, roughly, a fourth area. He knew of the voyages of Columbus and the other sea captains who followed him. These men included the Italian Amerigo Vespucci, whose name in Latin was Americus Vespucius. He had made perhaps four voyages to explore the coasts of what are now called South and Central America, and possibly Florida.

Waldseemüller proposed a name for this large area:

> A fourth part [of the world] has been discovered by Americus Vespucius (as will appear in what follows). For that reason I think that nothing should prevent us from calling it Amerige or America, that is, the land of Americus, after its discoverer Americus, a man of brilliant mind [using a feminine ending], since both Europe and Asia are also named for women.

The proposal was adopted, although there are still those who argue persuasively that Columbia or Colombia would have been a more logical choice.

The name Europe, as Waldseemüller commented, seems to be the name of a woman (especially in its Latin form), Europa. Mythology tells us that Europa was a beautiful maiden whose father may have been Agenor, the king of Phoenicia. Zeus (Jupiter), king of the gods, whose all-seeing eyes liked to concentrate on feminine pulchritude, observed her and determined to possess her. He changed himself into a handsome white bull and, as Thomas Bulfinch says in *The Age of Fable*, "mingled with the herd as Europa and her maidens were sporting on the sea-shore. Encouraged by the tameness of the animal, Europa tried to mount his back; whereupon the god rushed into the sea, and swam with her to Crete."

Alfred, Lord Tennyson, described the trip sensuously:

> Sweet Europa's mantle blew unclasp'd,
> From off her shoulder backward borne;
> From one hand droop'd a crocus; one hand grasp'd
> The mild bull's golden horn.

Once in Crete, Zeus assumed human form, and eventually Europa bore him three children. It was this Europa for whom the continent was supposedly named.

But reality is seldom so poetic. The word *europa* was once thought to mean ⟨sunset⟩ and to have been applied by the Greeks to the lands to the west of them. Now, however, scholars believe that it meant ⟨mainland⟩. "It appears," says the *Encyclopaedia Britannica*, "to have suggested itself to the Greeks, in their maritime world, as an appropriate designation of the broadening, extensive northerly lands that lay beyond, lands with characteristics but vaguely known."

Asia, too, has a feminine-sounding name, but apparently it is only an indicator of a direction—east. In Greek the word meant ⟨region of the rising sun⟩, which may be related to an Assyrian word *asŭ* ⟨east⟩. It is also possible that at one time it referred only to what is now called Asia Minor, and then gradually reached out to encompass the whole continent.

The Romans were responsible for the naming of Africa. The word apparently comes from Latin *aprica* ⟨sunny⟩, which is similar to the Greek *aphrike* ⟨without cold⟩. Two other hypotheses, though, have been advanced. One is that the Romans called the relatively unexplored southern two thirds of the continent Afriga ⟨land of the Afrigs⟩, who were Berber tribes from south of Carthage. The least plausible explanation is that Africa means ⟨ears of corn⟩ and was used to denote fertile land in what is now Tunisia.

Scholars of ancient history have encountered occasional references to a *terra australis incognita* ⟨unknown southern land⟩, and starting in the twelfth century A.D. there were more and more rumors of the existence of such a land. But it was not until the seventeenth century that exploration and settlement actually began. Since the Dutch were the earliest explorers, the landmass was at first named New Holland. But the Dutch did not persist in settlement, and the English did. One of their explorers, Matthew Flinders, who had demonstrated that the landmass was indeed a separate continent, argued in 1817 that because this appeared to be the most southern of the continents, the old word for ⟨south⟩ should be revived and that Australia should replace the outdated New Holland. This view soon prevailed.

We now know that an even more southerly continent exists, Antarctica. The etymology of *arctic* is explained in the *American Heritage Dictionary*:

> Middle English *artik*, from Medieval Latin *articus*, alteration of Latin *arcticus*, from Greek *arktikos*, from *arktos*, bear, hence the northern constellation Ursa Major, the Great Bear, hence "north."

So *arctic*, by way of that great bear in the sky that points the way to the north star, gave the Arctic Ocean and the Arctic Islands their names. The *Ant* in *Antarctica* is short for the prefix *anti-* ⟨opposite⟩. Antarctica is opposite the Arctic—opposite the north.

STATE NAMES
AND NICKNAMES

About half of our states' names are from Indian sources, although the original meanings are often uncertain and the pronunciations dubious.

Of the other half, several come from names of English royalty or other persons of high rank, some from places in England, one from a Greek Island (Rhodes), three from French sources, five from Spanish, and one (Washington) from a president.

Some states have, or have had, more than a single nickname. The ones that appear to be most generally used are listed here.

Alabama, the Yellowhammer State: said by some to be Choctaw for ⟨thicket-clearers⟩ or ⟨vegetation-gatherers⟩, but George R. Stewart says it is from the name of a Creek tribe, the Alibamu or Alabamons. AL.

Alaska, the Land of the Midnight Sun, or the Last Frontier: from an Aleut word for ⟨sea-breaker⟩ or ⟨mainland⟩. AK.

Arizona, the Grand Canyon State: Indian Arizonac, for ⟨little spring⟩. AZ.

Arkansas, Land of Opportunity: a Quapaw name of a tribe, the Arkansea or Arkansa, then applied to the river and the territory. AR.

California, the Golden State: name in a Spanish poem, *Las Sergas de Esplandián*, by Garcia Ordoñez de Montalvo, c. 1500, California being an imaginary, rich island with Amazons as rulers. CA.

Colorado, the Centennial State (admitted to the Union in 1876): Spanish for ⟨red⟩ or ⟨ruddy⟩. CO.

Connecticut, the Nutmeg State: Indian word early recorded as Quinnehtukqut ⟨beside the long tidal river⟩. CT.

Delaware, the Diamond State, or the First State (first to ratify the U.S. Constitution, 1787): Delaware river and bay, named for Sir Thomas West, Lord De la Warr, the first governor of colonial Virginia. DE

Florida, the Sunshine State: Spanish ⟨feast of the flowers⟩ (Easter). FL.

Georgia, the Peach State, or the Empire State of the South: named to honor George II of England. GA.

Hawaii, the Aloha State: uncertain origin, but the islands' discoverer is said to have been named Hawaii Loa. The traditional home of Polynesians was also called Hawaii or Hawaiki. HI.

Idaho, the Gem State, the Panhandle State, or the Spud State: origin obscure, but may be from the Kiowa-Apache name for the Comanche tribe (Idahi); or may be from a word meaning ⟨gem of the mountains⟩. ID.

Illinois, the Prairie State: an Indian tribe (Illini), with a French affix. Said to mean ⟨tribe of superior men⟩ or simply ⟨the men⟩. IL.

Indiana, the Hoosier State: *Indian* + *a*, said to mean ⟨land of Indians⟩. IN.

Iowa, the Hawkeye State, or the Land Where the Tall Corn Grows: Indian for ⟨the beautiful land⟩ or ⟨this is the place⟩; early spelling recorded as Ouaouiaton, shortened to Ouaouia. IA.

Kansas, the Sunflower State, or the Jayhawk State: Siouan for ⟨people of the south wind⟩; Spanish wrote the name as Escansaque, French as Kansa, then Kansas. KS.

Kentucky, the Bluegrass State: Iroquoian Ken-tah-ten ⟨land of tomorrow⟩ or Ken-ta-ke ⟨meadow land⟩. KY.

Louisiana, the Pelican State, or the Creole State: for King Louis XIV of France; Spanish changed the French Louisiane to Louisiana. LA.

Maine, the Pine Tree State: sometimes considered a compliment to Queen Henrietta Maria, wife of England's Charles I, who was associated with a French province, Mayne, but more likely means ⟨the main⟩, i.e., the mainland in contrast to nearby islands. ME.

Maryland, the Free State, or the Old Line State: for Henrietta Maria, queen of Charles I of England. MD.

Massachusetts, the Bay State, or the Old Colony State: Algonquian (Natick) words meaning ⟨great mountain place⟩. MA.

Michigan, the Wolverine State: Algonquian words meaning ⟨great lake⟩; early reported as Machihiganing. MI.

Minnesota, the North Star State, or the Gopher State, or the Land of 10,000 Lakes (actually about 22,000): Dakotah word for ⟨sky-blue water⟩ or a Siouan word for ⟨water-cloudy⟩. MN.

Mississippi, the Magnolia State: Algonquian for ⟨father of waters⟩ or ⟨big river⟩; early form Messipi. MS.

Missouri, the Show-Me State: Missouri Indian tribe, the name said to mean ⟨place of the large canoes⟩; but more likely ⟨big and muddy⟩; early recorded as Ouemessourit. MO.

Montana, the Treasure State: Latinized Spanish word, chosen by Representative J. M. Ashley of Ohio; means ⟨mountainous⟩. MT.

Nebraska, the Cornhusker State: Oto or Omaha for ⟨flat water⟩; early reported as Nibthaska. NE.

Nevada, the Sagebrush State, or the Silver State, or the Battle-born State (for the Mexican War): Spanish for ⟨snow-capped⟩. NV.

New Hampshire, the Granite State: English county of Hampshire. NH.

New Jersey, the Garden State: Channel Isle of Jersey. NJ.

New Mexico, the Land of Enchantment, or the Sunshine State: from the country of Mexico (Nehuatl Mexihco). NM.

New York, the Empire State: for the English Duke of York. NY.

North Carolina, the Tar Heel State: named to honor England's King Charles I (in Latin, Carolus). NC.

North Dakota, the Sioux State, or the Flickertail State: from the name of the Dakotah tribe, meaning ⟨allies⟩. ND.

Ohio, the Buckeye State: Iroquoian for ⟨great river⟩. OH.

Oklahoma, the Sooner State, for settlers who arrived sooner than officially permitted: Choctaw words for ⟨red people⟩. OK.

Oregon, the Beaver State: origin unknown, but may be Indian; place-name authority George R. Stewart said it came from a misprint in a French map of 1715. OR.

Pennsylvania, the Keystone State: honors its founder, William Penn; means ⟨Penn's woods⟩. PA.

Rhode Island, the Ocean State: from the Greek island, Rhodes. RI.

South Carolina, the Palmetto State: honors England's Charles I. SC.

South Dakota, the Sunshine State, or the Coyote State: from the name of the Dakotah tribe, meaning ⟨allies⟩. SD.

Tennessee, the Volunteer State: Cherokee town name, meaning obscure; early recorded as Tanasqui, much later as Tinnase. TN.

Texas, the Lone Star State: from Indian *teyas* ⟨friends⟩, which the Spaniards mistook for a tribal name. TX.

Utah, the Beehive State: named for the Ute tribe, said to mean ⟨the people of the mountains⟩. UT.

Vermont, the Green Mountain State: French *vert mont* ⟨green mountain⟩. VT.

Virginia, the Old Dominion State, or the Mother of Presidents: name honors Elizabeth I, called the Virgin Queen. VA.

Washington, the Evergreen State, or the Chinook State: for George Washington. WA.

West Virginia, the Mountain State: same as Virginia. WV.

Wisconsin, the Badger State: French version of an Algonquian name, meaning uncertain; early reported as Mescousing or Mesconsing, later Ouisconsin(g). WI.

Wyoming, the Equality State: named for the Wyoming valley of Pennsylvania; meaning may be ⟨alternate mountains and valleys⟩ or, more likely, ⟨big-flats-at⟩; early recorded as Mauwauwaming or Meche-weami-ing. WY.

THEY MERGE AT THE BORDER

These border towns or cities share parts of the names of two or more states:

Arkoma, OK (AR, OK)
Calexico, CA (a state and a country: CA, Mexico)
Delmar, DE (DE, MD)
Kanorado, KS (KS, CO)
Kenova, WV (KY, OH, WV)
Mardela Springs, MD (MD, DE)
Moark, AR (MO, AR)

Tennga, GA (TN, GA)
Texarkana, AR (TX, AR, LA)
Texhoma, OK, TX (TX, OK)
Texico, NM (TX, NM)
Vershire, VT (VT, NH— about fifteen miles from the border)

Mexicali, Mexico, shakes hands across the border with Calexico, CA.

Oklahoma and Texas also share a lake called Texoma.

Other combined names also exist or have existed but do not have post offices. They include Arkana (AR, LA), Calneva (CA, NV), Calzona (CA, AZ), Dahoming (Dakota and WY), Nosodak (ND, SD), Nypenn (NY, PA), Pen-Mar (PA, MD), and Viropa (VA, OH, PA).

Delmarva or the variant Delmarvia is a name sometimes used for the states of Delaware, Maryland, and Virginia as a group. Usually, though, Delmarva refers only to the peninsula between Chesapeake Bay and the Atlantic, consisting of most of Delaware and parts of Maryland and Virginia.

MOST CONSECUTIVE VOWELS

On a French map of the central part of North America, printed in 1693, was the name Ouaouiaton, spelled with seven consecutive vowels. Later, shortened to Ouaouia, the name was applied to the Indian tribe that subsequently was called Iowa. Iowa next was attached to the river, then to the territory, and now to the state.

Apparently no other American place name has been written with so many consecutive vowels.

AROUND THE WORLD IN ARKANSAS

With a little zigging and zagging, you can visit all these places without leaving Arkansas: Athens (including Parthenon), Carthage, Damascus, Egypt, England, Formosa (not yet called Taiwan), Genoa, Hamburg, Havana, Jerusalem, London, Manila, Moscow, Oxford, Palestine, Paris, Scotland, and Ulm.

If you prefer not to leave the United States, in Arkansas you can find (if you look carefully) Augusta, Bismarck, Charleston, Cleveland, Columbus, Concord, Danville, Decatur, Denver, Evansville, Fargo, Fulton, Helena, Houston, Monticello, Nashville, Omaha, Poughkeepsie, Tupelo, Waterloo, and about fifty other places that you probably thought were in other states.

In Arkansas you can even find Romance, and a Sweet Home, as well as Success.

IS THE UNITED STATES, OR *ARE* THE UNITED STATES?

President John Adams used to say "The United States are…" and so did a few lesser American dignitaries and many Britishers (who also say "the government are…" and report cricket matches in headlines like "England Defeat Wales").

Most Americans, though, regard the nation as a unit and therefore treat the name as a singular. Carl Sandburg said what should have been the last word—but wasn't—in 1958: "The United States *is*, not *are*. The Civil War was fought over a verb."

Problems arise when someone—usually a member of Congress or some other political orator—puts *these* before the name. Obviously one can hardly say "*These* United States *is*…" with a plural at one end and a singular at the other. The solution is simple: The speaker is not talking here about the place as a nation, but rather as a group of states that are united in some way or ways. In print the construction should be spelled without capitals: "These united states are determined..."

AROUND THE WORLD IN
MAINE

A postcard that travelers used to enjoy sending—perhaps still do—showed signboards at a crossroads pointing the way to Athens, Belfast, Belgrade, Bremen, China, Denmark, Dresden, Frankfort, Limerick, Lisbon, Madrid, Mexico, Naples, Norway, Oxford, Palermo, Paris, Peru, Poland, Rome, and Vienna.

All those places are within about fifty miles of a spot north and west of Portland, Maine.

17

HOW PLACES
GET THEIR
NAMES

NAMING PLACES IN THE
TWENTIETH CENTURY

Suppose that the North American continent had somehow been concealed from the rest of the world until the twentieth century, but that in other respects civilization had moved along as it has. What kinds of names might have been chosen for places in the newly developing country?

There may be some clues in the names that actually have been chosen in the past fifty or seventy-five years.

Perhaps most famous of these was adopted from a radio show in 1950. The proprietors of that show went to a place in New Mexico and offered to hold an annual fiesta there if the townspeople would change the name from Hot Springs to the name of the program. It sounded like good publicity, and business people argued for a yes-vote. Hot Springs had never before had so much excitement and such lively discussion. In the election a considerable majority approved the change, and so Truth or Consequences came into being. It was confirmed by a second vote in 1964. The radio show has long been gone, and the name is awkward. People in the area shorten it to T or C, and signs often say merely Truth or C.

Other twentieth-century entertainment has influenced names. An Oklahoma town in 1942 named itself Gene Autry, after a popular singing star in western movies. Children and sometimes adults talk excitedly about going to Disneyland or Disney World, using those as place names and sometimes unaware that they will really have to buy their plane tickets to Anaheim, CA or Orlando, FL, both of which have grown remarkably in population because of being entertainment centers. The name of the Paramount motion picture company was attached to the boulevard on which the huge movie lot was built, and later to the town of Paramount. Singer Elvis Presley's name has been given to streets and business establishments, especially in his native Memphis. Jiggs, NV was named for the leading character in a comic strip, and Dog Patch (from the habitat of the redoubtable Yokum family and other denizens such as Marryin' Sam, Senator Phogbound, and Moonbeam McSwine) is applied at least facetiously to many places.

The name of Jim Thorpe, an Indian who was one of America's greatest all-round athletes, is now the name of a Pennsylvania community formerly called East Mauch Chunk and Mauch Chunk (which means ⟨bear mountain⟩).

In Colorado in 1936 a place was named Uravan because uranium and vanadium were mined there. In Indiana, near a reactor testing station, is Atomic City.

TV Mountain, MT, is so called for the television transmitter built there in 1954. Somewhat older is Twenty Mule Team Canyon, CA, which became best known after a brand of borax was named Twenty Mule Team; the box showed the mules pulling a heavy wagon. Tin Mountain, CA, and Tin Mine Canyon, CA, celebrate one part of the mining industry, and Tin Can Branch, KY, memorializes a more immediate source of much of America's food supply (although, it seems, not much if any tin is now used in tin cans). The word Coal or a derivative appears in close to a hundred settlement names, some of them pre-twentieth century, and other things that are mined (Silver, Gold, Lead, and Copper, for instance) have their own namesakes. Cyanide County, MT, received the name of this deadly poison because it is a chemical used in treating ore. Several towns have Gas as a part of their names.

A California area renowned for experimentation with computers, silicon chips and the like, is publicized by journalists as Silicon Valley. Neon, Krypton, and Xena (for xenon) are near one another in Kentucky. Munition and Nitro in West Virginia got their names during World War I. Herpoco, CA, is an acronym for Hercules Powder Company.

Motorists entering Arizona may have their cars searched for illegal fruit; the official inspection station has been nicknamed Gripe.

Twentieth-century events and people are sometimes memorialized. In 1901 two Wyoming mountain climbers, reaching the top of a peak, celebrated by drinking a bottle of Pabst beer. That's how Pabst Mountain got its name. And in 1946 Phil D. Smith climbed another Wyoming mountain, which he modestly named Philsmith Peak. A well-liked Chinese consul in Seattle, named Goon Dip, died in 1936, and someone in Alaska remembered him in 1939 by naming Goon Dip Mountain for him.

One or another of the Roosevelts has frequently had places named for him, and in Colorado are some rocks called Teddys Teeth, probably because political cartoonists liked to feature TR's toothy grin. Hoover Dam, formerly Boulder Dam, was renamed in 1947 to honor the former president (and Democrats persist in calling an economic depression by his name). Other presidents have been honored in other places.

If we had indeed started afresh with naming in the twentieth century, names like those mentioned suggest the probable emphases—names taken from entertainment, science, war, industry, and both little-known and famous people.

Gone would be almost all our Indian names—gone Chicago, gone Massachusetts, gone Utah, gone many hundreds more. There would be no Washingtons, Franklins, Lincolns. Most French and Dutch names would probably be missing. Old names based on incidents, legends, or jokes might be replaced by names from newer happenings, imaginings, or humor.

A few of the idealistic and patriotic names might appear here and there. Assuming English as the language, maybe some Libertys, some Unions, a few Harmonys would still be here. Some places in the old world might again be remembered— perhaps London, Paris, Stockholm, Vienna, Canton.

There would still be many names describing the shape or

general appearance of natural features, still names from the trees and flowers and animals found here. There could still be Great Lakes or something similar, still the Rocky Mountains. Some things last better than others.

SOURCES OF PLACE NAMES

Unfold any state road map and you can see the names—long and short—of once nationally prominent people and of other people you've never heard of, pretty names and ugly names, names of rivers and mountains, names from the Old World and from farther east in the New, names that seem foreign, a few names that sound funny, some that seem inexplicable. Who named all these places, and what did they base their decisions on?

Naming practices varied somewhat from state to state, for historical reasons and especially because of differing patterns of immigration, but the thirteen sources of place names described by Ronald L. Baker and Marvin Carmony in *Indiana Place Names* are representative. The percentages attributable to each of the thirteen are different in other states, but the similarities are considerable. For instance, in every state a high percentage of place names are derived from people's names.

1. *People's names.* Eighty-five percent of Indiana's county names (e.g., Adams, Kosciusko, Warren) are those of people, usually "non-local people, especially military heroes." Thirty-seven percent of the names of cities, towns, and villages are also from people's names, although local people rather than national figures are usually the ones thus honored—sometimes through use of a Christian name or a nickname rather than a surname. Of Indiana streams and lakes, about 21 percent have people's names.

2. *Names of other places.* Eleven percent of Hoosier county names are for other places—sometimes far away (Switzerland, Orange) but more often local rivers or lakes (Ohio, Tippecanoe, Lake). Twenty-eight percent of town names are from other place names (Bunker Hill, Salem), with about half of those being names of natural features (Lakeville).

3. *Names indicating direction or position.* Two percent of settlement names (North Liberty, West Terre Haute) are of this sort, and 4 percent of natural features (East Fork Tennessee Creek).

4. *Descriptive names.* One county, La Porte ⟨the door⟩, has a descriptive name, referring here to a natural forest opening that was a good place for a trail or a road. Eight percent of settlement names are descriptive (Badger Grove, Cloverdale, Edgewood, Quakertown, Pleasant Ridge); 20 percent of streams and lakes have descriptive names (Blue Lake, Butternut Creek, Buck Creek).

5. *Inspirational names.* This source includes idealistic, classical, literary, biblical or religious, and commendatory names— the last being most numerous. In all, 7 percent of Indiana settlement names fit these categories (Harmony, Mt. Olympus, Waverly, Palestine, Acme, Fairfield, Prosperity). Union is the only county and St. Joseph the only stream or lake classed as inspirational.

6. *Indian and pseudo-Indian names.* The eastern and southern parts of the nation have more Indian names than do the midwest and west. In Indiana only two counties owe their names to Indians, and fewer than 2 percent of settlements. However, 33 percent of Indiana stream and lake names are of Indian origin (Big Shawnee Creek, Iroquois River, Kickapoo Creek, Shipshewana Lake, etc.). As is true elsewhere, the Indian names are often distorted from what the Indians probably said; thus the village of Mongo seems once to have been Mon-go-quin-ong ⟨big squaw⟩, and Baugo Creek was Baubaugo ⟨devil river⟩.

7. *Humorous names.* "Hoosier namers apparently were a sober lot," the authors complain, and although they relate humorous anecdotes about places called Pinhook, Popcorn, and the like, they say that only one name, Santa Claus, "clearly reflects humorous motivations."

8. *Names from languages other than English.* New York has more Dutch names than Indiana has; Illinois, Louisiana, and several other states have more French names; and the southwest has far more Spanish names. Three Indiana counties (La Porte, which is also descriptive, and Fayette and La Grange) are French, and a few settlements are, too (Terre Haute, Vincennes). Only

here and there can one find a trace of any other language, such as German Haubstadt, Greek Eureka, and Spanish Plano.

9. *Incident names.* Local happenings inspired no Indiana county names, and the names of only five settlements (including Battleground and Cyclone), and just three streams (creeks named Hurricane, Poison, and Treaty).

10. *Folk etymology.* People sometimes mishear or misinterpret an unfamiliar word, and then they pronounce it like a different, more familiar word—a process called folk etymology. Fewer than 1 percent of Indiana place names arose in this way. Examples include Koleen, which comes from kaolin, a kind of clay; Russiaville, which was actually named for a Miami Indian chief with the unlikely name of Richard; and Weasel Creek, from Wesaw, another Miami chief.

11. *Coined names.* Coinage also is responsible for fewer than 1 percent of Indiana names. Kyana and Michiana Shores blend parts of Kentucky and Michigan with parts of Indiana. Elwren uses parts of the names of four resident families: *El*ler, *Wh*aley, Bak*er*, and Breed*en*.

12. *Mistake names.* Again, fewer than 1 percent. Moores Mill was once the name of a town, but perhaps the second M looked like an H on the application for a post office. So for over a century the little town has been Moores Hill.

13. *Legends and anecdotes.* For about forty Indiana names, Baker and Carmony supplied unverifiable anecdotes or legends to account for the origin—a little over 1 percent of the settlement names and a similar proportion for lakes and streams. Limberlost Creek and Swamp, for instance, are said to owe their name to "Limber Jim" McDowell, who went bear hunting and was lost in a swamp for three days.

IT HAPPENED RIGHT HERE:
Names from Incidents

In the winter of 1873–74, Alfred Packer and five companions were snowbound on a plateau of the Rocky Mountains in Colorado. Their food was soon gone, and the men were weakening. The remaining details are skimpy and not well authenticated, but according to local accounts Packer killed the other men and lived off their flesh until the winter was past. The place where that incident occurred has since been called Cannibal Plateau.

Switch to ten years later—1883. Packer was arrested in a canyon in Wyoming. Its name, as a result, is Man-Eater Canyon. But Packer's guilt, and therefore the accuracy of the two names, is still contested.

Several hundred American place names—certainly many more if very local names are counted—are derived from incidents, some unquestionable, others probably invented. Most of the incidents are relatively trivial: someone fell into a creek and so the creek was named for him, a deer was seen and so a place was called Deer Lake or Buck Creek, a climber in Alaska in 1931 called the mountain Shivering Mountain because he was shivering from cold as he climbed, and similarly two other climbers of a small peak in Wyoming in 1959 called it Mount Quiver because the dangers they faced made them quiver. Some Nebraska cowboys ran out of supplies except for beans, and Bean Soup Lake remembers their temporary discomfort. Two flocks of sheep became hopelessly intermingled at Mixup Spring, Oregon. And so on.

However, other name-creating incidents may be a little less hohum than those.

In a lake in New Mexico the body of a man was found floating, pierced by several arrows. He was identified as a man named Ambrosio, and so the lake was called in Spanish "the lake of the dead Ambrosio." But Ambrosio was soon confused with *ambrosia*, the food of the gods, alleged to impart immortality. Today the place is Lake Ambrosia, and in a way Ambrosio has immortality.

At what was afterward called Bloody Point, California, Indians in 1852 killed sixty-three whites. But a creek in Nebraska got its name because a group of surveyors anticipated an Indian attack that did not materialize, so they called it Bloody Creek as a joke.

Bones of prehistoric mastodons and mammoths were found at the salt deposits thereafter named Big Bone Lick, Kentucky.

There was plenty of brandy aboard a schooner that went aground on an Oregon reef one nightfall in 1850. Making the best of their troubles the passengers and crew spent the night carousing, but were still able to free the boat sometime later.

The place was then called Brandy Bar. Jim Jam Ridge, CA marks the location of a longer spree in 1890—one so bad that the three miners involved got the jimjams, an old slang term for *delirium tremens*. The number of pink elephants they saw was beyond counting.

Governor John Winthrop had only cheese for dinner on February 7, 1632, because his servant had been neglectful. He named the Maine spot where he had his unaccustomed light meal Cheese Rock.

A half dozen or more places are named Christmas because of big or small events that happened on that day. For example, at Christmas, Florida, a military post was established on Christmas Day, 1837.

Conquest, NY got its name because one faction defeated another in an attempt to create a new settlement, but the names Union Ridge, North Carolina, Union County, South Carolina, and Union Grove, Minnesota, all celebrate not separation but the uniting of two formerly rivalrous church groups.

A creek in Wyoming was named Damfino because someone who asked a local what its name was, got the reply, "Damn if I know."

A cooperative postman in a little place in Texas reportedly liked to do favors for people but thought he should be paid at least a token amount. He put up a box into which people could drop dimes to pay him for his trouble. The place is now known as Dime Box.

Disaster Peak in Nevada commemorates a group of prospectors attacked by Indians in 1856. In contrast, John Vancouver escaped an Indian attack on an Alaskan point in 1793, and the name Escape celebrates his safety.

The gondola from a stratospheric explorer balloon landed in South Dakota in 1935. The landing place was afterward named Gondola Lake.

No one seems to know for sure who needed help in or near an Alaska creek. But the name Goshelpme suggests that someone must have been in trouble there. Helpmejack Creek in the same state also hints at some perilous occasion. But Oh-Be-Joyful Gulch, Colorado, proclaims a lucky strike. Nil Desperandum Gulch in Arkansas was apparently an erudite message of hope for someone who needed cheering up; it is Latin for ⟨Don't despair⟩.

In 1812 or 1813, Jack Storm's horse got mired in the mud of a little Indiana stream that flows into Beanblossom Creek. Jack had great difficulty in extricating himself and his mount. A sign, Jack's Defeat Creek, marks the spot at the edge of Ellettsville, where some natives may tell you a much-embroidered version of the story, complete with an exciting love affair and competing suitors.

In parts of South Dakota the roads go uphill a short distance, then down, then up, and so on for miles and miles. In the 1840s a slang term for alternating ridges and depressions in a road was kiss-me-quicks—probably to suggest the need for a quick kiss before the next bump. Travelers in South Dakota at that time or perhaps later translated the term into a name, the Kiss-Me-Quick Hills.

A South Dakota cowboy who couldn't spell very well found a calf with characteristics of both sexes. He named the place Morphradite Creek, by which he meant ⟨hermaphrodite⟩.

The name Lovers Leap is attached to dozens of places, memorializing one or two lovers, oftentimes Indians, who in despair jumped from a high place to certain death. A touching, beautiful, romantic tale, but, says George R. Stewart, "No authentic story is recorded."

During the years of Queen Victoria's reign in England, many American women became linguistically squeamish. Tables and chairs, for instance, no longer had legs (a naughty word), but only limbs; and *bull* was a word that no lady would utter. So when in 1890 a young California woman was chased by a bull and had to take refuge on a large rock, the place was named, not Bull Rock, but Man Cow Rock.

A geologist in Alaska in 1950 became greatly concerned when other members of his party did not show up when they were expected. After they came, he decided that the creek where he had awaited them should be called Panic Creek.

On June 1, 1778, James Cook displayed the British flag on a point in Alaska and "took possession for Great Britain." The point became Possession Point.

A party of explorers in Nevada in 1846 needed water badly. They finally found a spring by following rabbit trails, for rabbits know where to go when they're thirsty. They attached the name Rabbithole Spring.

We began with a gruesome incident of alleged cannibalism

and will end with something no more pleasant. Once the Apache and Maricopa Indians fought a bloody battle in Arizona and left their dead behind them. Some of the skulls were found many years later by white Americans. They called the place Skull Valley. Then, in 1866, Indians and whites fought there, and the whites left behind the bodies of the Indians who had been killed. Thus the accuracy of the name Skull Valley was recertified. If you are so inclined you can still visit the town, a few miles west of Prescott. (The skulls have been picked up.)

BRINGING THE HOLY LAND
TO AMERICA

John Leighly reported in 1979 an analysis of biblical place names that he found among 61,742 United States place names.

In all there were 803 (1.3 percent) that were clearly biblical in origin—101 *different* names.

Salem, as Jerusalem was anciently called, was the top choice, with ninety-five namings. Salem, MA, was the first town in North America to be given a biblical name.

In colonial times, New England and Pennsylvania made more use of biblical names than did other colonies. Before the Revolutionary War, New England had already chosen twenty-one such namings (twelve different names).

Areas that now have the greatest density of biblical place names, in addition to New England and southeastern Pennsylvania, are southeastern Ohio, northeastern South Carolina, and central and west central Georgia.

Here are the most common biblical place names in the U.S., as counted in Leighly's research:

Salem-95	Zion-24
Eden-61	Antioch-18
Bethel-47	Paradise-18
Lebanon-39	Shiloh-18
Sharon-38	Beulah-17
Goshen-33	Bethlehem-16
Jordan-27	Canaan-16
Hebron-26	Mount of Olives

(various forms)-15	Carmel (Mount Carmel)-13
Bethany (Bethania)-14	Smyrna-13
Corinth-14	Tabor (Mount Tabor,
Palestine-14	Taber)-12

Leighly's figures demonstrate the relative popularity of each of these names, but the actual total for each must be much higher, since the research covered only 61,000 of the estimated several hundred thousand U.S. place names.

THE ONLY VIRGIN

Virgin, UT, is the only Virgin in the United States that has a post office.

There is, however, a Virginville in Pennsylvania. Also, a western river, originally called Virgen by Spaniards, is now spelled Virgin.

Las Virgenes Creek, CA, is probably a religious name derived from a story about Saint Ursula and her 11,000 virgins who reportedly made a pilgrimage to Rome in the fourth century, but were slaughtered by Huns as they were returning to England. The Virgin Islands take their name from the same story; they were earlier called Santa Ursula y las Once Mil Virgenes. The Ursuline nuns, who devote themselves to the education of girls, are named for this Saint Ursula, whose feast day is October 21. Unfortunately, the details of the story about the pilgrimage have not been proved true, and Ursula is no longer sanctified.

Most geographical features called Virgin are named after families, but a few others may refer to unspoiled nature or to the Virgin Mary. Virginville, PA is said to be a translation of Indian words.

TWO BUNCH PALMS

The United States Army, experimenting with its Camel Corps, found it just right for surveying and mapping desert areas south of Los Angeles. One place, ten miles from what is now Palm

Springs, the Corps leaders named Two Bunches of Palms, because two small palm groves grew at an oasis there.

Indians had, of course, known the spot earlier and had believed that the oasis waters, which are about 100° F in temperature, had curative value. Whites who later bathed in the waters shared that belief and started a resort spa there, with nude sunbathing, saunas, massages, tennis, and a barbecue, as well as a tremendous white owl that reportedly lives in the largest palm tree but is not likely to be seen by visitors.

Nobody says "Two Bunches of Palms" any more. Like many other facets of language, long names are often shortened and simplified. So the resort is known as Two Bunch Palms.

MANY *MINNE'S*

Minne is the way we spell a Sioux word for ⟨water⟩. Blended with Greek *-polis* for ⟨city⟩, it gave us Minneapolis, although that name was suggested in part by Minnehaha, which means ⟨water falls⟩ and not ⟨laughing waters⟩, as Longfellow asserted in *Hiawatha*. (Minnehaha Falls, by the way, is redundant, because it means ⟨water falls falls⟩.)

Minnesota is ⟨water cloudy⟩ rather than the wishfully invented ⟨land of the sky-blue waters⟩. The state has other *Minne's*, too, including Minneota ⟨much water⟩, Minneola (with the same meaning), Minnesota City, Minnesota Lake, Minnetonka Beach and Lake Minnetonka ⟨water big⟩, Minneopa ⟨water falling twice⟩, Minneiska ⟨water white⟩, Minnetrista (in which *trista* may come from English *twist*, so that the name means ⟨crooked water⟩), and Minnewashk(t)a ⟨water good⟩, which is simplified in New York to Minnewaska.

Other states share *Minne*, although Minneola, KS, and Minneola, TX, commemorate girls named Minnie and Ola. North Dakota has Minnewaukan ⟨water spirit bad⟩, and its sister state to the south has the Minnechadusa ⟨water swift⟩ River and Minnesela ⟨water red⟩ Creek, now translated to Redwater Creek; the spelling of Minniesechi ⟨water bad⟩ Creek adds an *i*. In New Hampshire is the Minnewawa River, an Algonquian name that perhaps means ⟨many waters⟩. Minnequa, PA, may mean ⟨to drink⟩. Minnehaha Springs, WV, was named for the Indian girl in *Hiawatha*.

TOO LITTLE MUSIC

A superficial glance through lists of place names suggests that a fair number of them are related to music:

Alto (towns in five states)
Bass, AR
Bow, KY, WA; Bow Creek, AK, NE
Drum, KY; Drums, PA; Drum Bridge, CA; Mt. Drum, AK
Fiddletown, CA; Fiddle Creek, OR; Fiddlers Creek, NE
Fife (towns in three states)
Fluteville, CT; Fluted Rock, AZ
Horner, WV; Hornersville, MO

Organ, NM; Organ Cave, WV; Organ Mountains, NM; Organ Pipe Cactus National Monument, AZ
Singer, LA; Singers Glen, VA; Singing Mountain, NV
Solo, MO
Triangle (towns in three states)
Trio, SC
Tuba City, AZ
Viola (towns in nine states)

But not all is as it seems. Tuba City, it turns out, was named for an Indian chief, Viola is from the girl's name, Alto is a Spanish word for ⟨high⟩, Bow and Solo and Trio and Fluted are not applied here with reference to music, Triangle is a mathematical figure rather than a percussion instrument, Bass can be either a fish or a person, and Drum, Horner, and Singer are from surnames of early settlers. Fife is for a county in Scotland.

Fiddle does a little better. Fiddletown and probably Fiddlers Creek got their names from the numbers of fiddlers who once lived there, and Fiddle Creek is said to commemorate an injured man who played while recuperating. Drum Bridge has pillars with ends resembling drums. Fluteville was once a center for flutemaking. The names with Organ all apparently relate to rock formations that look like organ pipes. Singing Mountain is a dune where wine-driven sand sometimes makes the sound of weird singing.

Those are slim pickings, however, and hardly impressive to the musically minded. Where are the Pianos, the Violins, the Cellos? (Monticello doesn't count; the word is Italian for ⟨little mountain).) Where are the Piccolos, the Oboes, the Bassoons, the Timpani? There's not a Cornet or a Trumpet, and of course not a Clarinet, a Saxophone, or a Sousaphone. Nor a Guitar and, surprisingly, not a Banjo. Where can one find a Symphony, a Concerto, a Fugue? There's not even a Waltz or a Polka among our thousands of towns and cities.

More important, what places are named for musical performers or composers? Here and there a street perhaps, such as Presley Boulevard in Memphis or Mozart Street in Chicago. Why in our town names do we almost exclusively honor military men, early settlers, and politicians? Have they contributed more to civilization than Beethoven, Brahms, and Chopin, or even than Gershwin or Charles Ives?

Musicians join other prominent people in being neglected by those who choose names. Poets are seldom commemorated, although John Greenleaf Whittier made the grade in California. Is Eugene O'Neill remembered in any place name? Walt Whitman has a bridge. Doesn't he deserve more? What painters are memorialized? What architects, except in their own buildings? Outside the arts, what scientists are found on maps? What great teachers? What doctors and medical researchers? People who save thousands of lives—Jonas Salk, for instance—deserve to have their names on a few maps, right up next to Beethoven and Orchestra.

PENNYRILE GETS INTO
THE BASEBALL HALL OF FAME

"I'm a Pennyrile feller," said Albert B. (Happy) Chandler. "Born a mile from town, not in a town. I'm a country boy." The occasion of his remark was a gathering of ex-Kentucky New Yorkers who assembled in the summer of 1982 to honor the former baseball commissioner, U.S. senator, and Kentucky governor. He had just been inducted into the baseball hall of fame, at eighty-four the oldest living man to be honored. As commissioner he had been one of the two men most responsible for bringing black players into the big leagues.

"Pennyrile" is one pronunciation of *pennyroyal*, a member of the mint family (*Mentha pelegium*) that grows widely in the eastern half of the United States. It is a short plant with oval, mint-scented leaves and bluish lavender flowers. It was written about in New England as early as 1630, when it was called an "excellent Pot-herb." Its leaves have been made into tea and prepared as a laxative, a tonic, and an insectifuge. In the mid-nineteenth century some people sang "pennyroyal hymns," described as combining "unction and vivacity."

One area of Kentucky is known as "the Pennyroyal," or locally "the Pennyrile," and that is where Happy Chandler came from. The *Chicago Tribune* in 1892 named others: "Abraham Lincoln, Jefferson Davis...and Adlai E. Stevenson [U.S. vice-president, 1893–97] all came from what is locally known as the 'Pennyrile deestrict' of Kentucky." A later writer defined the area thus: "One of the lovers of Kentucky said to me that the State is divided into three parts. To the east we have the Mountains. Moving westward we come to the Blue Grass. Following the setting sun we come to the 'Pennyrile.'" What geologists called the Pennsylvania Plateau is called by some Kentuckians the Pennyroyal Plateau. A superhighway officially called the Pennyrile Parkway runs north and south near the western edge of Kentucky.

Happy Chandler never forgot his Pennyrile beginnings. To the transplanted Kentuckians at the banquet honoring him he sang a song, as he did at any meeting where he could find an excuse. His choice on this night was "Down the Trail to Home, Sweet Home."

THE COLDEST-SOUNDING NAMES

The most amusing frigid name didn't start out to be funny. It's for a New Jersey creek called Shiver-de-Freeze. During the Revolutionary War, poles were driven at angles in the Delaware River to obstruct boats, in a crisscross form known by the French name *cheval-de-frise*. By folk etymology this later became Shiver-de-Freeze, and was applied to the creek.

A more legitimate use of *shiver* is Shivering Mountain, AK. Alaska also has, unsurprisingly, a Snowcap Mountain and an Icy Cape. Ice appears as three Ice Mountains in West Virginia, although one of those was named for a man rather than for congealed water. Colorado has an Ice Lake, Washington an

Iceberg Point, and both Montana and California boast an unlikely Iceberg Lake.

There's a Snow Hill as far south as North Carolina, and a slightly misplaced Polar in Wisconsin. Idaho understates its winter temperatures with Chilly and Chilly Buttes, but also has a more realistic Blizzard Mountain. Michigan has Coldwater; Virginia, a Cold Harbor; and California both a Cold Mountain and a nearby Cold Canyon. Frio County, TX, uses the Spanish word for ⟨cold⟩.

Freezeout, AZ, and Freezeout Creek, CO, both recall incidents when the temperature was far below comfort. Two South Dakota creeks are called Frozen Man because someone froze to death beside each, and at Frozen Run, WV, a man saved his life by wrapping himself in the skin of a recently killed buffalo; even so, his friends had to thaw it to get him out.

Most places called Winter(s) are named for people, and a few, such as Winterhaven, FL, suggest refuge from the cold. However, explorer John Frémont gave Winter Ridge, OR, its name because it seemed so much colder than nearby Summer Lake.

California is usually thought of as a warm state, but it once held and perhaps still holds the championship for a cold-sounding name. Siberian Outpost, in Sequoia National Park, was given that name in the winter of 1895 because to the park developers the area seemed excessively cold and unpleasant. Now it's just called Siberia.

18

WHIMSY
AND
HUMOR

WE LAUGHED ALL THE WAY
TO CUCAMONGA

"Mention chickens and people laugh. Substitute hens in the
same joke and die. Kokomo is funny; Muncie, fifty-five miles
away, isn't. Brooklyn and the Bronx get laughs; Manhattan
draws a respectful silence. Pickles are funnier than relish, and
a porcupine is funny but a wolverine, with the same rhythm,
isn't."

So says Jack C. Horn in a brief filler in *Psychology Today*.
Comedians Mel Brooks and Buddy Hackett (each of whom
coincidentally has a *k* in his name) once told talk-show host
David Susskind that the *k* sound is the greatest laugh-getter.
Podunk (the name of small but real places in New York, Connecticut, and Maine) is a favorite among comics. Hackett and
Brooks might also have mentioned Keokuk and Kankakee, which
get their share of yucks. If the little old lady from Dubuque
had been from Davenport or Dyersburg, we probably would
never have heard of her. Kalamazoo also stretches the risible

muscles. Comedians haven't yet done much with Kaskaskia, IL, and too few people have ever heard of Keosauqua, IA.

Other comedians say P can also cause laughter. Podunk starts with it, and Peoria sounds much funnier than nearby Springfield. Poughkeepsie, like Podunk, has the hilarious good fortune to have both *k* and *p*—two p's, in fact. Pago Pago (pronounced like pong-go pong-go) is often taken lightly. Pippa Passes, KY, named by a teacher familiar with Robert Browning's poem of that name, seems funniest to people who have never read Browning. Punxutawney, PA, is famous for its watchful groundhog, but is blessed by the *p* and *k* sounds in its name. Has any Johnstown groundhog ever become so widely known? All the publicity that Johnstown ever got was for a flood.

Little or nothing has ever been written about the funniest vowel. The "long *u*" or "oo" sound is hereby nominated. It helps to make poodle jokes funnier than German shepherd jokes (if there are any), and it assists the *k*'s in Dubuque and Kalamazoo.

On the old Jack Benny shows a train announcer proclaimed a departure for "Anaheim, Azusa, and Cucamonga," a combination put together by a comic genius. It starts with the bland Anaheim, builds to a drawn-out "oo" in Azusa, and climaxes with the two *k* sounds surrounding the even more elongated "oo" in Cucamonga. The unimportant last syllables give the audience time to laugh.

WHIMSY IN PLACE NAMES

Although most places are solemnly named by serious-minded people, some seem to have arisen because the namer had tongue firmly planted in cheek.

Surveyors in Maryland in 1774 made a mistake, marking off some land "by accident." So, someone must have said, why not immortalize the error? The town named Accident is still on the map. Mistake Peak, AZ, and Mistaken Creek, KY, commemorate other goofs. They were confused with a different peak and a different stream.

Once there was an Elk Cove Canyon, CA, but no elk have been seen there for years. In the oral language Elk Cove sounds like Alcove, although the canyon has not many more alcoves than it has elk. So Alcove it became.

Where should Aloha be? In Hawaii, of course. But when the song "Aloha Oe" ⟨farewell to thee⟩ swept into national popularity after Queen Liliuokalani composed it in 1898, at least three places—in Louisiana, Oregon, and Washington—decided that Aloha should be their name.

Was Bayou des Amoureaux ⟨the amorous ones⟩ named for a pair of lovers, star-crossed or otherwise, or as George R. Stewart says, "Probably for des muriers 'of the mulberry trees'"? We can't be sure, but maybe it was the latter and then—maybe—someone noted the similarity of pronunciation and changed the name to the more romantic term.

Whimsy crosses the centuries. A Spanish explorer, Viscamo, discovered a previously unknown point on the California coast. The time was the start of a new year, January, 1603. So he called the point Ano Nuevo ⟨new year⟩.

Another explorer, the British Sir John Franklin, was afraid that he and his men would be prevented by bad weather from reaching a point on the Alaskan coast. They did reach it (in 1826), and he commemorated his worry by calling the place Anxiety Point.

"This soil is so sandy it looks like the Sahara," an early Nebraska settler complained. "At least somewhere in Arabia," his neighbor agreed. So they called the place Arabia.

Aromatic Creek in Texas may once have been called Stinking Creek, but who would want to live near such a place? A creek by any other name would smell more sweet.

There's a little place in central Texas called Art (not far from Grit). Ask a resident how the town got its name and you may be told, "Well, it's not for Arthur or Artesian, and far as I know people here weren't ever especially arty. We've heard they picked it just because they wanted a real short name."

The first postmaster in Avert, MO, may just have been rather uneducated, or he may have been a smart aleck. The U.S. Post Office Department told him to choose a village name that would avert confusion, and Avert probably did just that. But it didn't avert the later loss of the post office.

There's a Babel River in Alaska, named in 1956 by the author of *Dictionary of Alaska Place Names*, D. J. Orth. He chose that name "because of the 'confusion of tongues' (see Genesis 11:7) among authorities with respect to the name of this stream."

That's a good place to stop these examples of whimsy, even though we're only at the beginning of the B's. Readers of Stewart's *American Place-Names,* on which these explanations are loosely based, can find and label dozens more in that fascinating book.

"VERY LIKE A WHALE"

Hamlet: Do you see that cloud that's almost in shape like a camel?

Polonius: By the mass, and it's like a camel, indeed.

Hamlet: Methinks it is like a weasel.

Polonius: It is back'd like a weasel.

Hamlet: Or like a whale?

Polonius: Very like a whale.

Rock formations, particularly in the American West, are often named for real or fancied resemblance to something else. Guides in hilly or mountainous areas may cause tourists to ooh and ahh by pointing out faces or perching eagles or grieving Indian maidens or unicorns, all in stone. Nathaniel Hawthorne entitled one of his best short stories "The Great Stone Face," after an actual formation in the White Mountains of New Hampshire. "There was the broad arch of the forehead, a hundred feet in height, the nose with its long bridge, and the vast lips, which, if they could have spoken, would have rolled their thunder accents from one end of the valley to the other."

Here are some of America's place names for which geological quirks, slow erosion by wind and water, or the relentless movement of glaciers have been responsible.

AB Mountains, AK: when the snow melts you can read the two letters

The Alligator, AZ: a long, low ridge

Angel Terrace, WY: a white peak, especially beautiful in sun-
    light
Angleworm Lake, MI: long, narrow, and crooked
Anvil Rock, WA, WV
Bell Rock, AZ
Belt Mountains, MT: beltlike white rock goes around a butte
Bird Rock, CA
Biscuit Mountain, AZ
Book Cliffs, UT: resembling a set of books on a shelf
Boot Pack, AZ: several Boot Lakes, and other bootlike shapes
Bosom, WY: two peaks
Bottle Pinnacle, WY
Box Butte, NE
Bread Loaf Mountain, VT
Breast Mountain, AK
The Brothers and the Sisters, CA: two rocks on each side of a
    channel
Buddha Temple, AZ: one of many "Temples," "Pyramids,"
    "Towers," etc., in the Grand Canyon
Camelback Mountain, AZ
Charlies Bunion, NC: a comparatively small hill or mountain.
    Also Ropers Bunion, OR
Chetlo, OR: Chinook for ⟨oyster⟩, from the shape of this lake
Chickenbone Lake, MI: wishbone shape
Chimney Rock, NE: one of many chimney-shaped formations
    in various states
Chinese Wall, WY: long, wall-like formation
Churn Creek, CA: long, churn-shaped pothole in a rock
Cockscomb Crest, Cockscomb Peak, CA: sawtooth ridge on top
Corkscrew Peak, CA: curving layers of rock
Courthouse Rock, NE: a landmark for covered-wagon travelers
Cowhorn Mountain, OR: two pinnacles
Cross Mountain, AZ
Demijohn Mountain, CO
Mount Derby, CO: hat shape
Dumpling, MA
Eagletail Mountains, AZ: oddly shaped, like tailfeathers
Einanuhto Hills, AK: an Aleut word for ⟨three breasts⟩
Elephants Playground, CA: large boulders lying in a meadow
Face Rock, OR

Valley of Fire, NV: bright red rocks

Fishtail Canyon, AZ: upper end veed like a fishtail

Fluted Rock, AZ: looks like organ pipes

Fryingpan Lake, OR

Gooseneck Harbor, AK

Haystack: used often for buttes, hills, and rocks

Heckletooth Mountain, OR: rocks at the top look like a heckle, used to comb flax

Hole-in-the-Wall Falls, MT

Hook Arm, AK: shaped like a hook or a bended arm

Hump Mountain, WV

Lake Italy, CA: boot shape

Kidney Lake, UT

The Knobs, IN, NY: small hills

Longboat Key, FL: long, narrow island

Lumpy Ridge, CO

The Maiden's Breast, AZ

Mesa, AZ, Mesa Peak, CA: Spanish for ⟨table⟩

Mitten Butte, AZ: a pair of mittenlike formations

Moose Lake, CA: shaped like the head of a moose

Music Mountain, AZ: rock strata look like a musical staff

Natural Bridge: the most famous one is in Virginia, but Natural Bridges and Natural Arches are numerous in the west

Night Cap, CA: a mountain

Nipple Mountain, CO: the father of one girl named a particular formation Clara Bird's Nipple

Owlhead, AZ; Owl's Head, ME; Owlshead Mountain, CA

Packsaddle, TX

The Palisades of the Hudson, NJ, NY; The Palisades, CA; Palisade Canyon, NV: palisades were originally pales (poles) used in fencelike fortifications

Peapod Rocks, WA

Petticoat Mountain, CA

Preacher's Head, NM: the head of a serious-looking man

Ribbon: used for several narrow waterfalls

Rockcastle, KY

Saddle Mountain: widely used in the West

Sail Rock, NM, WA

Saw Buck Mountain, AZ: shaped somewhat like the X of a sawhorse

Table: often used to indicate a flat top. See also Mesa

Tepee Mountain, MT, OK; Tepee Buttes, SD
Tit Butte: common in the West
Tooth Back Mountain, AZ
Turtle Lake, MI
Wetauwanchu Mountain, CT: Algonquian for ⟨wigwam⟩
Whaleback Mountain, CA; Whale Tail Lake, MN

HEAVEN AND HELL

Some half a hundred hills, streams, canyons, or other natural features in California are named Paradise. Near the town of that name in Butte County is a supposedly contrasting place named Hell Town. But maybe Paradise itself wasn't always so heavenly. An early spelling was Paradice, which *may* have meant ⟨pair of dice⟩ but was possibly only the result of limited literacy.

In South Dakota one early settler was named Adam and another, nearby, was Eve. There was no intermarrying between the two families, but even so, with such residents, the place had to be called Paradise.

Eight Paradises are listed by the U.S. Postal Service, as well as a Paradise Valley, NV, and a Paradis, LA. That Pelican State town, however, was named for a man rather than for the Garden of Eden.

Eden itself is an even more popular name than Paradise, with post offices in fourteen states, although at least the one in Texas, and possibly others, are named for a man; Fred Eden owned the first store in the Texas town. There's an Eden Mills in Vermont, and there are Edentons in Ohio and North Carolina, the latter named for a onetime royal governor.

Heaven fares badly in the United States, although there's a Heavener, OK, probably named for a person. A few Horse Heavens, the Turkey Heaven Mountains of Alabama, and a Hog Heaven Branch in Georgia are obviously only facetiously descriptive.

Hades has no post office, nor does Hell, although there's a Hell station in Michigan. (Hell does freeze over every winter, the natives say.) New York has a Hell Gate station, and Wyoming a Hells Half Acre. The name Hell Gate, from Dutch Helle-Gat, was objectionable to some nineteenth-century New Yorkers, who renamed it Hurlgate, but author Washington Irving raised so much uh—fuss that Hell Gate was revived. The Hell Gate railway bridge, from Long Island to the Bronx, was opened in 1917.

Hell has been in North America much longer than that. The Hell Creek formation is what geologists call a division of Upper Cretaceous rocks that date back over 100 million years. The formation got its name from Hell Creek, not far from Jordan, MT, where there is an outcropping, but it shows up also in Wyoming and North and South Dakota. Remains of the Tyrannosaurus and the Triceratops have been found in the Hell Creek formation, as well as some of the most ancient primate bones known to man.

There's a Devil's Lake, ND, a Devils Slide, UT, a Devils Tower, WY, and somehow the Devils Elbow got away from him in Missouri. Angels Camp, in California, does what it can to cope with those of the other persuasion, but obviously the largest collection of earthly angelic beings is in Los Angeles, over four hundred miles away.

19

NAMING
IN THE
WILDS

I THINK THE IZAAK WALTON LEAGUE
SHOULD OUTLAW NAMES
LIKE MATTAWAMKEAG

Although I've fished in sun and rain,
I've never gone to fish in Maine.
The water's fine, the fish will pounce,
But the names of their lakes I can't pronounce.

The simple ones like Allagash
And Umbagog I say with dash,
But I need to take a second look
At any word like Chiputneticook.

Another one that always stops us
Is Upper or Lower Sysladobsis.
The thought of a trout in the Magagnavic River
Creates in my heartbeat nary a quiver.

(Nor does Lake Pattagumpus raise much of a rumpus.)

Medunkeunk is sunk by Nesowadnehunk.
When I see Pennamaguan I keep right agoin'.
Even Walloquoik is too much like woik.
And I never give more than a crass empty look
At such a place as Chimquassabamticook.
But on the map of old Conn. I get really agog
At Chargoggagaugmanchaugagoggchaubunagungamaugg.

Since New England's place names get my goata,
I'll confine my fishing to Minnesota,
For how can I brag how I hooked 'em and fought 'em
If I can't say the name of the place where I caught 'em?

Actually, Minnesota may cause problems of a different sort. According to one count it has ninety-nine lakes named Long, ninety-one named Mud, and a dozen or a few dozen named Round, Rice, Sandy, or Gull.

Incidentally, people who live near Lake Chargogg...and the rest of those forty-four letters, have solved the problem of pronunciation, according to the late Odell Shepard. They call it Webster.

THE NAMELESS ONES

Pioneers here and there, either trying to be funny, or unable to agree on a name, or only unimaginative and honest, have called a number of places across the country Nameless.

William Trogdon, writing in the *Atlantic Monthly* under the name William Least Heat Moon (and there's a tale behind that, too), tells about his search for Nameless, TN, which when he found it turned out to be "a dozen houses along the road, a couple of barns, same number of churches...." He gets the story of the naming of Nameless from a couple of elderly residents who say that after going for years without a name, the community was told by the Post Office Department that it could have mail deliveries if it would just choose a name.

"The community met; there were only a handful, but they commenced debating. Some wanted patriotic names, some names from nature; one man recommended, in all seriousness, his own name. They couldn't agree, and they ran out of names to argue about. Finally, a fellow tired of the talk; he didn't like the mail he received anyway. 'Forget the durn post office,' he said. 'This here's a nameless place if I ever seen one, so leave it be.' And that's just what they did."

The woman told Trogdon, "You think Nameless is a funny name....Well, you take yourself up north a piece to Difficult or Defeated or Shake Rag. Now them are silly names."

At a South Dakota cave, people who visited were invited to write down their suggestions for a name. The final tally showed Nameless Cave as the first choice, and so it was called that.

A creek and an island in Alaska bear the name, but usually Nameless eventually gets a different name. No post office town is Nameless. George R. Stewart says that there was once a Nameless in Texas and that some North Dakota visitors liked the Nameless name so well that they used it back home—but both places, apparently, are now called something else or have reverted to the post officeless state of the community in Tennessee.

There's also a Nonames Hill, NY, but that's misleading, for the name is based on that of an Indian chief who probably pronounced it very differently and to whom it had a different meaning.

When the crew of a British ship, the *Herald*, was surveying the coast of northern Alaska, a draftsman wrote *?Name* opposite one cape. A second man thought that *Name* was the name and wrote it as Cape Name. His *a* was not clearly formed, however, and Name was read by others as Nome. And so Nome, AK, once nameless and then Name, became what it is called today.

LIFE IN DEATH VALLEY

A party of emigrants named it in 1849, when they suffered dehydration and even death in heat that has been known to reach 134° F (57° C) in the shade, and 190° F (88° C) where the sun mercilessly burns the already scorched earth.

Death Valley, CA, is now a national monument. It is close to the Amargosa ⟨bitter⟩ range of mountains, which include the Black and Funeral Mountains, named for their funereal black volcanic rocks. Volcanic ash covers much of the almost waterless

earth—in some years no measurable rainfall has been recorded
in the valley, and the average for a year is less than two inches.
Near Bad Water is the lowest point in the United States, 282
feet below the level of the sea. Modern travelers who disregard
thermometers may visit Furnace Creek Inn and Dantes View
and the Devils Golf Course.

The travelers seldom see any desert life except for noisy
ravens which may croak to them "Nevermore," or they may see
a lizard skittering toward a crevice. But the few residents and
the more numerous geologists, pathologists, botanists, zoolo-
gists, and other scientists whose professional zeal drives them
to such an apparently godforsaken place, tell us that living
things are in truth not rare. There is much life in Death Valley.

A survey in the 1890s reported seventy-eight species of
birds, and later ornithologists, counting passers-through or
passers-over as well as inhabitants, tripled that number. Tiny
pupfish (*Cyprinidon*) live in Salt Creek and elsewhere; some of
them belong to the species *diabolis* ⟨devil⟩, so named because
they thrive best in hot climates. Now and then a snake may be
seen searching for small prey or perhaps the egg of a bird.

Many of the animals avoid exertion in the searing daylight
hours, but after dark a few rabbits venture out, as do desert
wood rats or kangaroo rats with their long hind legs. Occasionally an antelope squirrel appears, a ground squirrel whose
tail is white underneath; when the tail is lifted the white rear
resembles the white rump of a retreating antelope.

And there are larger mammals, too: wild burros whose
ancestors strayed from the campsites of prospectors or miners;
cute little kit foxes; coyotes, which can survive almost anywhere;
bobcats, sometimes crying shrilly from a distant ledge. Bighorn
sheep from the nearby mountains infrequently descend into
the valley.

Some people have brought in tamarisks, whose roots drill
deep for the scanty moisture; the bushlike trees provide meager
shade and pink-blossomed beauty near a few springs. Saltgrass
and other salt-enduring plants grow in or near some of the hot,
brackish water. Desert holly lies low in the valley. Creosote
bushes, from which an acidulous gum resin called Sonora gum
may be obtained, grow in many gravel fans; in season they
produce bright little yellow flowers.

Spring rains, when they come, may make much of the

valley bloom—less luxuriantly, though, than in the desert scenes from nearby Arizona made familiar to Easterners in the vivid pictures in *Arizona Highways*, but enough blossoms to completely dispel the notion that Death Valley is really dead.

THE WORST PUN?

Paul Ryan, reviewing George R. Stewart's *American Place-Names* for *Life* in 1971, wrote:

> The namers of countless Bridal Veil Falls were poets more in the intention than in the act, and the man who called a body of water in Maine Coffee-Los Lake because of nearby Telos Lake (Tealess, get it?) was one of the most pathetic punsters on record. Place names have to be lived with for years or even centuries, and no contrived joke is welcome as a lifelong companion.

THE LONGEST
AND SHORTEST U.S. PLACE NAMES

In Wales a few place names may total thirty or forty or more letters. In the late 1950s a twenty-foot sign bearing the name of a railroad station was stolen. The reason for such a large sign? The name on it was:

Llanfairpwllgwyngyllgogerychwyrndrobwllllandyssilogagoch
(fifty-six letters)

Americans seem to be shorter of breath than the Welsh. George R. Stewart says that probably the longest word among our place names is the name of some dunes in Alaska—a word of uncertain meaning that was taken over from the Eskimo. It is:

Nunathloogagamiutbingoi
(twenty-three letters)

Stewart says nothing about the name of a New England lake reported several decades ago by Odell Shepard and included in this book in the verse on page 211. The name is so ungainly that almost certainly no one now uses it. It is:

Chargoggagaugmanchaugagoggchaubunagungamaugg
(forty-four letters)

Candidates for the shortest place name include L, a lake in Nebraska, and T, a gulch in Colorado, each named for its shape.

NO SUBMACHINE GUNS?

Many creeks are near Little Soldier Mountain, ID. They include Pistol, Automatic, Winchester, Colt, Luger, Thirty-eight, Forty-five, and—of small value to the soldier—Popgun.

PANCAKES HARD AS ROCKS

Villages called Pancake, in Pennsylvania and Texas, are named for George Pancake and J. R. Pancake, early settlers.

But Pancake Rock, AK, is shaped like a stack of pancakes, and George R. Stewart says that the name Pancake Summit, NV, "is probably of similar origin."

WHEN THE NAMES
WELL RAN DRY

In 1927 two geologists, responsible for naming some of the numerous small streams in Alaska, found themselves without inspiration. Their well of names had run dry, yet there was still another river to name. So that's what they called it: Another River.

20

IMPROPER (?) NAMES

"NOT ALL NAMES ARE CONSIDERED TO BE PROPER"

"While names are classified as proper nouns, not all names are considered to be proper." So said Lester F. Dingman, Executive Secretary, Domestic Geographic Names, U.S. Board of Geographic Names.

One of the responsibilities of the Board (not the only one) is to determine which names are "proper" enough to be considered official and to appear in print on maps. For example, although Whorehouse wasn't taboo as part of the title of a long-running Broadway play (the Board has no jurisdiction over such things), it was disallowed in the geographic name Whorehouse Meadow, AZ, which on maps appears with the approved name Naughty Girl Meadow.

Just how such decisions are arrived at is not entirely clear. The same Board approved Cat House Creek, MT, and Pleasure House Creek, VA. Maybe the rules for creeks are different than for meadows.

Compromises, the Board has found, are often necessary. For S.O.B. Rapids, UT, it disallowed both the complete expression and the version with periods, changing he-man profanity to the tearful Sob Rapids.

Sometimes a name is originated with no salacious intent at all, the pure-minded namer being unaware of or at least not recalling a second meaning that will offend some people. For example, a mountain in Virginia with a treeless summit was called, in all innocence, Nakedtop; a locally well-known Oregonian named Peter was bald, but the Board obviously couldn't accept Bald Peter as an official name; Wee Wee Hill, IN, makes the prurient think of something other than small size; and The Broads of New Hampshire, named for The Broads of England (a low-lying, marshy area) might sound to some folks like the title of a ribald musical comedy. Rocky John Canyon was changed to Rocky Canyon after the Board found that John in the name didn't refer to a person.

One type of name that the Board consistently frowns on is that which suggests an ethnic or racial slur. So Chink Gulch became Chinese Gulch, and other place names containing words like Jap, Gook, Dago, Nigger, and even Yankee are banned, although somehow the post office address Yankeetown, FL, did get approved.

ONE RUN, ONE MISS, ONE ERROR

In Virginia, at a place where staves for whiskey barrels were once made, a stream was called Whiskey Barrel Run. It was changed to Stave Run by the U.S. Board on Geographic Names, but somebody misread or miswrote one letter. It began appearing on maps as Stare Run.

THE FRENCH BROAD

Crossing the French Broad River in North Carolina, sexist male travelers are likely to attempt a witticism: "French Broad? Let's stop and visit her," or "Is it true what they say about French broads?"

The stream flows westward 205 miles from the Blue Ridge Mountains, joining the Holston near Knoxville, TN, to form the Tennessee River. It was originally called the Broad River, but since North Carolina already had another stream with that name, the word *French* was added to differentiate the two. At the time, a number of French settlers lived in the western part of the area through which the river flows.

A LETTER TO THE GOVERNOR
ABOUT MISS NELLIE'S ANATOMY

When Ronald Reagan was the governor of California, he received the following letter from a woman in Omaha:

> Your Excellency:
> I was looking at the map of California, looking for "Bellflower" where an old school mate of mine lives. I never did find Bellflower, but saw a mountain that I do not like, and wondered if you could change the name? It's called "Nellie's Nipple." Since I have an Aunt Nellie, I don't think this is very nice, or fit for children to study about except in Medical School! I hope to visit your beautiful State some day, if I'm lucky. But in the meantime will you please change the mountain's name at once; it seems rather scandalous.

INDELICATE NAMES?

Most of the town names mentioned here are derived from people's names, and all had perfectly innocent beginnings. But the ignorant, the crude, or the prurient have found double entendres in each.

For example, after the word *gay* came to refer to homosexuality, some people made remarks that they considered funny about Gay, GA, MI, WV; Gays, IL; Gay Hill, TX; Gays Creek, KY; Gays Mills, WI; Gayville, SD; and Gaysville, VT. Each of these towns actually bears the name of a person or persons. Gay Hill, for example, is called that because of two pioneer settlers, G. H. Gay and W. C. Hill.

Equally innocuous explanations can be found (by the pure in heart and the clean in hand and mouth) for these:

Bloomer, WI
Bullsgap, TN
Cherry Grove, NY, WV;
　Cherry Hill, AR; Cherry
　Valley, AR, IL, NY;
　Cherryville, MO, NC, PA
Doctors Inlet, FL
Eros, LA
French Lick, IN
Hooker, KY, OK;
　Hookerton, NC
Idamay, WV

Letcher, KY, SD
Lolita, TX
Lovejoy, GA, IL
Lovelady, TX
Maiden, NC; Maidens, VA;
　Maidsville, WV
Mangohick, VA ("Man
　drink too much, man go
　hick.")
Ova, KY
Pansey, AL

FROM HEAD TO FOOT

Let's check on anatomy as revealed in U.S. town names.

There's Indian Head, MD, as well as Headland, AL, Bull-head, SD, Horseheads, NY, and Head of Grassy, KY (where, however, it means ⟨source of a stream⟩). Louisiana's Grosse Tete means ⟨large head⟩. Arkansas gives us Birdeye. There are no Ears except two little Earlings (IA and WV).

The various heads are supported by Indian Neck, VA, Dutch Neck, NJ, Colts Neck, NJ, and Great Neck, NY, besides an entire Neck City, MO.

There's a Chest Springs, PA, but obviously one finds only a spelling coincidence in the various Chesters, Chesterfields, Chestnuts, and similar names. The word *breast* is apparently taboo in town names, although it or less delicate equivalents may be found in mountainous regions as names of mountains or hills.

Several hearts exist, as in Crowheart, WV, Heart Butte, MT, and Heartwell, NE. A heart is disguised in the spelling of Elkhart, IN, said to have been named for a heart-shaped island in the nearby river.

We have Big Arm, MT, Devil's Elbow, MO, and Elbow Lake, MN. Handshoe, KY, reminds us of the German word for glove, *handschuh*. There's only a Left Hand in West Virginia. Tennessee has a single Finger, which is apparently outnumbered in South Carolina's Fingerville.

Kiester, MN, nothing to do with *keister*, a slang term for ⟨buttocks⟩.

Kneeland is in California, but Footville is in Wisconsin. Between them (anatomically but not geographically) are Shinrock, OH, and a fascinatingly named place, Shinhopple, NY. ("Probably Algonquian, meaning uncertain," says Stewart's *American Place-Names*.) Kentucky appears to suffer from a Cutshin.

The anatomy of our four-legged friends is recalled specifically in Paw Creek, NC.

Muscle Shoals, AL, gives strength to the whole body, and the osteal system is suggested by Bonecave, TN, Boneville, GA, and Bonetraill, ND, although there is a Bone Gap in Illinois. No post office town is named Skeleton, but the West commemorates in other names some locations where human skeletons were found: Skeleton Canyon, AZ, Skeleton Creek, OK, Skeleton Gulch, CO, Skeleton Ridge, AZ, and Skeleton Springs, SD.

Blood is likewise avoided in town names. Stewart, however, mentions a Blood Gulch, CA, in which early gold miners saw blood flowing and traced it upstream to the corpse of a murdered man. And between Blood Mountain and Slaughter Mountain in Georgia, which commemorate an Indian battle, we find Blood and Slaughter Gap.

SMALL TOWN NAMES
IN HEADLINES

Some of the following headlines are genuine, others contrived. Each contains two or more actual names of small towns.

Sports headlines
(AL)   Chestnut Upsets Canoe
(AZ)   Bumble Bee Overcomes Mammoth
(AR)   Bigflat Travels to Pea Ridge
(CA)   Crows Landing at Blue Lake Tonight; Feather Falls Falls

(NY)   Big Indian Succumbs to Stella Niagra
(IA)   Imogene Draws Stanley; Amelia Gets Tingley; Nora
       Springs Meets Waterloo; Rose Hill Travels to Loveland

Society news
(IL)   Oblong Man Marries Normal Girl
(IA)   Fertile Girl Weds Manly Man
(PA)   Visitors Enjoy Intercourse; Paradise Next Stop

21

ON THE
BIG APPLE
AND
SMALLER APPLES

HOW "THE BIG APPLE"
GOT THAT NAME

Some people say that baseball players, who are great coiners of nicknames and slang, are responsible for the nickname "The Big Apple." But it appears more likely that jazz musicians deserve the credit.

Musicians of the 1930s, playing one-night stands, coined their own terms not only for their music and its components but also for their travels, the people they met, the towns they stayed in. A town or city was an "apple."

At that time a man named Charles Gillett was president of the New York City Convention and Visitors Bureau. Learning of the jazz term, he bragged, "There are lots of 'apples' in the U.S.A., but we're the best and the biggest. We're The Big Apple."

The name did not catch on widely for some time, but in

the 1970s, perhaps earlier, it became used as a tourist-attracting slogan, referring not only to New York's musical attractions but also its plays, ballets, athletic events, and convention facilities.

OF COURSE THERE'S ONLY ONE NEW YORK

"What town and city name do you think is most frequently used in the United States?"

Pause. "I don't know. Is it Washington?"

"Good guess. Washington is tied for second. It's used in twenty-six of the states."

"Springfield?"

"No, but it's near the top."

"I give up."

"Try another president."

"Lincoln?"

"No. Only sixteen Lincolns. The winner is Madison."

Here are the winning numbers, along with the usual source(s) of each name.

Madison (27)-President
Clinton (26)-Personal name
Washington (26)-President
Franklin (25)-Statesman
Greenville (24)-Personal name; description
Marion (24)-Revolutionary War General, nicknamed "the Swamp Fox"
Salem (24)-Biblical place
Manchester (23)-English city; personal name
Monroe (22)-President
Springfield (22)-Description
Troy (22)-Literature; history

Ashland (21)-Tree; home of Henry Clay
Milford (21)-English town; ford near a mill
Clayton (20)-Description; personal name
Fairfield (20)-Description
Jackson (20)-President
Jamestown (20)-English king; personal name
Jefferson (20)-President
Newport (20)-Description
Oxford (20)-English city or shire
Cleveland (19)-President; other personal name

Lebanon (19)-Biblical place
Plymouth (19)-English city
Canton (18)-Chinese city;
   French or Swiss district
Dover (18)-English cliffs
   and port; a religious
   report of 1832
Farmington (18)-Description

Glenwood (18)-Description
Hillsboro (18)-Description;
   personal name
Milton (18)-English place;
   poet; other personal
   name
Windsor (18)-English place;
   English nobleman

Most large American cities have to share their names with much smaller places. The list above shows that Washington, DC has twenty-five name-alikes. Here are the numbers of name-alikes for some other cities:

Cleveland, OH-18
Dayton, OH-17
Buffalo, NY-16
Columbus, OH-16
Oakland, CA-16
Rochester, NY-13
Portland, OR-12
Atlanta, GA-11
Denver, CO-10
Newark, NJ-9

Louisville, KY-9
Boston, MA-8
Dallas, TX-8
Houston, TX-8
Akron, OH-7
Miami, FL-7
St. Paul, MN-7
Memphis, TN-6
Omaha, NE-6

There's only one New York, of course. Also standing in lonely grandeur are Chicago, San Francisco, New Orleans, Pittsburgh (with an *h*), Seattle, Cincinnati, Indianapolis, Fort Worth, Oklahoma City, Honolulu, Jersey City, and Tulsa.

For what it's worth,

Oxford beats Cambridge, 20 to 12.

Columbia wins the Ivy League, 17 to Princeton's 16. Also ran:

Yale 6, Cornell 5, Harvard 4, Brown 1, Dartmouth 1, Pennsylvania 0 (although Pennsylvania Furnace scores 1).

Athens defeats Rome, 15 to 7, but loses to Troy, 22 to 15. Sparta scores 11, Carthage *delenda est* with 10.

Antelope play in five states, but Deer only in Arkansas.

The only Arctic village, not unexpectedly, is in Alaska.

THE BRITISH DON'T PRONOUNCE
GOTHAM CORRECTLY

Gotham, a village in Nottinghamshire, is pronounced GOT-um. In medieval times, to keep King John from taking up residence there, the inhabitants are said to have pretended to be stupid. For instance, they tried to drown eels.

In the United States, Gotham is a nickname for New York City that Washington Irving and some of his contemporaries made famous. On this side of the water it is pronounced GŎTH-um, and the residents do not need to pretend to be stupid.

British place-name pronunciation often differs from American by being more economical. Similarly, the British chop sounds or syllables out of some words, such as *secretary*, which they call SEK-ruh-tree. It's well-known that in England, Gloucester sounds like GLOS-ter, Leicester like LES-ter, Worcester like WOOS-ter, Greenwich like GREN-ij, Thames like TEMZ, Derby like DAR-be, and Cholmondeley like CHUM-lee.

Here are some other place names and a few personal names that many British people pronounce in ways that seem odd to Americans, although some modern Britishers come closer to the sounds suggested by the spellings.

Spelling	Pronunciation
Ayscough	ASK-you or ASK-o
Banbury	BAN-bree
Berkeley	BARK-lee
Berkshire	BARK-sher
Bicester	BIS-ter
Boleyn	BULL-un
Bottomley	BUM-lee
Burghley	BUR-lee
Cirencester	SIS-uh-ter
Claverhouse	CLAV-ers
Colquhoun	CO-hoon
Daventry	DAIN-tree
Falconer	FAWK-ner
Hawarden	HAR-dun
Heathcote	HETH-kut
Kirkcudbright	ker-KOO-bree

Leominster	LEM-ster
Mainwaring	MAN-uh-ring
Marjoribanks	MARSH-banks
Marlborough	MAWL-bruh
Ponsonby	PUN-sun-bee
Pontefract	PUM-fret
Pulteney	POLT-nee
Raleigh	RAW-lee or RAL-lee
Scone	SKOON
Seymour	SEE-mer
Shrewsbury	SHROZ-bree
Slaithwaite	SLO-it
Sotheby	SUTH-uh-bee
Stanhope	STAN-up
St. Clair	SIN-clair
St. John	SIN-jun
Strachan	STRAWN
Teignmouth	TIN-muth
Trotterscliff	TROS-lee
Warwick	WOR-ik
Whitefield	WHIT-field
Wriothesley	ROTS-lee, ROX-lee, or RIS-lee

THE NOWHERE CITIES

In an editorial the *New York Times* objected to an ad prepared for the Diors, designers and makers of French clothing. The ad asked, "What would New York be without the Diors?" It answered its own question: "Newark."

Other cities besides Newark have been the target of jokesters who like to ridicule what they consider an out-of-it, nowhere place. One old joke says that the first prize in a contest is "A week in Philadelphia." Second prize: "Two weeks in Philadelphia."

The president of the AFL-CIO, Lane Kirkland, made the mayor of Hoboken unhappy when he said, "Everything outside the AFL-CIO is Hoboken."

Decades ago Gertrude Stein expressed her opinion of Oakland: "When you get there, there isn't any there there."

"The little old lady from Dubuque" has become a stock phrase to caricature not only naive and prissy or puritanical old ladies, but also Dubuque and other communities like it as supposedly being out of date, not with it.

The *Times* answered the jokesters in this way:

> What all the jokes overlook...is that most of the cities on the list have in recent years proven through redevelopment of business and neighborhoods that they no longer deserve to be ridiculed [if they ever did]. That's what Newark is doing, and it doesn't need any help from the Diors.

YOU KNOW NAMES
FROM MAXWELL STREET

It smells. Since the early 1800s it has smelled. It has smelled of sweat and urine, herring and lox, hot dogs and Polish sausage, cheap cigars, spoiled vegetables and too-ripe fruit, carelessly washed used clothing. Maxwell Street, just southwest of Chicago's Loop, was once a mile long but was cut to half that in a spasm of change a couple of decades ago.

In its more than 150 years it has known thousands of small shops, many of them short lived, and more thousands of pushcarts. It escaped—was barely south of—the 1871 fire that consumed most of Chicago; many homeless victims found cheap lodging near or along Maxwell Street.

Ira Berkow in *Maxwell Street* (Doubleday, 1977), a book on which this account has relied extensively, has written:

> Irish and German immigrants who fled famine and depression in Europe were the earliest inhabitants of the area. With the Jewish influx [which occurred especially as a result of the Russian pogroms] the Germans and Irish moved out, just as several decades later the Jews would move when blacks and Mexicans moved in. Gypsies have long lived there. Italians and Poles and Lithuanians and Greeks and Scandinavians lived on the outskirts.

Berkow quotes Carl Sandburg, who wrote in *Chicago Poems* (1916):

> I know a Jew fish crier down on Maxwell Street...
> He dangles herring before prospective customers evincing a joy identical with that of Pavlova dancing.
> His face is that of a man terribly glad to be selling fish, terribly glad that God made fish, and customers to whom he may call his wares from a pushcart.

The street smelled. But many of its people worked or fought or bargained or studied and thought, and worked more and left Maxwell Street and its smells, its noise.

It is possible that no other mile-long street in America has produced a greater number of famous names. Boss of the leading television network. Champion boxers. Show biz folk. Gangsters. An internationally known ambassador.

You never heard of Muni Weisenfreund? Not surprising. His parents owned a little theater at Twelfth and Waller, just off Maxwell, and from the silent flickerings on the screen he learned to act. You know him from reruns on TV as Paul Muni, who starred in *The Good Earth, Louis Pasteur, The Last Angry Man*; if you're old enough and lucky, you saw him on Broadway in *Inherit the Wind*.

Al Capone's business manager, Jake "Greasy Thumb" Guzik, was prosperous enough to be convicted of evading $800,000 in income taxes. Small potatoes for a man the government said earned $970,302 in one year. Bootlegger, panderer, and inventor of the "Crime Syndicate," it was widely said. He claimed, "I never carried a gun in my life." But he knew how to keep the boss's books very well. And a Treasury Department official asserted that Guzik might have had as much as $150 million stashed away, back in the days when a million was worth several hundred thousand. His brother Harry owned brothels and unintentionally, said his friends and enemies, was instrumental in passage of the Mann Act.

William S. Paley, chairman of the Board of CBS, is the son of Samuel Paley who wrapped cigars in a storefront factory on Maxwell Street and eventually had fifty workers under him.

His brand was La Palina. Bill made use of his father's money and business instincts and attended the Wharton School of Finance. On the side, he was admired as a great ladies' man. He became president of CBS before he was twenty-seven.

John L. "Jack" Keeshin owned a horse and wagon, used for deliveries in the Maxwell Street area. Then another horse and wagon, a truck, more trucks. Later, *Fortune* magazine said, "Besides muscle and guts he has brains and persistence and ambition and prodigious energy. [That could be a theme song for Maxwell Street.] For these reasons he also has money, and he flaunts the title of Keeshin Transcontinental Freight Lines."

Barney Ross started out as Barnet David Rasofsky. Not a good name for a boxer. After boyhood fights in the streets, he used to be beaten by his father with a cat-o'-nine-tails. Al Capone told him, "You couldn't be a hood if you wanted to." So Barney continued fighting and went on to championships in three weight classes.

Jackie Fields, born Jacob Finkelstein on Maxwell Street, was a pretty good boxer, too. Undisputed welterweight champion. So was Maxwell Street's King Levinsky—pretty good. But he made the mistake of living at the time when Joe Louis was the undefeated heavyweight. Joe, from Detroit, knocked out the Chicagoan. But he was knocking everybody out.

Benny Goodman's father was a Maxwell Street tailor. In a synagogue Benny and two of his brothers were lent musical instruments and given lessons, and a little later they played in a band at Hull House. At age twenty-nine he played his clarinet in Carnegie Hall in its first-ever swing-jazz concert; among his orchestra members were Gene Krupa, Lionel Hampton, Harry James, and Count Basie.

Barney Balaban started by buying a nickelodeon (a tiny theater) for $750, raised by scraping together all the money his family and friends had. He went on to be co-owner of the huge Balaban and Katz theater chain, and president of Paramount Pictures. His father had run a small grocery-delicatessen close to Maxwell Street, and the big family had lived in four rooms behind it.

U.S.A.F. Major Sidney Barnett was the first American to bomb Berlin in World War II. He said about his boyhood on Maxwell Street, "I learned [to fight] the American way. Hit 'em first, knock 'em down, and make 'em know who's boss."

Born on Sangamon Street, just off Maxwell, Meyer Levin would become the author of *The Old Bunch,* a novel about Chicago's West Side. Better known: his dramatization of *The Diary of Anne Frank,* and his psychological book called *Compulsion* that was made into a hit Broadway play.

Natal name: Jacob Rubinstein. Birthplace: Fourteenth and Newberry, just south of Maxwell Street. Better known as Jack Ruby. You would never have heard the name if he hadn't killed Lee Harvey Oswald, the assassin of John F. Kennedy. At age eleven he had been referred to the Chicago Institute for Juvenile Research because of "truancy and incorrigibility at home."

Joseph Weil, in the archives of crime, is better known as Yellow Kid Weil, who learned on Maxwell Street how to be a confidence man, separating fools and sometimes wise men from their money. His total take has been estimated as eight to ten million dollars. He died, a pauper, at age one hundred.

Arthur Goldberg was born in the 1300 block of Washburne, about a block from Maxwell. "He recalls," Ira Berkow tells us, "the continuous street fights between Jews and the neighboring Irish. 'I used to fetch bricks for my brothers to throw.'" He graduated high in his class at Northwestern Law School. At age fifty-four he was named by President Kennedy to the United States Supreme Court. Three years later he became U.S. Ambassador to the United Nations. Not surprising, considering all the things that can happen to a bright boy from Maxwell Street.

THE INDIANAPOLITANS CARE
WHAT THEY CALL THEIR DOME

"I seriously hope the Council that decided 'Hoosier Dome' best suits Indianapolis' newest city-expansion project will reconsider.... If this was Missouri, would we call it the 'Show Me Dome'? If we were in Idaho, would it be called the 'Spud Dome'?"

That was typical of hundreds of letters received by the *Indianapolis Star* in 1982, when ground was being broken for a new sports or all-purpose structure. Samples from others:

"I submit a proposal that the d____d thing be

christened 'The Dumb Dome' in honor of [Mayor] Hudnut and his fellow pushers and shakers who are so self-satisfied and insensitive to the wishes of those who will eventually be called upon to bail out their big $ projects."

"If we have to have a rustic connotation, why not 'Hayseed Dome,' or 'Hick Dome,' or 'Strawstack Dome' or how about 'Country Syndrome' or 'Barn-drome' or 'Peasantdrome' or just plain 'Barn'—huh, fellers?"

"Apple is our middle name. Move over, New York. Make way for the big crabapple, or is it little crabapple? How about 'Appledome'?"

Incidentally, about fifteen hundred contestants submitted the name "Hoosier Dome" to the citizens committee that made the choice, and dozens of other names drew less support. A drawing had to be held to determine which of the fifteen hundred was the winner.

FROM SKUNK'S MISERY
ONWARD AND UPWARD

Scranton, PA has worked its way up. It started out as Skunk's Misery (perhaps the most unappealing name ever coined). That was followed by an unimaginative Harrison, a lazy-sounding Slocum Hollow, and a patriotic Unionville. Then to honor a prominent local family, it became Scrantonia and finally Scranton. Eventually one of the eponymous Scrantons (William) became governor of the state and a candidate for the United States presidency.

WHAT DO YOU CALL SOMEBODY
WHO LIVES IN MOSCOW?

That depends. Residents of the Russian Moscow (which they call Moskva) are Muscovites. But people in Moscow, ID aren't sure whether they are Moscovites, Moscovians, or Moscowites, with the majority apparently favoring the third choice.

There is disagreement about the most appropriate designation for many other Americans, too: Floridan, Alabaman, Arizonan, Indianan, and Oklahoman; or Floridian, Alabamian, Arizonian, Indianian, and Oklahomian? The *i* seems preferred in the first four, but Oklahoman is the winner in that state.

Is it Atlantan or Atlantian? The former, probably. Does one say, for New Orleans, an OrleANian or an OrLEENian? People who live in the Crescent City generally say the latter.

What does one call a person from Little Rock or Big Rock? Little Rocker and Big Rocker seem ambiguous. And are any names really suitable for residents of Elk River, Grand Junction, LaCrosse, Bumpus Mills? Most people from the hundreds of *-villes* want to avoid sounding like *-villains*. A person from Yellow Bluff, AL, might not like the designation Yellow Bluffer. The name Welcomer, for someone who lives in Welcome, LA, MD, MN, or NC, may appear too effusive to anyone who dislikes or distrusts strangers.

Years ago, in *American Speech*, George R. Stewart suggested these principles to designate residents:

1.   For places ending in *-a*, add *n*: Oklahoman, Tacoman, Arkadelphian

2.   For the ending *-on*, add *ian*: Washingtonian, Bostonian

3.   For the ending *-i*, *-o*, *a* pronounced *-e*, or *-ie*, or *-ee*, add *an*: Miamian, Chicagoan, Albuquerquean, Poughkeepsian, Tuskegean

4.   For the ending *-y*, change to *i* and add *an*: Sanduskian

5.   For the ending *-olis*, change to *olitan*: Minneapolitan

6.   For a consonant ending or a silent *-e*, add *ite* or *er*, whichever sounds better: New Yorker, Brooklynite, Detroiter, Harlemite, Orangeite

Stewart's principles, although widely followed, are not accepted everywhere. So we have, in violation of the principles, Akronites, San Franciscans and San Diegans and Sacramentans, Angelenos, Cantabrigians (from Cambridge, MA), and Trojans (from any of the Troys). In Taos, NM linguistically meticulous men call themselves Taoseños, and the women are Taoseñas.

Sometimes, of course, nicknames are applied, whether affectionately or derisively: Hoosiers (from Indiana), Jayhawks (Kansas), Cornhuskers (Nebraska), Tarheels (North Carolina), Crackers (Georgia), and Blue Hen Chickens (Delaware), but heard less now than a century or so ago are intentionally insulting names such as Maniacs (Maine), Bugeaters (Missouri), Leatherheads (Pennsylvania), and Crawthumpers (Maryland).

WHY KANSAS CITY ISN'T CALLED FONDA

If Abraham Fonda hadn't insisted that he was a gentleman, one of the nation's large cities might have been named for him.

In the frontier days of Missouri a man was expected to be a "real man"—loud-swearing, hard-drinking, gun-toting, unafraid to soil his hands. But Abraham Fonda wore fancy clothes and soft leather gloves, preferred wine to whiskey, had a jeweled stickpin, and when he wrote a letter he signed it "Abraham Fonda, Gentleman." He was one of the few self-styled gentlemen in the young state in the late 1830s.

Fonda had some money, and he and ten or twelve others pooled their funds to buy a ferryboat landing and a couple of hundred acres on the banks of the Missouri River. It was not far from the mouth of the Kaw and also near a trading post for western overland expeditions, set up earlier by a French fur trader, François Chouteau. The buyers got together after their purchase to discuss the name of the settlement, then only a few log cabins. They intended to promote it as a river port and as a gateway to the West.

One of Fonda's few friends suggested Port Fonda, arguing that Fonda had put up a considerable share of the money. But another partner, Henry Jobe, wasn't having any of that. Inspired by the whiskey passed around, he ranted and swore and patted his gun to signify what might happen to anyone who supported the soft-spoken Fonda.

The partners turned to other possibilities, leaving Fonda looking uncomfortable but probably relieved. They discussed Kawsmouth because of the proximity of that stream, and one orated facetiously on the merits of Possum-trot. A few Kansas Indians still lived in the area and across the river, and Indian names were being selected here and there for other towns. "Why not call the place Kansas instead of the less pleasant-sounding Kawsmouth?" someone asked. (At the time there was not even a Kansas Territory, and the state by that name would not be admitted to the Union until 1861.) So the Town of Kansas was what the settlement became in 1839, the City of Kansas in 1853, and Kansas City in 1889.

By the way, Kansas and Kaw are alternative names for the Indian tribe, so if Kawsmouth had been selected, it might conceivably later have become Kansasmouth. Maybe the verdict of history was best.

NICKNAMES
OF PLACES

Most places, especially if they have long names, are familiarly or facetiously called by shorter ones: Frisco for San Francisco, LA for Los Angeles, P-town for Provincetown, MA, Hamp for Northampton, MA, Burgy for places ending in -burg (especially Williamsburg, VA), Philly for Philadelphia, Indy for Indianapolis, the Hut for Terre Haute.

Sometimes publicists use nicknames longer than the name of the place itself. New York's relatively few years of use of The Big Apple has reportedly brought in billions of tourist dollars. Less inspired and less profitable are The Windy City for Chicago, and The Hub City for Boston. (Reportedly so called because some of its leading residents once considered Boston the hub of the universe; perhaps a few still do, such as the wealthy dowager who refused to travel, saying, "Why should I? I'm already here.") Incidentally, there has been at least one other Hub City: Stoughton, WI, because wagons and hubs for wagon wheels were once made there; it was also called Wagon City, but perhaps both terms became less frequent when it switched to making auto bodies.

Two-word names such as Cedar Grove, Green Bay, Wichita Falls, Cedar Swamp, Great Neck, Grand Rapids, and Walnut Point are likely to be known in the surrounding area as "the Grove," "the Neck," etc.: "I'm going down to the Point tomorrow."

Also usually restricted to local and occasional use are names related to local industries. For instance, the communities of Mount Clare and nearby Wilsonville, IL, were long called Number Three (or just Three) and Number Four (or Four) because coal mines with those numbers were the chief employers in the area.

Nicknames that are critical or opprobrious are likely to be mainly local, too:

Lake Quana-polluted (Lake Quanapowitt, MA)
Louseville (Louisville)
Merrimuck (Merrimack River)
Northwest Distressway (Expressway)
Sandy Kitty (Kansas City)
Sin Valley (Sun Valley, CA, ID)
Slumberland (Cumberland, MD)
Taxachusetts (Massachusetts)

The bigoted apply nicknames to places largely inhabited by any ethnic group other than their own, although that practice appears to be diminishing as general educational levels rise. There may still be occasional local references, however, to Swedetown, Little Italy, Frenchman's Flats, Hunkytown, Niggertown, Greaser Gulch, the P.V. (Polish Village), Dago Creek, and others for almost any place where "they" live and "we" don't.

DON'T TELL HIS WIFE

William Safire recalled an old bilingual place-name pun in this way:

A peccadillo is a minor fault or petty sin, from the Latin *peccare*, to sin. Its use recalls one of the great diplomatic code messages based on a pun, from Sir Charles Napier, who had been sent to gain control of the Indian province of Sind in the 1840s. After the battle of Hyderabad, the British general sent back his report in a single word: *Peccavi*. At the Foreign Office, his Latin-speaking colleagues immediately knew its import: "I have Sind."

22

THIS IS A LOVELY LITTLE TOWN, WASN'T IT?

RISING CITY RISING FAST

Several U.S. places are Rising. Montana's Rising Wolf Mountain is named not for a lupine revolution but for a Blackfoot Indian chief. California's Rising River makes a sudden appearance from a large spring.

A few miles from Champaign, Illinois, is a sign that says Rising Road. Actually the road lies perfectly still. Its name is that of an early settler.

Indiana and Maryland each have a Rising Sun, and Ohio has a Risingsun, all so named because of a clear view to the east. For the Indiana town, which is a county seat overlooking the Ohio River, the formal explanation is this: "The name was suggested by the grandeur of the sunrise over the Kentucky hills above the town of Rabbit Hash, across the river."

A Texas community wanted to be a Rising Sun also, but

for some reason the request was denied, so the residents now live in Rising Star.

About seventy miles west of Omaha is a community named Rising City. From 1970 to 1980 Omaha, like many other U.S. cities, declined in population, dropping almost 36,000 during the decade. Meanwhile, Rising City was living up to its name, as these population figures show:

	1960	*1970*	*1980*
Rising City	308	344	392
Omaha	301,598	347,328	311,681

In the unlikely event that both Omaha and Rising City populations continue to fall and rise at the same numerical rates as in the decade of the 70s, in less than ninety years Rising City will have more people.

HOW REMOTE IS REMOTE?

Is Remote, in southwestern Oregon, well named? Some would say so. It nestles in the Coast Range of mountains some thirty miles from the Pacific Ocean.

But in 1887, when Remote was named, neighbors weren't crowded in on all sides as they are now. Today the Remote postman serves sixteen families, and some of them wish they had as much elbowroom as their great-grandparents did.

You see, there's a place called Bridge only seven miles away. Not a big place. Not big enough to have a post office, but anyhow that's pretty close, almost within spittin' distance. Broadbent and Myrtle Point are each about eighteen miles, and Norway is twenty-one, but Sitkum is just over a few mountains some ten miles for anybody with a helicopter, and only a little farther than that are Lookingglass and Riddle.

Some residents think that Remote should change its name.

LOCAL LEGENDS
ABOUT TOWN NAMES

When the history of a place is unknown or at least forgotten by most of the present residents, someone is likely to make up a story to account for it. Although sometimes the stories are possible, other origins are more probable.

For instance, Galveston, Indiana, was probably named for the place in Texas. But local legend has it that its founder looked out the window and saw "a gal with a vest on" and that she inspired the name. (Sexist males loafing on Galveston's busiest corner used to make ribald remarks about Galvestoff.)

A similar story is told about Roann, Indiana. A father saw his daughter in a boat in a dangerous current and kept shouting at her, "Row, Ann! Row, Ann."

Slightly more amusing is the story of an earlier name of Lorane, another Indiana village. First called Steam Corners for the steam-operated sawmills there, it was later named Buzzards Glory. The local legend says that a traveler crossed a little stream late one day, saw some beautiful scenery, and was then invited to spend the night with a family named Lord. "The next morning," the legend continues, "he said he crossed the river Jordan, went through Glory, and stayed all night with the Lord, and from that time on the little place was called Glory. Someone added the name Buzzard. Why, no one knows." Maybe the stranger's name was Buzzard.

No legend about the name Lorane, though. It appears to be only a simplified spelling of Lorraine, a French province.

SOME OF THE BEST POSTMARKS

Best rhyme: Solo, MO

Most affirmative: Okay, OK

Best refrain for a song: Walla Walla, WA

THE TOWN WHOSE MAYOR CAN'T PRONOUNCE ITS NAME

Imagine a town with only eleven people but about 40,000 visitors each summer. Its annual budget is $350. It has no crime at all, but it has a police chief nevertheless. The town council consists of a woman and her two sons. It has a Slovenian name but a mayor of Italian descent. All town officials are unpaid.

The mayor, since he is not Slovenian, cannot pronounce the town's name, which is Slovenska Narodna Podporna Jednota. One of the ways in which that name appears unique is that its origin may be different from any other—no person's name, no description, none of the usual sources. The name means Slovene National Benefit Society.

Here's how it happened. The Benefit Society, which is a fraternal organization that provides insurance and other services for its members, wanted to open a recreation area to which members might come for overnight stays or short vacations. In 1963 it located a 500-acre tract in Lawrence County in western Pennsylvania that included a small lake and seemed ideal. One drawback: North Beaver Township, where the land lies, allowed no liquor, and some Slovenians (originally a Yugoslovian group) have been known to want a drink occasionally.

So the little area of less than a square mile seceded and became an independent municipality. The Society installed a swimming pool, a nine-hole golf course, tennis courts, a picnic area, a little restaurant and of course a bar, a water tower, and five dozen small cabins.

In November 1981, Pat Chiaro, of Italian descent, was elected mayor of Slovenska Naroda Podporna Jednota by a vote of 10–0. (He chose not to vote for himself.) And even though he can't pronounce the name of the town, few others pronounce it either. Almost everybody calls it S.N.P.J.

A MISNAMED MINNESOTA TOWN

The town of Mountain Lake, in southwest Minnesota, has neither a mountain nor a lake.

WHY NOT SNOWBIRD?

In Alaska, people tell how a place named Quail got its name. The settlers liked very much a local bird called a ptarmigan, a partridge-like grouse that thrives in cold areas. So they decided to name the place Ptarmigan.

"How do you spell it?" someone asked. Nobody knew. So they settled on Quail, which several of them could spell.

OKAY, NOKAY

There are villages called Okay in Arizona and Oklahoma, the latter having been named for the OK Truck Company.

There's a Nokay Lake in Minnesota, from the name of an Indian chief of the Ojibway tribe.

IS THE HOLE GONE, TOO?

A place called Hole-in-the Wall in Talbot County, Maryland, was renamed Hambleton, but now Hambleton has disappeared from highway maps of the area. Did it go into the hole?

THE NAME IS NOW CORRECT

When a post office was to be established in a village a few miles south of Versailles, Indiana, in the nineteenth century, Versailles postmaster William Will (so the story goes) was asked to suggest a name, a not-uncommon practice in those days. Because of a current and rather widespread interest in comets, Will recommended Comet. His handwriting was not clear, however, so the U.S. Post Office Department sent him a card with "Comet" on it and asked him to verify it. He wrote "Correct" on the card, and today's state maps still show Correct as the village name.

The name of another Indiana village, Siberia, is the result of another Post Office Department error—also based on good intentions. Father Isidore Hobi had named it Sabaria for the place where Saint Martin of Tours was born. A Post Office Department employee assumed that the priest could not spell well, and designated the place as Siberia.

Clerical errors by other folks resulted in the names of Perkinsville and Taswell, two other Indiana villages. The original intention had been to name them for early settlers William Parkins and James Laswell.

However, Scircleville, another Hoosier village, is not erroneous. It was named for George Scircle. (The first two syllables of the village name are pronounced like *circle*.)

THE TWENTY-FOUR
NOISIEST TOWNS IN THE
UNITED STATES

Bangor, CA, ME, MI, PA, WI	Guntown, MS
Bangs, TX	Hammer, SD
Bigbee, AL	Roaring Branch, PA
Big Falls, MN	Roaring Gap, NC
Bighorn, MT	Roaring River, NC
Boomer, NC, WV	Roaring Spring, PA
Cannon Falls, MN	Roaring Springs, TX
Drum, KY	Rumbley, MD
Drums, PA	Storm Lake, IA
Falling Rock, WV	Stormville, NY
Falling Waters, WV	Thunderbolt, GA
Good Thunder, MN	Yellville, AL

THE MODEST ONES

The town names given here suggest—rightly or not—that the inhabitants are or were modest, even self-deprecating. Although the modesty may sometimes have been genuine, often any unfavorable implication may have been unintentional.

Dinkey Creek, CA, for instance, does not belittle either the town or its creek: it memorializes a dog named Dinkey that unwisely tangled with a grizzly bear. And Ordinary, VA isn't said to be an ordinary town. An old word for *tavern* or *inn* was *ordinary*, and near one such ordinary the town grew up. (In the same state there is also a Smoky Ordinary.)

Here are some other apparently modest or even self-accusing town names:

Acorn, KY, VA	Cheapside, TX
Bland, MO	Cloudy, OK
Blanks, LA	Crum, WV, and
Boca Raton, FL ⟨mouse	Crummies, KY
mouth⟩	Dink, WV
Boring, MD, OR, and	Dowdy, AR
Boreing, KY	Drifting, PA
Burden, KS	Dwarf, KY

Lower Peach Tree, AL
Lowpoint, IL
Little, KY (and about 60
   more with Little as part
   of the name, such as
   Littleton [7 states] or
   Little Silver, NJ)
Maybe, MI
Micro, NC
Mousie, KY*
Muddie, IL
Novice, TX

Nuttsville, VA
Odd, WV
Oldenburg, IN
Peculiar, MO
Plain, WI, Plain City, OH,
   Plainfield (12 states),
   Plainview (6 states),
   Plainville (6 states)
Rowdy, KY
Shadow, VA
Weed, CA, NM, and
   Weedville, PA

---

*The source of this name is delightful. Postmaster Clay Martin, at the turn of this century, had two daughters, Kitty and Mousie. When he was asked to suggest a name for the post office (and thereby the village), he flipped a coin to see which of his daughters should be honored. The younger daughter won.

TOWNS THAT BRAG
ABOUT THEMSELVES

The namers of some towns (if the names are taken at face value) appear to have been boastful, and sometimes they were. Often, however, the names are deceiving. Ace, Texas, for example, which seems to refer to itself as the highest-ranking card in the deck, was actually named for its first postmaster, Ace Emmanuel.

The following names are among those that seem to boast about the characteristics of the land or the scenery.

Broadlands, IA
Buena Vista (10 states)
Fairview (13 states)
Frostproof, FL (but oranges
   have frozen there)
Goodland (6 states)
Good Water, AL
Grand Island (3 states)
Grand Meadow, MN
Grandview (8 states, plus 2
   Grand View)
Levelland, TX

Lovely, KY
Majestic, KY
Marvel, AL, CO
Nice, CA
Paradise (8 states)
Plentywood, MT
Pretty Prairie, KS
Richfield (fourteen states)
Scenic, SD
Waterproof, IA (but it was
   muddy when we were
   there)

Here are some that superficially, at least, appear to commend the early inhabitants or their life style:

Algood, TN; Allgood, AL
Brave, PA
Carefree, AZ
Champion (3 states)
Cornucopia, WI
Fairplay or Fair Play (5 states)
Goodwine, IL
Hardy (5 states)
Jolly, TX
Leader, MN
Lively, VA
Loyal, OK, WI

Niceville, FL
Noble (5 states)
Pleasant Unity, PA
Plush, OR
Rich, KS
Rising Star, TX
Smartt, TN
Smartville, CA
Star (4 states)
Superior (7 states)
Swift, MN
Valiant, OK

This last group includes some of the names that seem to praise miscellaneous virtues:

Aroma Park, IL
Balm, FL
Belle (40, usually with another word)
Blessing, TX
Bliss, ID
Bold Spring, TN
Bonnie, IL
Cool, CA
Darling, MS, PA
Diamond (4 states)
Dunmor, KY; Dunmore, WV
Faith, NC
Felicity, OH
Fine, NY

Gem (3 states)
Liberty Center (3 states, plus 3 Liberty and 24 others with Liberty as part)
Mammoth (4 states)
Marvel, OH, CO
Metropolis, IL
Miracle, KY
New Freedom, PA
New Haven (11 states)
New Hope (4 states)
Optima, OK
Premium, KY
Radiant, VA
Tiptop, VA

THE MOST MILITANT NAMES

Bellicose Peak, AK
Cannon, KY (also Cannon

Beach, OR; Cannon Falls, MN; Cannonsburg, MI)

Guntown, MS
Powderhorn, CO
Rifle, CO

Salvo, NC
War, WV

NAMES OF ADVICE,
ENTREATY, OR COMMAND

Commenting on Do Stop, Kentucky, George R. Stewart called it "one of the few hortatory advertising names to have received recognition on an official map."

Many other names, however, appear to give advice, to entreat, or to command. Actually the appearance is usually false, for the names are often derived from personal names. For example, Dare, Virginia, which seems to be exhorting Virginia to be bold, was really named in memory of Virginia Dare, the first child born of English parents in North America.

But let's forget factuality for a few moments and have a little fun. Read this first group with a pause at the comma, so that you seem to be advising the people of the state—maybe on the Fourth of July or other patriotic occasion.

Advance, Indiana!
Duck, West Virginia!
Fly, Ohio!
Hustle, Virginia!
Huzzah, Missouri!
Muse, Oklahoma!
   (Pennsylvania!)
Ponder, Texas!
Reform, Alabama!
   (Mississippi!)

Rule, Arkansas! (Texas!)
Rush, Colorado!
   (Kentucky!) (New York!)
Smile, Kentucky!
Stay, Kentucky!
Switchback, West Virginia!
Wade, Mississippi! (North
   Carolina!) (Oklahoma!)
Zigzag, Oregon!

We'll read the names in this group without commas. In Bluff Utah, for instance, we are advising someone to make Utah think we have a royal flush.

Admire Kansas
Chase Alabama (Kansas,
   Louisiana, Maryland,
   Michigan)
Cook Minnesota (Nebraska,
   Washington)

Crown Kentucky
   (Pennsylvania, West
   Virginia)
Cut Off Louisiana
Dent Minnesota
Divide Colorado

Dodge Nebraska (North Dakota, Texas, Wisconsin)	Revere Minnesota (Missouri, Pennsylvania, West Virginia)
Honor Michigan	Shock West Virginia
Hurt Virginia	Slaughter Louisiana
Mix Louisiana	Surprise Nebraska (New York)
Peel Arkansas	
Purchase New York	Tell Texas

"SOME FELLOW OUT IN SOUTH SUCCOTASH"

A public figure must be careful about the illustrative names he or she chooses. President Ronald Reagan was complaining in 1982 about TV news emphases, saying that "constantly downbeat" stories from the networks were delaying economic recovery. "Is it news," he asked, "that some fellow out in South Succotash has just been laid off that he should be interviewed nationwide?"

The sarcastic choice of name infuriated residents of countless small towns, as well as many other people who happened to be out of work. Editorials critical of the president's "thoughtlessness" and "lack of sensitivity" appeared here and there for weeks.

Jobless Andy Hjelmeland, for instance—he was from Maple Plain, MN, a midwestern representative of the South Succotashes, perhaps—wrote to *Newsweek*:

> I wish the President could be that unemployed guy in South Succotash for just one month. I'd be curious to know what his view would be on the greater need for warheads than for jobs if the window of vulnerability were situated on the front porch of his home.

AFL-CIO President Lane Kirkland decided to equate South Succotash with unemployment. In a Labor Day pronouncement he said:

> South Succotash, with its population of nearly 11 million, must be a considerable place. It's bigger than

New York and Los Angeles combined. It's bigger than Pennsylvania or Ohio, bigger than all of Sweden, twice the size of Denmark and three and one half times the size of New Zealand.

SEXISM IN
THE NAMES OF TOWNS

We can find Guys in Tennessee and a Guy in Arizona or Texas, as well as Guys Mills in Pennsylvania and Guysville in Ohio, but there are no Gals anywhere. There aren't any Dolls either.

DYING TO HAVE A PLACE
NAMED FOR YOU?

The Board on Geographic Names, which was created by federal law as an interdeparmental agency, decides which names are approved for federal use. You can't name a new village, for instance—not if you want to get mail delivery—unless the name has Board approval.

If the name you recommend is that of a person, the person must be dead. So you can't flatter your father-in-law, reingratiate yourself with your husband or wife, or immortalize your bright-eyed child by assigning that person's name to your village.

GOODNIGHT, ROSEANN.
GOODBYE, GOLDEN POND.

Every year, as population in some places dwindles and as the U.S. Postal Service tries to cut costs, post offices are closed. Most often the terminated offices are branches and substations, but sometimes post offices classified as Independent or Community are affected.

The 1982 Post Office Directory reported that in the preceding two-year period a total of 234 "postal units" were closed.

So goodnight, Roseann, VA—love letters to Roseann must now go to Grundy.

Goodbye, Golden Pond, KY. Cadiz is where the old folks now buy their stamps.

Goodbye, Valle Crucis, NC. The Postal Service says you belong to Boone.

The Apple Ridge, MI, and the Powderly, AL, substations are closed, and so are those called Echo Park, CA, Cherrelyn, CO, Pinehurst, TX, and about twenty in Puerto Rico with musical Spanish names such as Altamesa, Plaza Cortada, Villa Prades, Tiendas Deco, and branches called Las Flores and Barrio Cantito.

Send your mail not to the CPO (Community Post Office) in Saint Bernard, AL, but to Cullman, not to Jacob Lake, AZ, but to Fredonia (and don't forget that your zip code is changed to 86022). Farewell to once-ambitious Hope Valley, CA, and to Colorado Sierra, CO, although perhaps Golden is no less attractive. Goodbye to Round Oak, GA, and to Twin Lakes and Stonewall. Naf, ID, is so tiny it lost out to Malta, which itself is printed in the smallest road map type.

Chester, MN, succumbed to big brother Rochester, and Clearwater, MO, folks now get their mail from the little office in Sainte Genevieve, and so do those in Lake Forest. Do you feel abandoned—lost in nowhere—when you no longer have a post office?

Goodbye, six branch offices in New Jersey. Bosque Farms, NM, loses twenty-six points from its zip code by shifting to Peralta. High Rock, NC, may lose altitude by its change to Denton. People addressing mail to Geneva on the Lake, OH, save time by sending it now to Geneva, unadorned. Ormsby, PA, mail—will it be blown away in Cyclone? Snowflakes are somewhat uncommon in southern Virginia; perhaps that's why the Snowflake CPO no longer exists.

And what should we make of this? The Downtown station in Helena, MT, now has its mail delivered to the station called Last Chance.

23

CHANGING
TIMES,
CHANGING
NAMES

URPAIGN? ONO!
MINNEHAHA? WYNOT!

People in Lebanon County, PA, and Shasta County, CA, like to tell strangers how the town called Ono in each of those places got its name. It seems that years ago when the village was to be incorporated there was much discussion in village meetings as to what the name should be. Whenever a new suggestion was made, someone would say "Oh, no!" At last someone said, "All right, let's give you what you want. We'll call it Ono." And so they did.

In all probability the story isn't true. The good settlers in each place knew their Bible, and some of them wanted a biblical name but not a frequently used one such as Goshen or Hebron. In one of the begat chapters of I Chronicles (8:12) there is a passing reference to a place called Ono, which is not mentioned again. So it is almost certainly the source of that name which graces the two little towns as well as a few other, even smaller ones.

There is apparently some truth in a story told about Wynot, NE, and Whynot, MS and NC. This time, when in a name-discussion someone said, "I don't like that name," someone else asked, "Why not?" And eventually those three places settled on Wynot and Whynot.

No place in the Bible has those names.

Other squabbles over place names, it is said locally, once helped to prevent the merging of Champaign and Urbana, IL, separated by only a street, and Minneapolis and St. Paul, MN, also right next to each other.

The Illinois merger talks aroused much interest, and general principles seemed reachable concerning the combination of governments, fire and police departments, tax assessments, and so on. But Elm Street in Champaign runs north and south, and in Urbana east and west, and the two don't come close to meeting. The avenue named Florida in Urbana becomes Kirby in Champaign, and residents on neither side of the dividing line wanted to change addresses. Even if those problems and other similar ones were soluble, what should the merged city be called? Chambana seemed a good choice, but residents of Urbana urged that because their city was older, it should come first; they didn't want to be the tail of an onomastic dog. And Urpaign didn't arouse anyone's enthusiasm, particularly after a professor discoursed learnedly on the sad fate of an ancient city named Ur.

The proposed merger of Minneapolis and St. Paul also ran afoul of the naming problem, a favorite local story says. A proponent of the plan suggested Minnehaha—the name of an attractive waterfall, creek, and park. A St. Paulite who opposed the merger saw his chance.

"Fine!" he said. "That's exactly what I thought someone would propose. "It's *Minne* for Minneapolis and *haha* for St. Paul!"

WHAT THE ENGLISH DID
TO THE FRENCH LANGUAGE

In parts of North America, especially in what is now called the midwest, French explorers and sometimes settlers preceded the English. Since the best-educated of the English usually knew some French, many French names remained intact, so that we find, for instance in Wisconsin or Minnesota, places named Eau Claire ⟨clear water⟩, Fond du Lac ⟨foot of the lake⟩, and Lac Qui Parle ⟨the lake that talks⟩, ⟨one of the loveliest of place names⟩. That last name, however, has deteriorated in pronunciation to something like "lackeyparl."

Larger changes occurred in other French names—sometimes enough to hide the original. Here are some examples:

Bob Ruly, MI: *Bois brûlé* ⟨burned wood⟩ was what the French called a place where there had been a forest fire. To the English that sounded like a man's name.

Dishmaugh: a well-traveled Indian trail led to this lake in Indiana, which the French called *lac du chemin* ⟨lake at the road⟩. The English converted *du chemin* to Dishmaugh.

Glazypeau: a creek and a small mountain in Arkansas. *Glaise* was the French word for a salt lick, a deposit where animals could lick the salt they craved. One such lick was *glaise à Paul* ⟨Paul's lick⟩. The name went through various stages (Glazypool, Glazypole, Glazier Pole, Glacierpeau) and finally settled into Glazypeau.

Gnaw Bone: a village and a short creek in Indiana. Although local legends attribute the name to a person or persons who because of deep snow or other reasons were reduced to gnawing bones, the probable explanation is that early French settlers had called the place Narbonne, after a French town.

Lemon Fair: a Vermont river. Said to be an anglicization of *les monts verts* ⟨the green mountains⟩.

Loose: a Missouri creek. Possibly from *l'ours* ⟨the bear⟩. The same explanation has been offered for Louse Creek in Oregon, but George R. Stewart says that an early camp there was badly infested by lice.

Low Freight: an Arkansas creek. Originally *l'eau froide* ⟨the cold water⟩. Understood by later English settlers as "low freight." Now it is officially L'Eau Fraise ⟨fresh water⟩, although *frais*, Stewart points out, should be *fraiche*.

Meredosia, a town in Illinois: A *marais* was ⟨a pool or spring⟩, and *marais d'osier* was a pool near willows. Perhaps influenced by Greek names such as Theodosia, English speakers reworked the French. In other places, *marais* has taken other forms, as in Marie Saline Landing in Arkansas, from *marais saline* ⟨salty pool⟩, or in Mary Delarme Creek in Indiana, corrupted from *marais de l'orme* ⟨elm spring⟩.

Ozark Mountains in Missouri and adjoining states: the French referred to *Aux Arks* ⟨at the Arks⟩, from the Arkansa Indian tribe. Ozark is basically a respelling of the earlier name.

Picketwire, a Colorado creek: officially Purgatoire, but Picket-wire is much easier for English-trained tongues. Originally a Spanish name, El Rio de las Animas Perdidas en Purgatorio ⟨the river of lost souls in Purgatory⟩, in memory of some Spaniards who were killed by vengeful Indians before they could receive absolution, it was for obvious reasons shortened to Purgatorio and then translated by Frenchmen into Purgatoire.

Skilligallee, in Michigan: from *Ile aux Galets* ⟨pebble island⟩.

Smackover, a town in Arkansas: the French called it Chemin Couvert ⟨covered road⟩, perhaps because of overhanging tree branches. Try saying shuh-MAA cuh-VAIR a few times rapidly, and you too may come out with Smackover.

Swashing, a creek in Missouri: the French named it for Joachim, perhaps Saint Joachim. By folk etymology the pronunciation changed to Swashing.

Tar Blue is only one of a number of names in which French *terre* ⟨earth⟩ was changed to *tar*; *blue* is obviously from French *bleue*. Stewart has also mentioned Pumly Tar from *Pomme de Terre* ⟨earth apple, potato⟩; Movestar from Mauvaise Terre ⟨bad earth⟩; and Turnwall, an Arkansas creek, from *Terre Noire* ⟨black earth⟩.

Zumbro, a stream in Minnesota: In small streams French voyageurs frequently encountered tangled tree trunks and tree limbs and other barriers to easy passage. They called these *les embarras* ⟨obstructions⟩. The Embarras River in Illinois is named for them and is called EM-brah or EM-braw by the knowledgeable, em-BARE-us by strangers. In Minnesota *les embarras* or *aux embarras* became Zumbro. A town on its banks is Zumbrota, which combines the revised French with a Siouan ending *-ta* ⟨on, at⟩.

Many French names were merely replaced by other names that the English preferred. Lac Saint Sacrement, for instance, became Lake George; Fort Carillon, Fort Ticonderoga; and Au Sable, Sandy Creek. La Rivière de la Famine was translated to Famine River.

HOW THE EUROPEANS
CHANGED INDIAN NAMES

Novelist Thomas Wolfe wrote in *Of Time and the River*:

Where can you match the mighty music of their names?—The Monongahela, the Colorado, the Rio Grande, the Columbia, the Tennessee, the Hudson (Sweet Thames!); the Kennebec, the Rappahannock, the Delaware, the Penobscot, the Wabash, the Chesapeake, the Swannanoa, the Indian River, the Niagara (Sweet Afton!); the Saint Lawrence, the Susquehanna, the Tombigbee, the Nantahala, the French Broad, the Chattahoochee, the Arizona, and the Potomac (Father Tiber!)—these are a few of their princely names, these are a few of their great, proud, glittering names, fit for the immense and lonely land that they inhabit.

We tried to imitate the sounds the Indians made when they talked of rivers, lakes, and mountains, and we used imitations of what we heard to name hundreds of our towns, a score of our large cities, about half of our states.

The Indians could not write the names, and white men's ears were sometimes faulty, white men's vocal organs untutored in forming the gutturals and other strange (to them) sounds that Indians had learned to form with ease.

So when we say that a place has an Indian name, all we can mean is that a modern word represents what white men once thought the Indians were saying. Often, assuredly, today's name would be incomprehensible to an Indian of two hundred or so years ago if he or she could now be brought back to life.

Consider some of the Indian names that Wolfe included in his rhapsodic list.

French voyageurs encountered a rather small river that the Indians seemed to call Ouaboukigon, which may or may not mean ⟨shining white⟩. The Indian name seemed ungainly, and the French shortened and altered it to Oubache. To the English that sounded like Wabash, and so it appears on modern maps. In the old books of favorite songs, the Hoosier brother of novelist Theodore Dreiser, who called himself Paul Dresser, has written sentimentally of "the banks of the Wabash." Could he have written—would he have written—"On the Banks of the Ouaboukigon"?

Kennebec ⟨long-reach⟩ was recorded in 1609 as Kinebeki. Apparently Penobscot ⟨sloping-arch-at⟩ was originally just one small stretch of the stream above Bangor, Maine, but the name was extended by whites to the whole river. The same seems true of Monongahela ⟨high-banks-falling-down⟩, a word of which Walt Whitman said, "It rolls with venison freshness on the palate." The name of North Carolina's Nantahala seems to mean ⟨noonday sun⟩, so called because in some places, although not along the whole river, the cliffs are so steep and high that sunlight reaches the water only at midday.

The Spanish wrote a Cherokee name as Tanasqui more than four centuries ago, and the English 150 years later thought it was Tinnase. For years it was the Cherokee River, but some secession-minded western North Carolinians in the late eighteenth century chose to call their new state, and the river, Tennessee.

In 1585 Chesapeake was first written by the English as Chesepiooc, which may have meant ⟨big-river-at⟩ (*che* definitely meant ⟨big⟩ in Algonquian). Susquehanna hasn't changed much from Sasquehanough, as John Smith wrote it as early as 1608, although the deleted final letters in effect deleted "men" from the meaning ⟨Sasque-tribe-stream-men⟩ (*hanna* was ⟨stream⟩ to the Algonquians).

Alabama's Tombigbee River of course has nothing to do with large makers of honey. The Choctaw was earlier written as *itombiikbi*, then respelled to appear more English and more pronounceable. It means ⟨coffin makers⟩, after a tribe who scraped the bones of their dead and made boxes to keep them in.

Virginia's Rappahannock ⟨back-and-forth stream⟩ was called that because it rises and lowers with the tides; Rapidan, a tributary, is a shortened form.

John Smith and other early settlers recorded Potomac as

Patawomeck or Potowanmeac, which shortcutting Englishmen quickly reduced to Potomack and then dropped the *k*. Among the earliest written versions of Niagara were Unéaukara and Ongniaahra, shortened by the French to Ongiara and then to the present form.

What happened to the Indian names of the rivers that Wolfe wrote about so lovingly is similar to what has happened to countless other names borrowed from the native Americans. Here are early spellings of a few other familiar places:

Illinois: Eriniouai, later Aliniouek, Iliniouek. The French provided the final *s* to make it look more French.

Arizona: Ali-shonak ⟨place of the spring⟩ in Papago; then Arizonac. (A recent theory, though, says that Arizona is a Basque name, not Indian, and that it comes from the Basque *aritz* ⟨oak⟩, which appears in a number of western place names.)

Milwaukee: Milo-aki

Wisconsin: Mescousing or Mesconsing, French Ouisconsing

Kansas: the name of the Indian tribe was written as Escansaque by the Spanish.

Manhattan: Manna-hatta, possibly the same as a name by which Mohicans were sometimes called, Manhecan or Manahegan.

Schenectady: written Scheaenhechstede by the Dutch

Hoboken: Hopoakan-hacking

Roanoke: Rarenawok

Missouri: Ouemessourit

Michigan: Machihiganing

Eventually an anglicized version of an Indian name may be still further shortened. Thus the Swatara, a creek with its name based on an Iroquoian word, is informally called the Swatty in southeastern Pennsylvania.

Walt Whitman, who loved most American names, and in particular names of Indian ancestry, said, "What is the fitness— What the strange charm of aboriginal names?—They all fit. Mississippi!—the word winds with chutes—it rolls a stream three thousand miles long."

Maybe so. But American settlers were seldom content with a name that seemed three thousand miles long. They modified the long names, the hard-to-pronounce names, cutting a corner off here, a syllable there, often dispensing with endings or supplying endings that were more familiar. Inevitably in diminishing the Indian names they diminished the meanings, too—sometimes to no-meaning.

But who is alive to know the difference?

THE POWER OF LOVE
IN GOLD RUSH COUNTRY

In Amador County, CA, are places named Fiddletown, Kit Carson, Pioneer, River Pines, Sutter Creek, and Volcano.

But the most interesting onomastically is Ione—not because of what it is but because of what it was. The place used to be called Bedbug. Girls, however, could seldom be induced to marry men whose permanent address would be Bedbug, so the citizens got together and changed it to Ione—a girl's name said to mean ⟨violet⟩.

Such feminine influence or other forces of civilization resulted in other name changes in the gold-mining areas of California. Growlersburg, in El Dorado County, probably sounded too grumpy and so became Georgetown, and Hangtown became Placerville, and Gouge Eye, in nearby Sutter County, is now the charming little town of Pleasant Grove.

Others of the once-flourishing gold towns have vanished or at least crumbled. Once there was Tin Cup, where miners boasted they could find that much gold daily. Whiskeytown is now a tiny village (some fifty places had Whiskey in their names). Stories are still told about other spots with such names as You Bet, Shirttail (a prospector carried his new-found gold in his shirttail), Tinkers Knob (teamster J. A. Tinker had a big nose), and Tinkers Defeat (which took place on a sharp curve), and Pinchemtight (where a pinch of gold was the price of a drink and a Swedish bartender, Big-Thumb Ole, was threatened when he didn't pinch his fingers tight enough—or so one version of the legend goes).

Bret Harte immortalized Poker Flat, but he didn't turn his genius loose on Cheese-Marie (perhaps from Jesus Maria), Hell

Hollow, Murderers' Bar, Jackass Hill, Squaw Hollow, Sucker Flat, Humbug, and the Rattlesnake Bar and the Frogtown Bar. And Mark Twain reached California a little too late, although he did enlighten us about jumping frogs in Calaveras County, where Angel's Camp has been restored.

SHOULD PIKES PEAK
BE JAMES'S PEAK?

Who deserves the honor of having a mountain named for him— its discoverer or the man who first climbs it?

In November 1806, Zebulon Pike, an army officer and explorer, led an exploring party to the southwest. West of what is now Colorado Springs, he found a previously unknown mountain over 14,000 feet high. He attempted to climb it, but cold weather and snow prevented him and his party from reaching the top. Nevertheless, his followers and then other people who went to the area began to call the mountain Pikes Peak.

Fourteen years later, in July 1820, an expedition led by Stephen Long was exploring the area. One mountain that he discovered he named for himself, Longs Peak. He sent a team to try to climb another, which was the peak that Zebulon Pike had been unable to master. The team members were Edwin James, J. Verplank, and Z. Wilson. After they successfully completed the ascent, Long said that the mountain should be named for James.

Since Long was an official of the U.S. Corps of Topographical Engineers, James's Peak would apparently be the accepted name. But to the people of the area it was Pikes Peak, and that's what they continued to call it, regardless of Topographical Engineers. Eventually officialdom gave in, and today Pikes Peak, although less tall than thirty other Colorado mountains, is probably best known of them all.

STREET NAMES
IN HOUSING DEVELOPMENTS

The term *housing development* has been defined as ⟨a place where they cut down all the trees and then name the streets after them⟩.

ON THE STREET
(CIRCLE, DRIVE, LANE, TRAIL)
WHERE YOU LIVE

Are there fashions in street names as in clothing and other things? John Algeo found that there are—at least in Athens, Georgia.

In 1859 about three quarters of the forty-six street names in Athens were names of people prominent in the early days of the community or the university. The others were often directional: Oconee (for the river, which everyone would presumably know about), Factory (because there was a factory there), College, School, Rock Spring, Foundry, and so on.

But by 1978, although the early names for the most part still existed, the names of the rest of the 850-plus streets were generally "chosen for their pleasant associations and hence for their commercial value."

So modern Athens has street names such as Homestead Drive, Doe Run, Orchard Circle (no orchard there), Indian Lake Court (no lake), Deertree Drive (What's a deertree?), Woodstock Drive, Spruce Valley Road (no valley), Ravenwood Court, Arborview Drive (no arbors in sight), Mockingbird Circle, Horseshoe Circle (not shaped like either a horseshoe or a circle), Jockey Club Drive (no club, probably no jockeys).

As these names suggest, even the words *street* and *avenue* may now be superseded by other terms. In Athens, Algeo found eighteen Drives, ten Courts, eight Circles, three Places, two Roads, two Runs, one Way, one Lane, and one Trail.

In other cities many of the early names were those of national figures, other states, and trees. But their modern names resemble those that Algeo found in Athens, although sometimes they include more or less prominent, living, local people, not forgetting the developers and members of their families.

An example, from Gary Jenning's *Personalities of Language*: A street in Stamford, CT, was called Bubsey Lane, reportedly the nickname of a child of the tract developer. The residents petitioned to have the name changed to Club Circle.

PART IV

"The time has come," the author said,
"To talk of other names.

Of cars-and pets-
and baseball teams-
Of suffragettes-
and games."

24

ALL
OF THE
ABOVE,
AND MORE

CRICKET, CROESUS, BROWNIE CAR,
YOU DIDN'T TRAVEL VERY FAR

People who are old enough to have listened to Jack Benny can remember his vintage car called a Maxwell. Most of us at displays of so-called antique cars may have seen a Stanley Steamer, various electrically powered cars, and a Reo (named for R.E. Olds, whose other namesake was more enduring), Hupmobile, Moon, Sun, Star (once a rival of Ford and Chevrolet), Marmon, Lafayette, Elwood, and—not nearly so old—Nash, Packard, and Studebaker.

In all, though, there have been over 2,200 makes of automobiles manufactured in the United States. Phillip R. Rutherford has uncovered more than 1,500 of these names. Eight of the cars, he says, were named for U.S. presidents: Washington, Monroe, Jackson, Lincoln (still in existence), Johnson, Grant, Roosevelt, and Harding.

Some of the other names memorialized the inventor or the man who put up the money, or they described the car's chief claim to innovation, associated it with a place, hinted at something classical about it, or praised it highly. Here are some names culled from Rutherford's long list of automobiles:

Auto-Bug	Fwick	Punge Finch
Best	Hazard	Red Bug
Blood	Hercules	Rickenbacker
Brown Burtt	Ideal	Savage
Brownie Car	Klink	Sprite Cycle Car
Bugmobile	Klock	Storms
Centaur	Norwalk Underslung	Terwilliger
Cricket	Okay	Twombley
Croesus	Only	Vestal
Dan Patch	Ottomobile	Wasp
Diana	Pawtucket Steamer	Wildman
	Peter Pan	

LICENSE PLATES
CAN BE GOOFED UP, TOO

Arizona is one of those states in which for a fee one may order a personalized auto license plate. Heidi Hansen decided to get one as a Christmas present for her mother, Mrs. Alice Hansen, who is a reading resource teacher in the Mesa Public Schools.

The instructions said to list two choices. Heidi wrote:
1.–Read
2.–Books
The plate arrived in time for Christmas. It said:
2 BOOKS

Another instance was reported by broadcaster Paul Harvey. A Floridian named Dave Burton was asked by his wife what he wanted for a birthday present. He replied, "I'd like some personalized license plates with my name on them." A couple of weeks later the license plates arrived, on each of them the words
MY NAME

NAMELY BLOOPERS

Disc jockey: "Here's the last record for tonight's show, played by Les Bastard and his orchestra—I mean Baxter."

Announcer: "This medicine must still be approved by the Pure Drum and Fugg Administration."

Newscaster: "The people of Cuba are beginning to form anti-Castrate forces."

Quebec announcer: "This is the Dominion network of the Canadian Broad Corping Castration."

Durward Kirby: "The Blonde Bed Breakers are on the air—I mean Bond Bread Bakers."

Golf announcer: "Johnny Tee is now on the pot—uh, that's Johnny Pott."

PALINDROMES

Ava is a palindrome—it's the same whether you read it backward or forward. Others include Anna, Hannah, and—a rare masculine example—Otto.

If a surname can be successfully inverted to suggest a given name (not many can), a two-word palindrome results. A professor of classics at the University of Illinois in Urbana-Champaign was named Revilo Oliver.

If his middle name had been Otto, his name would have been a three-word palindrome: Revilo Otto Oliver.

When most surnames are spelled backward, the result either is unpronounceable or sounds like a character in science fiction: Senoj, Strebor, Sirrom, Nameloc, Zepol, Nadroj, Nodrog, or Rednaxela. (Try your own name. Is it as good as Kooh?)

REAL OR FICTIONAL?

Does each of these names represent a real or a fictional person?

Johnny Appleseed   Billy the Kid
King Arthur   Daniel Boone

John Brown	Jack the Ripper
Buffalo Bill	Jesse James
Paul Bunyan	Casey Jones
Crazy Horse	Captain Kidd
Davy Crockett	Jean Lafitte
Robinson Crusoe	Pecos Bill
Febold Feboldson	Peter Pan
Frankenstein	Pocahontas
Lemuel Gulliver	Long John Silver
John Henry	Sitting Bull
Sherlock Holmes	Rip Van Winkle
Robin Hood	

Johnny Appleseed. Real. Actual name John Chapman (1774–1845). He did not scatter apple seeds randomly, but did plant apple orchards from the Alleghenies westward.

King Arthur. Uncertain, although there may have been a Welsh Arthur who won important battles from the Saxons. Most of the Round Table stories, however, were made up centuries later.

Billy the Kid. Real. Actual name William H. Bonney (1859–1881). A bandit in the Southwest.

Daniel Boone. Real (1734–1820). American explorer and pioneer.

John Brown. Real (1800–1859). American abolitionist leader who was executed.

Buffalo Bill. Real. Actual name William Frederick Cody (1846–1917). Frontiersman and showman.

Paul Bunyan. Basically fictional, although there appears to have been a French Canadian named Bon Jean whose exploits were greatly exaggerated in the tales.

Crazy Horse. Real. Actual name Tashunca-Uitco (c. 1849–1877). Sioux leader who participated in the Battle of Little Big Horn.

Davy Crockett. Real (1786–1836). Frontiersman, Congressman. Killed at the Alamo.

Robinson Crusoe. Fictional, although author Daniel Defoe got his idea and some of his facts from the story of the marooned Alexander Selkirk.

Febold Feboldson. A fictional Paul Bunyan-like "Big Swede" of Nebraska, developed by Don Holmes and Wayne T. Carroll.

Frankenstein. Fictional. A mad scientist created by Mary Wollstonecraft Shelley (wife of the poet Percy Bysshe Shelley). Trivia question: What was Frankenstein's first name? (Victor)

Lemuel Gulliver. Fictional. The leading character in Jonathan Swift's satire *Gulliver's Travels.*

John Henry. Uncertain. The exploits of the powerful black railroad worker, "a steel-drivin' man," have been celebrated in countless stories and songs, some of them possibly based on fact.

Sherlock Holmes. Fictional, although author Sir Arthur Conan Doyle fashioned the character in part on Dr. Joseph Bell (1837–1911), under whom Doyle had studied medicine.

Robin Hood. Mainly fictional, although some scholars say that he actually lived in the twelfth century, that his true name was Robert Fitz-Ooth, and that he was reputed to be the Earl of Huntingdon.

Jack the Ripper. Real, although the actual name of this vicious murderer of London prostitutes (1888) is unknown.

Jesse James. Real (1847–1882). American outlaw.

Casey Jones. Probably real. A popular ballad was written about this self-sacrificing railroad engineer, whose original name may have been John Luther Jones. There had been, however, a somewhat similar earlier ballad about a black fireman, Jimmie Jones.

Captain Kidd. Real. Actual name William Kidd (1645?–1701). Scottish-born pirate who was hanged.

Jean Lafitte. Real (1780–1826). French pirate who was an American hero in the War of 1812.

Pecos Bill. Fictional Southwestern hero, credited among other things with digging the Rio Grande.

Peter Pan. The fictional boy who never grew up, created by Sir James Barrie.

Pocahontas. Real. Original name Matoaka (1595?–1617), later called Lady Rebecca. In Captain John Smith's account (which some historians say was romanticized), when Powhatan's men were "ready with their clubs, to beate out his [Smith's] braines, Pocahontas, the Kings dearest daughter...got his head in her armes, and laid her owne upon his to save him from death."

Long John Silver. The fictional one-legged pirate leader in Robert Louis Stevenson's *Treasure Island.*

Sitting Bull. Real. Indian name Tatanka Iyotake (1834–1890). Dakota-Sioux Indian chief who annihilated General George Custer's forces in 1876.

Rip Van Winkle. The fictional creation of Washington Irving, whose story of the famous long sleep shows how many changes may occur in twenty years.

THE OLD NAMES FOR OUR MONTHS

The Anglo-Saxons, an agricultural people, used names for the months which were much more descriptive than our Latin-derived ones.

January was Wulf-mōnaþ ⟨wolf month⟩, when people had to be especially fearful that hungry wolves might invade their villages.

February, Sprote-kalemōnaþ ⟨sprout cabbage month⟩

March, Hlyd-mōnaþ ⟨boisterous month⟩, because of the wind

April, Ēaster-mōnaþ

May, Primilce-mōnaþ ⟨month of three milkings⟩, because grass was then so lush that cows could be milked three times a day

June, Sēre-mōnaþ ⟨dry month⟩

July, Mäēd-mōnaþ ⟨meadow month⟩, when meadows were blooming

August, Wēod-mōnaþ ⟨weed month⟩, when weeds flourished

September, Hāērfest-mōnaþ ⟨harvest month⟩

October, Wīn-mōnaþ ⟨wine month⟩

November, Blōt-mōnaþ ⟨sacrifice month⟩, when a calf might be sacrificed; also Wind

December, Midwintra-mōnaþ; also called, by Christians after about A.D. 600, Hālig-mōnaþ ⟨holy month⟩

PETS' NAMES

The name given a pet may be decided by mutal agreement between owner and pet. An ordinary dog, for instance, may be satisfied with an ordinary name such as the conventional Spot, Brownie, Rover, or even Fido or Dog, but an extraordinary dog such as yours may demand or at least deserve something else.

Here are the names of one extraordinary dog and his parents, grandparents, and great-grandparents:

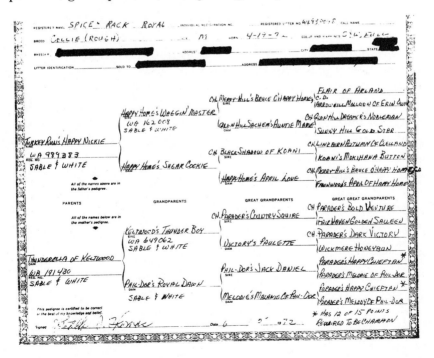

MRS. ALICE JONES,
MRS. JOHN JONES,
MS. ALICE JONES,
ALICE JONES

Until about 1750 in the United States, *Mrs.* (Mistress) was used for both unmarried and married adult females, and *Miss* was for some time regarded as a possible slur on the woman's moral standards. So Alice Jones in that early period would not have been Miss Alice Jones or Mrs. John Jones. She could have been, however, Mrs. (Mistress) Alice Jones.

But late in the eighteenth century and early in the nineteenth, conditions changed and it became customary to write Mrs. John Jones, Mrs. Washington Post, and so on. If the husband had a high position, a wife might reflect his glory and enhance her own by being known as Mrs. General Jones, or Mrs. Judge Jones.

Not everyone was happy with this situation. French author George Sand and English author George Eliot, for example, took those pseudonyms as disguises of both their gender and their possession of one or more mates.

Lucy Stone, while organizing women's rights conventions in the U.S., met and married Henry B. Blackwell in May 1855. For a year and two months she was either Mrs. Henry B. Blackwell or Mrs. Lucy Stone Blackwell, but then, with Henry's enthusiastic support, she reverted to Lucy Stone. He abetted her, too, in her extended campaign for women's rights, helping her to found and edit several suffragist publications. Lucy's reversion to her maiden name caused her trouble with Massachusetts authorities, who allowed women to vote in local elections but were reluctant to let Lucy do so unless she used her "legal" name, Blackwell.

Stone and Blackwell established the American Woman Suffrage Association in 1869, started *Woman's Journal*, a suffrage weekly, and published numerous *Woman Suffrage Leaflets*, frequently considering the question of the "right" name for married women.

Long after they were dead, a Lucy Stone League was revitalized (in 1969), mainly because so many women objected to being called the equivalent of Mrs. John Jones or Mrs. Henry Blackwell.

A group with a still more specific function was founded in 1973, the Center for a Woman's Own Name. In 1974 it published a *Booklet for Women Who Wish to Determine Their Own Names after Marriage*, which covered not only the emotional issues but also legal questions and possible problems with the names of children.

Karla Taylor, writing for the *Indianapolis Star* in 1982, reported the comments of several women and men concerning their experiments with married names.

Donna Bays-Beinart: "Just because I got married, Donna Bays didn't stop existing."

Nancy Hartman Scott (who puts her maiden name at the end): "If I was Mrs. Worth Hartman, I'd be losing part of myself....Sometimes people think he's my brother. And when people call me Mrs. Scott, I really feel like they're talking about my mother."

Worth Scott Hartman (who puts his wife's maiden name in the middle of his own): No other comment needed.

Teresa Adler-Phelps: "File it under Phelps, so Kevin and I can keep our records together."

Mary Beth Ramey, married to Rich Haily: "If we gave [our daughter] the name Ramey-Haily, God help her when she enters first grade and tries to learn to spell her name. And if it were Andrea Elizabeth Ramey-Haily and she married a Zabrowski—ugh!"

Genira Stephens-Hotopp: "What will they do if our son Brian Alexander Stephens-Hotopp grows up and marries, for instance, Katherine Anne Gallagher-Stewart? That will be up to them."

Bruce Stephens-Hotopp (who legally changed his name to include Genira's name and the hyphen): "For most men, the first reaction is 'Why in hell would you do a thing like that?' For me, it was based on an evaluation of who I feel like I am and my personal beliefs, which reflect that I enjoy my partner being equal with me."

Genira Stephens-Hotopp: "He's an exceptional human being."

Here are the names of the editor and publisher of *Womankind*:

Given name	Father's name	Stepfather's name	Former husband's name	Professional name
Judith	La Fourest	Gruner	Gilstrap	La Fourest

(She's married again, but her present husband's name appears nowhere.)

The statutes of most states say in effect that a woman (or a man) may use any name she (or he) wishes, provided that the choice is not made with the intent of defrauding anyone. The Supreme Court of Alabama, a state that was one of the last holdouts, ruled in 1981 that even for drivers' licenses and voter registration, a married woman should no longer be required to use her husband's name. Lucy Stone finally triumphed.

BECOMING FAMOUS
BY BECOMING COMMON

Sometimes the best way to become famous—maybe immortalized, in fact—is to have your name become a common noun, written without a capital letter. That, as is well-known, is what happened to the Fourth Earl of Sandwich (1718–92), who invented the sandwich so that he could eat without interrupting his gambling. And it's what happened to Governor Elbridge Gerry of Massachusetts who, to help his party in 1812, reshaped an election district that turned out to be salamander-shaped and gave rise to the noun (and verb) *gerrymander*.

Here are some other examples, some of which may be a little less known.

Electrical terms
ampere (amp)—André Marie Ampère (1775–1836), French mathematician and physicist, "father of electrodynamics"
joule—James P. Joule (1818–1889), British physicist
ohm—George Simon Ohm (1787–1854), German physicist
tesla—Nikola Tesla (1857–1943), Croatian-born American electrical engineer

volt—Count Alessandro Volta (1745–1827), Italian physicist

watt—James Watt (1736–1819), Scottish engineer and inventor

Flower names

begonia—Michel Bégon (1638–1710), governor of Santo Domingo

camellia—George Joset Kamel (1661—1706), Moravian Jesuit missionary

clivia—a Duchess of Northumberland, *nee* Clive

dahlia—Anders Dahl, eighteenth-century Swedish botanist

fittonia—Elizabeth and Sarah Mary Fitton, botanists

fuchsia—Leonhard Fuchs (1501–1566), German botanist

gentian—probably for Gentius, king of Illyria in second century B.C.

lobelia—Matthias de Lobel (1538–1616), Flemish botanist

magnolia—Pierre Magnol (1638–1715), French botanist

poinsettia—discovered by J.R. Poinsett (1799–1851), U.S. minister to Mexico

wistaria or *wisteria*—Casper Wistar or Wister (1761–1818), American anatomist.

zinnia—Johann Gottfried Zinn (1729–1759), German botanist

Miscellaneous

blanket—possibly for Thomas Blanket of England, said to have been the inventor in 1340; more likely, though, from French *blanc* ⟨white⟩

bobby—Sir Robert Peel (1788–1850), British prime minister who helped to establish London's police force

boycott—Charles C. Boycott (1832–1897), British land agent driven out by tenants when he refused to lower their rents

bowdlerization—Thomas Bowdler (1754–1825), English editor who expurgated Shakespeare

cardigan—Seventh Earl of Cardigan (1797–1868), British army officer

chauvinism—Nicholas Chauvin, nineteenth-century French soldier extraordinarily devoted to Napoleon

derrick—a hangman, Derick (c. 1600) at Tyburn, England; the gallows was named for him, then other suspension devices

diesel—Rudolf Diesel (1858–1913), German mechanical engineer

dunce—contemptuously used by opponents to ridicule followers of John Duns Scotus (1265?–1308), Scottish philosopher and theologian

fermium (a synthetic element)—Enrico Fermi (1901–1959), Italian-born American physicist

guillotine—Joseph Guillotin (1738–1814), French doctor who recommended its use

guy—Guy Fawkes (1570–1606), British conspirator whose effigies are burned each Guy Fawkes Day (November 5)

hoodlum—of doubtful origin, but sometimes said to be based on Muldoon, a ruffian on San Francisco's once notorious Barbary Coast

jimmy—Jemmy or Jimmy, a conventional name for an assistant in the late Middle Ages; a jimmy, to pry things open, is a "thief's assistant"

kaiser, czar, tsar—Julius Caesar and other dictators who followed him

lynch—Charles Lynch (1736–1796), Virginia planter and justice of the peace

masochism—Leopold von Sacher-Masoch (1836–1895), Austrian novelist who described the abnormal condition

maudlin—old pronunciation of (Mary) Magdalene, a symbol of tearful repentance

mausoleum—Mausōlus (d. 353 B.C.), king of Caria, whose widow built an elaborate tomb for him

maverick—Samuel A. Maverick (1803–1870), unconventional Texas cattleman who did not brand his calves

nicotine—Jean Nicot, sixteenth-century French ambassador credited with introducing tobacco to France

pants, pantaloons—Pantaleone, fourth-century Venetian doctor who was made a saint; later became a stock figure in comedies, wearing a garment including tight-fitting breeches and stockings

pap smear, pap test (sometimes still capitalized)—George Papanicolaou (1882–1962), American scientist of Greek descent

pasteurization—Louis Pasteur (1822–1895), French chemist who invented the process

pompadour—Marquise de Pompadour (1721–1764), mistress of French king Louis XV; she wore her hair brushed straight back

praline—invented by the cook of French Count du Plessis-*Praslin* (1598–1675)

ritz (putting on the)—César Ritz (1850–1918), Swiss hotelier

sadism—Comte Donatien de Sade (1740–1814), French novelist and libertine who praised sexual violence

saxophone—Adolphe Sax (1814–1894), German maker of musical instruments, who invented it in 1846

silhouette—Étienne de Silhouette (1709–1767), briefly a French controller-general, but no one is sure of what his association is with the word

sousaphone—in honor of John Philip Sousa (1854–1932), American bandmaster

spoonerism—William A. Spooner (1844–1930), English clergyman who frequently transposed sounds in his speaking, e.g., "well-boiled icicle" for "well-oiled bicycle"

tawdry—Saint Audrey (died A.D. 679), queen of Northumberland, whose throat tumor was blamed on her liking for necklaces

teddy bear—Theodore Roosevelt (1858–1919), whom some people ridiculed because he once refused to shoot a bear cub

varnish—Berenice II (c. 269–221 B.C.), queen of Egypt. The Greek city of Berenike, in Libya, was named for her, and a smooth, glossy finish for wood was developed there. The name was changed to Latin *veronix*, Old French *vernis*, Middle English *varnisch*, our *varnish*.

In all, the English language has about six or seven hundred of such persons' names made common. They are sometimes called *eponyms*, although that word has other meanings also. In addition, many personal names have been made into adjectives—e.g., *ritzy* and *sadistic*, from the same sources as *ritz* and *sadism*.

HOW DO AUTHORS NAME THEIR CHARACTERS?

Margaret Mitchell's Scarlett O'Hara originally had a blah name, but an editor insisted on a change. Beyond little doubt, *Gone with the Wind* owed part of its financial success to the inspired names of Scarlett O'Hara, Rhett Butler, and the saccharine-sweet Melanie.

Literary onomastics (the study of characters' names) is a growing part of literary criticism, probably because most profes-

sional authors do choose names with care. As one example,
Erwin C. Brody made an analysis of names used by Fyodor
Dostoevski in *Crime and Punishment* and another novel.

Raskolnikov's name, according to Brody, means ⟨schis-
matic, dissident, heretic⟩, and as readers of the novel will recognize, those words are a pretty accurate character sketch. (The
full name, incidentally, is the alliterative Rodion Romanovich
Raskolnikov.)

Marmeladov, a "tragicomical small government clerk," is
based on *marmelad* ⟨a candied fruit jelly⟩, and, says Brody, shows
the man's fundamental weakness.

Raskolnikov's sober, thoughtful friend, Razumiklin, has a
name derived from *razum* ⟨reason, intelligence⟩.

And Amalia Ivanovna Lippewechsel, who is of German
ancestry, is as her name suggests a "lip-changer," a gabble-
mouth.

Twentiety-century authors may not use names quite so
obviously to indicate character, preferring suggestiveness instead. A glamorous leading man is not likely to be named either
Mark Brown or Aloysius Heffelfinger, but he may be called—
well, how about Rhett Butler?

HOW DO YOU
NAME A BOAT?

Paddling his kayak in waters off the east coast of Florida, John
McNamara tallied and classified the names of one thousand
yachts, cabin cruisers, charter-fishing boats, and sailing vessels,
and whenever possible chatted with people aboard concerning
the boats' names.

The favored types of names, with examples, were these:

1. Picturesque (144)—Moonraker, Spindrift, Windchime
2. Sea-going (75)—Sea Angler, Sea Scamp, Sea Witch
3. Children (67)—Gekiven (*Ge*orge, *Ki*m, Ste*ven*)
4. Geographical (67)—Arkansas Traveller, Souix [*sic*] City Sue
5. Birds (63)—Flamingo, Ibis, Pelican
6. Man and Wife (62)—Dot-N-Mike, Jack-Lynn
7. Foreign (61)—(Italian names defeated Spanish, 25 to 23)
8. Whimsical (50)—Mi-Yot, Pade-IV, This-L-Du

9. Alcoholic (45)—Rheingold Express, B & B
10. Fictitious (40)—Davey Jones, Lorelei, Poseidon
11. Zoological (40)—Crashing Boar
12. Men (38)—Sneaky Pete

Other categories were Ethnic (Italian Stallion), Fish, Initials, Ladies (Fast Lady, Shady Lady), Numbers (Three Pals), Reversals (Rolyat), Risqué (Muffdiver, Rut Cry), Surnames, Unexplained (Fat City).

Under the heading of Wrong Assumption, McNamara reported a Full House, which turned out to refer not to poker but to the seven children in the family.

One name, selected as Dullest, was Investment Broker.

WE'RE NOT SUPERSTITIOUS, BUT...

For many years large numbers of British sailors have cherished the belief that Friday is an unlucky day, and as much as possible they try to avoid any unusual or innovative activities on that day.

Earlier in this century, British navy officials decided to disprove the superstition by providing a dramatic example of its falsity. They began building a ship on a Friday, never missed a Friday during its construction, finished it on a Friday, named it Friday, officially christened it on a Friday, and started it on its shakedown cruise on a Friday.

The ship was never seen again.

Sometimes numbers substitute for names. Pampa, TX numbers its police cars. Late in 1980 Car 13, in use only a few days, was in an accident. A little later, another; then another; five accidents in all, some of them serious enough to keep Car 13 off the street for weeks.

In April 1982, Police Chief J. J. Ryzman finally decided to take action. He changed 13 to 25.

In September he told United Press International, "We've got some superstitious people here. We haven't had an accident since."

I'M JUNE BUG—FLY ME

In stagecoach days the coach lines and the individual coaches had names. Some of the lines were called June Bug, Stocktons, Mail Pilot, and Good Intent. Among the coach names were Queen Victoria and Rough and Ready. A competitor of Stocktons advertised with this couplet:

> If you take a seat in Stocktons Line,
> You are sure to be passed by Pete Burdine.

HE CALLED THE STORM MARIA

One of the earliest best-selling novels in which a storm was the central character was *Storm*, by George R. Stewart, published by Macmillan in 1941. It concerns a storm, nicknamed Maria, that was born in the Pacific and brought tremendous damage and some injuries and deaths to the West Coast, and whose daughter, Little Maria, inundated New York before slipping off to die in the Atlantic.

The main human character in the novel is the Junior Meteorologist, or "the J. M." "Not at any price would the Junior Meteorologist have revealed to the Chief that he was bestowing names—and girls' names—upon those great moving low pressure areas. But he justified the sentimental vagary by explaining mentally that each storm was really an individual and that he could more than easily say (to himself, of course) 'Antonia' than 'the low pressure center which was yesterday in latitude one-seventy-five East, longitude forty-two North.'"

Today the United States National Weather Service echoes the J. M.'s reasoning: "Experience shows that the use of short, distinctive given names in written as well as in spoken communications is quicker, and less subject to error than the older more cumbersome latitude-longitude identification methods."

In the nineteenth century many hurricanes had been named after saints. For instance, Hurricane Santa Ana hit Puerto Rico a severe blow in 1825, and two vigorous San Felipes struck there, the first in 1876 and the second in 1928. And an Australian meteorologist, Clement Wragge, had begun using women's names in the late 1800s.

Stewart's widely read novel, however, popularized the custom, and both meteorologists and journalists began following the J.M.'s lead during World War II. The armed forces, though, still preferred Able, Baker, Charlie, etc., but gave in in 1953. After that, women's names were used by the National Weather Service until 1978, when it bowed to feminist complaints that the exclusive use of women's names was insulting.

After consultation at conventions of the World Meteorological Organization, the U.S. Weather Service and others agreed on the internationally flavored names listed here, with women's and men's names alternating. Since 1979 these names have been applied to all tropical storms (those with rotary circulation and wind speeds above thirty-nine miles per hour). The initial letters Q, U, X, Y, and Z are not included. The Atlantic names are repeated after a five-year cycle, the Eastern Pacific names after four years. Thus the 1988 Atlantic names will be the same as those for 1983.

If your name is, say Teresa or William, Sandra or Vicente, the chances are slim that a storm by that name will be spawned, since usually no more than twelve or fifteen hurricanes appear in either the Atlantic or the Eastern Pacific in a given year. But if your name is among the top ten in any list, the odds are fairly high that your friends will have something to tease you about. You may need to remind them that the National Weather Service says, with emphatic capital letters, "The Names of Particular Individuals Have Not Been Chosen for Inclusion in the List of Hurricane Names."

The Five-Year List of Names for Atlantic Storms

1983	1984	1985	1986	1987
1988	1989	1990	1991	1992
1993	1994	1995	1996	1997
Alicia	Ana	Allen	Arlene	Alberto
Barry	Bob	Bonnie	Bret	Beryl
Chantal	Claudette	Charley	Cindy	Chris
Dean	David	Danielle	Dennis	Debby
Erin	Elena	Earl	Emily	Ernesto
Felix	Frederic	Frances	Floyd	Florence
Gabrielle	Gloria	Georges	Gert	Gilbert
Hugo	Henri	Hermine	Harvey	Helene

Iris	Isabel	Ivan	Irene	Isaac
Jerry	Juan	Jeanne	Jose	Joan
Karen	Kate	Karl	Katrina	Keith
Luis	Larry	Lisa	Lenny	Leslie
Marilyn	Mindy	Mitch	Maria	Michael
Noel	Nicolas	Nicole	Nate	Nadine
Opal	Odette	Otto	Ophelia	Oscar
Pablo	Peter	Paula	Philippe	Patty
Roxanne	Rose	Richard	Rita	Rafael
Sebastien	Sam	Shary	Stan	Sandy
Tanya	Teresa	Tomas	Tammy	Tony
Van	Victor	Virginia	Vince	Valarie
Wendy	Wanda	Walter	Wilma	William

The Four-Year List of Names for Eastern Pacific Storms

1983	1984	1985	1986
1987	1988	1989	1990
1991	1992	1993	1994
Aletta	Andres	Agatha	Adrian
Bud	Blanca	Blas	Beatriz
Carlotta	Carlos	Celia	Calvin
Daniel	Dolores	Darby	Dora
Emilia	Enrique	Estelle	Eugene
Fabio	Fefa	Frank	Fernanda
Gilma	Guillermo	Georgette	Greg
Hector	Hilda	Howard	Hilary
Iva	Ignacio	Isis	Irwin
John	Jimena	Javier	Jova
Kristy	Kevin	Kay	Knut
Lane	Linda	Lester	Lidia
Miriam	Marty	Madeline	Max
Norman	Nora	Newton	Norma
Olivia	Olaf	Orlene	Otis
Paul	Pauline	Paine	Pilar
Rosa	Rick	Roslyn	Ramon
Sergio	Sandra	Seymour	Selma
Tara	Terry	Tina	Todd
Vicente	Vivian	Virgil	Veronica
Willa	Waldo	Winifred	Wiley

SKIING DOWN THE
SPIRAL STAIRS

Some of America's ski slopes seem especially well named. *Outside* magazine, identifying the twelve most difficult ski runs in America, included these four:

Elevator Shaft	(Aspen, CO)
Gunbarrel	(Heavenly Valley, CA)
Spiral Stairs	(Telluride, CO)
Exterminator	(Crystal Mountain, WA)

HAVE YOU NAMED
YOUR LAWNMOWER YET?

The two lawnmowers at the Interim Waste Treatment Plant in Mount Laurel, NJ are self-propelled. They need no gasoline, oil, or electricity. They cut more grass as they get older. They needn't ever be taken to the shop where mowers are repaired.

The employees of the plant are fond of their mowers and sometimes pet them. They have even given them names.

The names are Lamb and Chop. The two young ewes will be idle during the winter and will have to be fed corn.

A AS IN *ALFA*

The British military in 1898, when it was necessary to clarify which letter-sound was intended, began translating: "*A* as in *ack*; *b*, *beer*," and so on. Since that time many variations of pronunciation alphabets have been tried. In 1956 an International Telecommunications Union (ITU) list was promulgated, and it has since been adopted by some of the world's armed forces and many ham radio operators and air traffic controller groups. It is presented here along with a comparison list approved for use by operators with General Telephone of California (GTC), which like other phone companies makes almost exclusive use of personal names, in contrast to the mixed bag of the ITU.

ITU		GTC	
ITU	Mike	**GTC**	Mary
Alfa	November	Alice	Nellie
Bravo	Oscar	Bertha	Oliver
Charlie	Papa	Charles	Paul
Delta	Quebec	David	Quaker
Echo	Romeo	Edward	Richard
Foxtrot	Sierra	Frank	Sam
Golf	Tango	George	Tom
Hotel	Uniform	Henry	Utah
India	Victor	Ida	Victor
Juliette	Whiskey	John	William
Kilo	X-ray	Kentucky	X-ray
Lima	Zulu	Lewis	Zebra

DIDJA BRING YOUR SWITCHBLADE TODAY?

In the 1950s, New York City opened certain schools for tough kids only—not hardened criminals but disrupters who made life difficult for teachers and most other students. There was considerable discussion of what such a school should be called.

One suggestion was "a 600 school," because a teacher got an extra $600 a year as a combat bonus for teaching there. That became the most commonly used designation, but the cleverest suggestion came from William Riley Parker, who was executive secretary of the Modern Language Association. That background showed in his use of a bilingual pun in his recommended name: *P.S. de resistance.*

THE SHORTEST MOVIE TITLE

It's hard to imagine a movie title much shorter than that of a picture directed by Fritz Lang in 1931: *M.*

A RECORD FOR MOVIE-TITLE GOOFS?

How many errors can be made in a four-word movie title? Perhaps the record is held by a thriller called *Krakatowa, East of Java*, concerning the volcano that erupted disastrously in 1883. There are two errors. The conventional spelling of the volcano's name is Krakatoa, and it is west of Java, not east.

WHY OSCAR?

How did the Oscar, symbol of motion picture achievement, get its name? A frequent explanation is that in 1927 a secretary saw one of the earliest of the statuettes and exclaimed, "It looks like my Uncle Oscar!"

BEHIND THE
SILVER SCREEN

Would you suppose that a common preposition could be a forbidden word in titles of movies? When the Hays Office in the early 1930s was busy inventing things that movie makers must not do or allow to be said, one of the words not permitted in movie titles was *behind*.

A NEW SPELLING FOR
X

Some newspapers or local mores or ordinances require that titles of certain X-rated movies be modified in advertising. *Deep* or *Throat* may be acceptable, but *Deep Throat* may not. A gay film entitled *Stud Farm* was advertised as *Study Farm*. The theater probably lost money on that one.

THE BIBLE
THAT ORDERED
ADULTERY

Ever since printing was invented, printers have occasionally made mistakes and proofreaders have sometimes failed to notice them. Not even the Bible has escaped error-free.

Generally the errors are inconsequential. For instance, the first printing of the Authorized Bible, in Ruth 3:15, referring to Ruth's departure from Boaz, says "...and he went into the city." As a result that printing was nicknamed the He Bible. The next printing, called the She Bible, got it right: "...and she went into the city."

Another printing, in 1717, had vinegar instead of vineyard, and so was named the Vinegar Bible.

British Tories had a little fun when one edition appeared in which Matthew 5:9 said "Blessed are the *placemakers*" instead of *peacemakers*. Because the Whig leaders of the time were often accused of creating "places" ⟨easy jobs, sinecures⟩ for their party hacks, the Tories promptly nicknamed the version the Whig Bible.

One of the Ten Commandments, as several people know, says "Thou shalt not commit adultery." But in one version, called the Wicked Bible, Exodus 20:14 not only condones adultery but requires it: "Thou shalt commit adultery."

Other Bibles have been nicknamed not for printers' errors but for eccentric translations. For instance, the Breeches Bible (which officially is the Geneva Bible) says in Genesis 3:7 that Adam and Eve "made themselves breeches." The conventional translation is "made themselves aprons." Perhaps to the conservative British Puritans who were responsible for that translation, breeches seemed more decent, less revealing apparel than aprons for our ancestors to wear.

Another translator, whatever his reason, altered "strong drink shall be bitter to them that drink it" to "beer shall be bitter to them that drink it." His version was named the Beer Bible.

THE CDH
PICKS A LEMON

In Ireland, *Orange* signifies an Irish Protestant, and orange is therefore not the favorite color of many Irish Catholics.

In California one freeway is called the Orange Freeway, although the name has no reference to the Irish or to religion. But the CDH (California Division of Highways) was not notably tactful when in 1976 it opened a new 1.5-mile section of the Orange Freeway—on St. Patrick's Day.

WHO IS WALTZIN'
MATILDA?

Wrong question. The Matilda of Australia's enduringly most popular song is not a *who* but a *what*.

The composer of the song was Andrew Barton (Banjo) Paterson (1864-1941), an Australian lawyer and poet. Lawyer Paterson might long since have been forgotten, but the poet—or at least one of his products—lives on and on. As early as 1900 a British *Literary Yearbook* said of him, "No living English or American poet can boast so wide a public, always excepting Mr. Rudyard Kipling."

The Anzacs marched to World War I singing "Waltzin' Matilda," and their sons sang it in World War II. The British named a kind of tank "Matilda," while their little children at home were learning to sing the song in their nurseries.

Paterson, riding with a friend into Winton, Queensland, had heard the expression "Waltzin' Matilda" and learned that it refers to a pack or "tucker bag" such as a peddler, wandering worker, or tramp (a "swagman") might carry. The term fascinated him, and he improvised verses as they rode along. That evening, in Winton, he composed music to fit, not knowing that he was writing what has been called Australia's unofficial national anthem.

So a waltzin' Matilda is a pack carried by a swagman. This swagman stops in the shade of a coolibah tree (a kind of evergreen) and starts a fire under his "billy" (a kettle or pail used for cooking). Along comes a "jimbuck" (a sheep) to drink at the "billabong" (a water hole).

The swagman grabs the jimbuck "with glee" and shoves it into his tucker bag, singing, "You'll come a-waltzin' Matilda with me." But the jimbuck's owner—presumably a rancher but called a "squatter"—rides up with three troopers to arrest the itinerant thief. He refuses to give up his freedom, however:

> Up jumped the swagman and dived into the billabong.
> "You'll never take me alive!" cried he,
> And his ghost may be heard as you pass by that
>   billabong,
> Singing, "Who'll come a-waltzin' Matilda with me?"

The song owes its undying popularity in part to the rollicking tune, but perhaps more to the universal desire for freedom, for lack of regimentation, for independence of authority. Moralists rightly lament the swagman as a poor guide to conduct, but an Australian woman novelist, Kylie Tennant, declared, "There is no sweeter mutton than what has been stolen, killed, and hung in a fig tree overnight and cooked next morning."

Z FOR *ZANY?*

Why a Z-shaped bridge? An unproved guess is that midwestern bridges which approximated that shape were built in honor of Ebenezer Zane, who was responsible for clearing Zane's Trace, an important road for Ohio and Kentucky pioneers. More likely the Z shape, really closer to S, was intended to reduce the force of the water. (Zanesville, OH, named for Ebenezer Zane, gained renown for having what may have been the only Y-shaped bridge in the country.)

HENRY CLAY, PUNSTER

Statesman Henry Clay of Kentucky was in a stagecoach that upset close to Uniontown, PA. He was unhurt but got dirty. As he brushed off his clothes he said, "I'm mixing the Clay of Kentucky with the limestone of Pennsylvania."

MAYBE HE HAD A
POETIC LICENSE

"I'll Take You Home Again, Kathleen," generally supposed to be an Irish song, was actually written by a Virginian with the un-Irish name of Thomas Paine Westendorf.

His wife's name was Jennie.

MORE FIGGYHOBBIN, PLEASE

In Mineral Point, WI, tourists usually look for Shake Rag Street, so named because wives there used to shake rags from their doorways to signal working or gossiping husbands that it was time to come home to dinner. Not far away is Shake Rag Alley, where artisans now make and sell their products. And down at the Walker House tourists may enjoy Cornish pasties—pies made with meat, onions, and potatoes—and a dessert named figgyhobbin, a pastry with brown sugar, raisins, and a generous mound of whipped cream.

ON THE ADVANTAGES OF LEARNING FOREIGN LANGUAGES

A Chevrolet with the name Nova did not sell well to Hispanics. The reason: in Spanish, *no va* means ⟨It doesn't go⟩.

CUTIE-PIE COMMERCIAL NAMES

The Wearhouse (clothing store)

The Meating Place (butcher shop)

Den of Antiquity (antique shop)

Turtles Pantyhose—They Never Run

Wallpapers to Go

Merrys Little Lambs (David and Mary Merry, sheep raisers)

Evil People Lounge (Fort Pierce, FL. It advertised "the finest in topless entertainment" but would admit no one wearing jeans and no males in collarless shirts.)

TALL CORN

Places in Iowa we may have to patronize sometime:
Flatt Tire Service.
Little Charm Motel.

THE GREATEST
UNDERSTATEMENT
OF ALL TIME

The Enola Gay, a B-29 bomber named for the mother of the pilot, Colonel Paul Tibbets, flew straight west from Tinian Island toward its target on August 6, 1945. The twelve men on board were almost entirely silent during the six-hour flight.

The navigator was Captain Theodore "Dutch" van Kirk. The bombardier was Major Thomas W. Ferebee, twenty-four years old. Under his control was "Little Boy"—the greatest onomastic understatement.

Little Boy actually weighed 7,000 pounds. It lay in the bomb bay, and would be released automatically when the cross hairs of the Norden bomb sight showed that the plane was directly over the Aioi Bridge in the heart of Hiroshima. But if the automatic control failed, Major Ferebee had only to push a manual release.

The manual release was not needed. At 8:15:17 the bomb dropped, detonating at precisely 8:16.

Colonel Tibbetts turned hard right. The plane lurched, shuddered, bounced, bucked, and seemed for a few moments as if it might fall apart as the shock waves shook it like a rag.

Three days later, Little Boy's successor, nicknamed Fat Man, took a similar ride, this one ending in Nagasaki.

Little Boy and Fat Man, some people say, signaled the beginning of the end of civilization. But, as Ferebee said in 1982, "You just can't make a bomb and leave it. You must develop it to stay even with others."

That's the trouble.

ONE JOHN ISN'T
ENOUGH

The most often misspelled and misspoken name of a university may be that of the Johns Hopkins University. The reason for the *s* in *Johns* is that a large part of the original endowment for the university and hospital came from a Baltimore banker named Johns Hopkins.

The most often incorrectly worded name of a university is probably that of Indiana University. That's the official name, *not* the University of Indiana.

The, by the way, is an official part of the names of several universities and colleges, e.g., *the* Ohio State University.

MADE IN AMERICA?

The makers of Lionel trains once manufactured an HO-scale model of a famous train called the American Freedom Train, which had toured the country displaying historic documents and other American memorabilia.

The transformer of the model was marked "Made in Hong Kong." On the locomotive was the notice "Molded in Canada."

TAKE-OFFS

Name of an exotic dancer: Libby Ration.
Name of a very exotic dancer: Saki Tumi.
Name of a topless bar: The Body Shop.

HOW DID SHE CALL HER HUSBAND?

A woman named her dog Dammit. Sometimes her penetrating voice could be heard throughout the neighborhood as she called, "Dammit! Come here, Dammit!"

ANYBODY FOR USAN?

As is generally agreed, *American* is inappropriate as a designation of a resident of the United States. *United Statesian*, though listed in dictionaries, has never caught on. (Perhaps USan, pronounced you-esś-an, would be more manageable.)

THE MOST FAMOUS
AMERICAN EPITAPH

In the eighteenth and nineteenth centuries, long and sometimes flowery epitaphs were sometimes carved on tombstones. Perhaps the most famous is that composed by Benjamin Franklin for his own grave:

The Body

of BENJAMIN FRANKLIN

printer

Like the cover of an old book,

Its contents torn out,

And stripped of its lettering and gilding,

Lies here food for worms,

Yet the work itself shall not be lost

For it will, as he believed, appear once more

In a new

And more beautiful edition,

Corrected and amended

by

the Author